Exit from Globalization

Exit from Globalization moves from theory to practice: from questions of where incorrigible knowledge of substantive economic life derives and how that knowledge is put towards making a progressive, redistributive, eco-sustainable future of human flourishing.

Westra discards at the outset views that the root of current economic ills is the old devil we know, capitalism. Rather, he maintains the neoliberal decades spawned a "Merchant of Venice" economic excrescence bent upon expropriation and rent seeking that will scrape all the flesh from the bones of humanity if not stopped dead in its tracks. En route to providing a viable design for the human future in line with transformatory demands of socialists and Greens, Westra exorcizes both Soviet demons and ghosts of neoliberal ideologues past that lent support to the position that there is no alternative to "the market".

Exit from Globalization shows in a clear and compelling fashion that, while debates over the possibility of another, potentially socialist, world swirl around this or that grand society-wide scheme, the fact is that creative future directed thinking has at its disposal several economic principles that transformatory actors may choose from and combine in various ways to remake human economic life. The book concludes with an examination of the various social constituencies currently supporting radical change and explores the narrowing pathways to bring change about.

Richard Westra received his PhD from Queen's University, Canada. His current appointment is Designated Professor at the Graduate School of Law, Nagoya University, Japan. Among his numerous international publications, he authored *The Evil Axis of Finance*, (2012) and co-edited *The Future of Capitalism After the Financial Crisis*, (2015).

Routledge frontiers of political economy

1 **Equilibrium Versus Understanding**
   Towards the rehumanization of economics within social theory
   Mark Addleson

2 **Evolution, Order and Complexity**
   Edited by Elias L. Khalil and Kenneth E. Boulding

3 **Interactions in Political Economy**
   Malvern after ten years
   Edited by Steven Pressman

4 **The End of Economics**
   Michael Perelman

5 **Probability in Economics**
   Omar F. Hamouda and Robin Rowley

6 **Capital Controversy, Post Keynesian Economics and the History of Economics**
   Essays in honour of Geoff Harcourt, volume one
   Edited by Philip Arestis, Gabriel Palma and Malcolm Sawyer

7 **Markets, Unemployment and Economic Policy**
   Essays in honour of Geoff Harcourt, volume two
   Edited by Philip Arestis, Gabriel Palma and Malcolm Sawyer

8 **Social Economy**
   The logic of capitalist development
   Clark Everling

9 **New Keynesian Economics/ Post Keynesian Alternatives**
   Edited by Roy J. Rotheim

10 **The Representative Agent in Macroeconomics**
   James E. Hartley

11 **Borderlands of Economics**
   Essays in honour of Daniel R. Fusfeld
   Edited by Nahid Aslanbeigui and Young Back Choi

12 **Value, Distribution and Capital**
   Essays in honour of Pierangelo Garegnani
   Edited by Gary Mongiovi and Fabio Petri

13 **The Economics of Science**
Methodology and epistemology as if economics really mattered
James R. Wible

14 **Competitiveness, Localised Learning and Regional Development**
Specialisation and prosperity in small open economies
Peter Maskell, Heikki Eskelinen, Ingjaldur Hannibalsson, Anders Malmberg and Eirik Vatne

15 **Labour Market Theory**
A constructive reassessment
Ben J. Fine

16 **Women and European Employment**
Jill Rubery, Mark Smith, Colette Fagan and Damian Grimshaw

17 **Explorations in Economic Methodology**
From Lakatos to empirical philosophy of science
Roger Backhouse

18 **Subjectivity in Political Economy**
Essays on wanting and choosing
David P. Levine

19 **The Political Economy of Middle East Peace**
The impact of competing trade agendas
Edited by J.W. Wright, Jnr

20 **The Active Consumer**
Novelty and surprise in consumer choice
Edited by Marina Bianchi

21 **Subjectivism and Economic Analysis**
Essays in memory of Ludwig Lachmann
Edited by Roger Koppl and Gary Mongiovi

22 **Themes in Post-Keynesian Economics**
Essays in honour of Geoff Harcourt, volume three
Edited by Claudio Sardoni and Peter Kriesler

23 **The Dynamics of Technological Knowledge**
Cristiano Antonelli

24 **The Political Economy of Diet, Health and Food Policy**
Ben J. Fine

25 **The End of Finance**
Capital market inflation, financial derivatives and pension fund capitalism
Jan Toporowski

26 **Political Economy and the New Capitalism**
Edited by Jan Toporowski

27 **Growth Theory**
A philosophical perspective
Patricia Northover

28 **The Political Economy of the Small Firm**
Charles Dannreuther and Lew Perren

29 **Hahn and Economic Methodology**
Edited by Thomas Boylan and Paschal F O'Gorman

30 **Gender, Growth and Trade**
The miracle economies of the postwar years
David Kucera

31 **Normative Political Economy**
Subjective freedom, the market and the state
David Levine

32 **Economist with a Public Purpose**
Essays in honour of John Kenneth Galbraith
Edited by Michael Keaney

33 **Involuntary Unemployment**
The elusive quest for a theory
Michel De Vroey

34 **The Fundamental Institutions of Capitalism**
Ernesto Screpanti

35 **Transcending Transaction**
The search for self-generating markets
Alan Shipman

36 **Power in Business and the State**
An historical analysis of its concentration
Frank Bealey

37 **Editing Economics**
Essays in honour of Mark Perlman
Hank Lim, Ungsuh K. Park and Geoff Harcourt

38 **Money, Macroeconomics and Keynes**
Essays in honour of Victoria Chick, volume I
Philip Arestis, Meghnad Desai and Sheila Dow

39 **Methodology, Microeconomics and Keynes**
Essays in honour of Victoria Chick, volume II
Philip Arestis, Meghnad Desai and Sheila Dow

40 **Market Drive and Governance**
Reexamining the rules for economic and commercial contest
Ralf Boscheck

41 **The Value of Marx**
Political economy for contemporary capitalism
Alfredo Saad-Filho

42 **Issues in Positive Political Economy**
S. Mansoob Murshed

43 **The Enigma of Globalisation**
A journey to a new stage of capitalism
Robert Went

44 **The Market**
Equilibrium, stability, mythology
S.N. Afriat

45 **The Political Economy of Rule Evasion and Policy Reform**
Jim Leitzel

46 **Unpaid Work and the Economy**
Edited by Antonella Picchio

47 **Distributional Justice**
Theory and measurement
Hilde Bojer

48 **Cognitive Developments in Economics**
Edited by Salvatore Rizzello

49 **Social Foundations of Markets, Money and Credit**
Costas Lapavitsas

50 **Rethinking Capitalist Development**
Essays on the economics of Josef Steindl
Edited by Tracy Mott and Nina Shapiro

51 **An Evolutionary Approach to Social Welfare**
Christian Sartorius

52 **Kalecki's Economics Today**
Edited by Zdzislaw L. Sadowski and Adam Szeworski

53 **Fiscal Policy from Reagan to Blair**
The left veers right
Ravi K. Roy and Arthur T. Denzau

54 **The Cognitive Mechanics of Economic Development and Institutional Change**
Bertin Martens

55 **Individualism and the Social Order**
The social element in liberal thought
Charles R. McCann Jnr.

56 **Affirmative Action in the United States and India**
A comparative perspective
Thomas E. Weisskopf

57 **Global Political Economy and the Wealth of Nations**
Performance, institutions, problems and policies
Edited by Phillip Anthony O'Hara

58 **Structural Economics**
Thijs ten Raa

59 **Macroeconomic Theory and Economic Policy**
Essays in honour of Jean-Paul Fitoussi
Edited by K. Vela Velupillai

60 **The Struggle Over Work**
The "end of work" and employment alternatives in post-industrial societies
Shaun Wilson

61 **The Political Economy of Global Sporting Organisations**
John Forster and Nigel Pope

62 **The Flawed Foundations of General Equilibrium Theory**
Critical essays on economic theory
Frank Ackerman and Alejandro Nadal

63 **Uncertainty in Economic Theory**
Essays in honour of David Schmeidler's 65th birthday
Edited by Itzhak Gilboa

64 **The New Institutional Economics of Corruption**
Edited by Johann Graf Lambsdorff, Markus Taube and Matthias Schramm

65 **The Price Index and its Extension**
A chapter in economic measurement
S.N. Afriat

66 **Reduction, Rationality and Game Theory in Marxian Economics**
Bruce Philp

67 **Culture and Politics in Economic Development**
Volker Bornschier

68 **Modern Applications of Austrian Thought**
Edited by Jürgen G. Backhaus

69 **Ordinary Choices**
Individuals, incommensurability, and democracy
Robert Urquhart

70 **Labour Theory of Value**
Peter C. Dooley

71 **Capitalism**
Victor D. Lippit

72 **Macroeconomic Foundations of Macroeconomics**
Alvaro Cencini

73 **Marx for the 21st Century**
Edited by Hiroshi Uchida

74 **Growth and Development in the Global Political Economy**
Social structures of accumulation and modes of regulation
Phillip Anthony O'Hara

75 **The New Economy and Macroeconomic Stability**
A neo-modern perspective drawing on the complexity approach and Keynesian economics
Teodoro Dario Togati

76 **The Future of Social Security Policy**
Women, work and a citizens basic income
Ailsa McKay

77 **Clinton and Blair**
The political economy of the Third Way
Flavio Romano

78 **Marxian Reproduction Schema**
Money and aggregate demand in a capitalist economy
A.B. Trigg

79 **The Core Theory in Economics**
Problems and solutions
Lester G. Telser

80 **Economics, Ethics and the Market**
Introduction and applications
Johan J. Graafland

81 **Social Costs and Public Action in Modern Capitalism**
Essays inspired by Karl William Kapp's Theory of Social Costs
Edited by Wolfram Elsner, Pietro Frigato and Paolo Ramazzotti

82 **Globalization and the Myths of Free Trade**
History, theory and empirical evidence
Edited by Anwar Shaikh

83 **Equilibrium in Economics**
Scope and Limits
Edited by Valeria Mosini

84 **Globalization**
State of the art and perspectives
Edited by Stefan A. Schirm

85 **Neoliberalism**
National and regional experiments with global ideas
Edited by Ravi K. Roy, Arthur T. Denzau and Thomas D. Willett

86 **Post-Keynesian Macroeconomics Economics**
Essays in honour of Ingrid Rima
Edited by Mathew Forstater, Gary Mongiovi and Steven Pressman

87 **Consumer Capitalism**
Anastasios S. Korkotsides

88 **Remapping Gender in the New Global Order**
Edited Marjorie Griffin Cohen and Janine Brodie

89 **Hayek and Natural Law**
Erik Angner

90 **Race and Economic Opportunity in the Twenty-First Century**
Edited by Marlene Kim

91 **Renaissance in Behavioural Economics**
Harvey Leibenstein's impact on contemporary economic analysis
Edited by Roger Frantz

92 **Human Ecology Economics**
A new framework for global sustainability
Edited by Roy E. Allen

93 **Imagining Economics Otherwise**
Encounters with identity/difference
Nitasha Kaul

94 **Reigniting the Labor Movement**
Restoring means to ends in a democratic labor movement
Gerald Friedman

95 **The Spatial Model of Politics**
Norman Schofield

96 **The Economics of American Judaism**
Carmel Ullman Chiswick

97 **Critical Political Economy**
Christian Arnsperger

98 **Culture and Economic Explanation**
Economics in the US and Japan
Donald W. Katzner

99 **Feminism, Economics and Utopia**
Time travelling through paradigms
Karin Schönpflug

100 **Risk in International Finance**
Vikash Yadav

101 **Economic Policy and Performance in Industrial Democracies**
Party governments, central banks and the fiscal-monetary policy mix
Takayuki Sakamoto

102 **Advances on Income Inequality and Concentration Measures**
Edited by Gianni Betti and Achille Lemmi

103 Economic Representations
Academic and everyday
Edited by David F. Ruccio

104 Mathematical Economics and the Dynamics of Capitalism
Goodwin's legacy continued
Edited by Peter Flaschel and Michael Landesmann

105 The Keynesian Multiplier
Edited by Claude Gnos and Louis-Philippe Rochon

106 Money, Enterprise and Income Distribution
Towards a macroeconomic theory of capitalism
John Smithin

107 Fiscal Decentralization and Local Public Finance in Japan
Nobuki Mochida

108 The 'Uncertain' Foundations of Post-Keynesian Economics
Essays in exploration
Stephen P. Dunn

109 Karl Marx's Grundrisse
Foundations of the critique of political economy 150 years later
Edited by Marcello Musto

110 Economics and the Price Index
S.N. Afriat and Carlo Milana

111 Sublime Economy
On the intersection of art and economics
Edited by Jack Amariglio, Joseph W. Childers and Stephen E. Cullenberg

112 Popper, Hayek and the Open Society
Calvin Hayes

113 The Political Economy of Work
David Spencer

114 Institutional Economics
Bernard Chavance

115 Religion, Economics and Demography
The effects of religion on education, work, and the family
Evelyn L. Lehrer

116 Economics, Rational Choice and Normative Philosophy
Edited by Thomas A. Boylan and Ruvin Gekker

117 Economics Versus Human Rights
Manuel Couret Branco

118 Hayek Versus Marx and Today's Challenges
Eric Aarons

119 Work Time Regulation as Sustainable Full Employment Policy
Robert LaJeunesse

120 Equilibrium, Welfare and Uncertainty
Mukul Majumdar

121 Capitalism, Institutions and Economic Development
Michael Heller

122 Economic Pluralism
Robert Garnett, Erik Olsen and Martha Starr

123 Dialectics of Class Struggle in the Global Economy
Clark Everling

124 Political Economy and Globalization
Richard Westra

125 Full-Spectrum Economics
Toward an inclusive and emancipatory social science
Christian Arnsperger

126 Computable, Constructive and Behavioural Economic Dynamics
Essays in honour of Kumaraswamy (Vela) Velupillai
Stefano Zambelli

127 Monetary Macrodynamics
Toichiro Asada, Carl Chiarella, Peter Flaschel and Reiner Franke

128 Rationality and Explanation in Economics
Maurice Lagueux

129 The Market, Happiness and Solidarity
A Christian perspective
Johan J. Graafland

130 Economic Complexity and Equilibrium Illusion:
Essays on market instability and macro vitality
Ping Chen

131 Economic Theory and Social Change
Problems and revisions
Hasse Ekstedt and Angelo Fusari

132 The Practices of Happiness
Political economy, religion and wellbeing
Edited by John Atherton, Elaine Graham and Ian Steedman

133 The Measurement of Individual Well-Being and Group Inequalities
Essays in memory of Z.M. Berrebi
Edited by Joseph Deutsch and Jacques Silber

134 Wage Policy, Income Distribution, and Democratic Theory
Oren M. Levin-Waldman

135 The Political Economy of Bureaucracy
Steven O. Richardson

136 The Moral Rhetoric of Political Economy
Justice and modern economic thought
Paul Turpin

137 Macroeconomic Regimes in Western Industrial Countries
Hansjörg Herr and Milka Kazandziska

138 Business Ethics and the Austrian Tradition in Economics
Hardy Bouillon

139 Inequality and Power
The economics of class
Eric A. Schutz

140 Capital as a Social Kind
Definitions and transformations in the critique of political economy
Howard Engelskirchen

141 **Happiness, Ethics and Economics**
Johannes Hirata

142 **Capital, Exploitation and Economic Crisis**
John Weeks

143 **The Global Economic Crisis**
New perspectives on the critique of economic theory and policy
Edited by Emiliano Brancaccio and Giuseppe Fontana

144 **Economics and Diversity**
Carlo D'Ippoliti

145 **Political Economy of Human Rights**
Rights, realities and realization
Bas de Gaay Fortman

146 **Robinson Crusoe's Economic Man**
A construction and deconstruction
Edited by Ulla Grapard and Gillian Hewitson

147 **Freedom and Happiness in Economic Thought and Philosophy**
From clash to reconciliation
Edited by Ragip Ege and Herrade Igersheim

148 **Political Economy After Economics**
David Laibman

149 **Reconstructing Keynesian Macroeconomics, Volume 1**
Partial perspectives
Carl Chiarella, Peter Flaschel and Willi Semmler

150 **Institutional Economics and National Competitiveness**
Edited by Young Back Choi

151 **Capitalist Diversity and Diversity within Capitalism**
Edited by Geoffrey T. Wood and Christel Lane

152 **The Consumer, Credit and Neoliberalism**
Governing the modern economy
Christopher Payne

153 **Order and Control in American Socio-Economic Thought**
U.S. social scientists and progressive-era reform
Charles McCann

154 **The Irreconcilable Inconsistencies of Neoclassical Macroeconomics**
A false paradigm
John Weeks

155 **The Political Economy of Putin's Russia**
Pekka Sutela

156 **Facts, Values and Objectivity in Economics**
José Castro Caldas and Vítor Neves

157 **Economic Growth and the High Wage Economy**
Choices, constraints and opportunities in the market economy
Morris Altman

158 **Social Costs Today**
Institutional analyses of the present crises
Edited by Wolfram Elsner, Pietro Frigato and Paolo Ramazzotti

159 **Economics, Sustainability and Democracy**
Economics in the era of climate change
Christopher Nobbs

160 **Organizations, Individualism and Economic Theory**
Maria Brouwer

161 **Economic Models for Policy Making**
Principles and designs revisited
S.I. Cohen

162 **Reconstructing Keynesian Macroeconomics, Volume 2**
Integrated approaches
Carl Chiarella, Peter Flaschel and Willi Semmler

163 **Architectures of Economic Subjectivity**
The philosophical foundations of the subject in the history of economic thought
Sonya Marie Scott

164 **Support-Bargaining, Economics and Society**
A social species
Patrick Spread

165 **Inherited Wealth, Justice and Equality**
Edited by Guido Erreygers and John Cunliffe

166 **The Charismatic Principle in Social Life**
Edited by Luigino Bruni and Barbara Sena

167 **Ownership Economics**
On the foundations of interest, money, markets, business cycles and economic development
Gunnar Heinsohn and Otto Steiger; translated and edited with comments and additions by Frank Decker

168 **Urban and Regional Development Trajectories in Contemporary Capitalism**
Edited by Flavia Martinelli, Frank Moulaert and Andreas Novy

169 **Social Fairness and Economics**
Economic essays in the spirit of Duncan Foley
Edited by Lance Taylor, Armon Rezai and Thomas Michl

170 **Financial Crisis, Labour Markets and Institutions**
Edited by Sebastiano Fadda and Pasquale Tridico

171 **Marx and Living Labour**
Laurent Baronian

172 **A Political Economy of Contemporary Capitalism and its Crisis**
Demystifying finance
Dimitris P. Sotiropoulos, John G. Milios and Spyros Lapatsioras

173 **Against Utility-Based Economics**
On a life-based approach
Anastasios Korkotsides

174 **Economic Indeterminacy**
The dance of the meta-axioms
Yanis Varoufakis

175 **Freedom, Responsibility and Economics of the Person**
Jérôme Ballet, Damien Bazin, Jean-Luc Dubois and François-Régis Mahieu

176 **Reality and Accounting**
Ontological explorations in the economic and social sciences
Richard Mattessich

177 **Profitability and the Great Recession**
The role of accumulation trends in the financial crisis
Ascension Mejorado and Manuel Roman

178 **Institutions and Development After the Financial Crisis**
Edited by Sebastiano Fadda and Pasquale Tridico

179 **The Political Economy of Gunnar Myrdal**
A reassessment in the post-2008 world
Örjan Appelqvist

180 **Gender Perspectives and Gender Impacts of the Global Economic Crisis**
Edited by Rania Antonopoulos

181 **Hegel, Institutions, and Economics**
Performing the social
Carsten Herrmann-Pillath and Ivan A. Boldyrev

182 **Producer Cooperatives as a New Mode of Production**
Bruno Jossa

183 **Economic Policy and the Financial Crisis**
Edited by Łukasz Mamica and Pasquale Tridico

184 **Information Technology and Socialist Construction**
The end of capital and the transition to socialism
Daniel E. Saros

185 **Beyond Mainstream Explanations of the Financial Crisis**
Parasitic finance capital
Ismael Hossein-zadeh

186 **Greek Capitalism in Crisis**
Marxist analyses
Stavros Mavroudeas

187 **Of Synthetic Finance**
Three essays of speculative materialism
Benjamin Lozano

188 **The Political Economy and Media Coverage of the European Economic Crisis**
The case of Ireland
Julien Mercille

189 **Financial Cultures and Crisis Dynamics**
Edited by Bon Jessop, Brigitte Young and Christoph Scherrer

190 **Capitalism and the Political Economy of Work Time**
Christoph Hermann

191 **The Responsible Economy**
Jefferson Frank

192 **Globalization and the Critique of Political Economy**
New insights from Marx's writings
Lucia Pradella

193 **Exit from Globalization**
Richard Westra

Exit from Globalization

Richard Westra

Taylor & Francis Group
LONDON AND NEW YORK

First published in paperback 2016

First published 2015
by Routledge
2 Park Square, Milton Park, Abingdon, Oxon OX14 4RN

and by Routledge
711 Third Avenue, New York, NY 10017

Routledge is an imprint of the Taylor & Francis Group, an informa business

© 2015, 2016 Richard Westra

The right of Richard Westra to be identified as author of this work has been asserted by him in accordance with sections 77 and 78 of the Copyright, Designs and Patents Act 1988.

All rights reserved. No part of this book may be reprinted or reproduced or utilised in any form or by any electronic, mechanical, or other means, now known or hereafter invented, including photocopying and recording, or in any information storage or retrieval system, without permission in writing from the publishers.

Trademark notice: Product or corporate names may be trademarks or registered trademarks, and are used only for identification and explanation without intent to infringe.

British Library Cataloguing in Publication Data
A catalogue record for this book is available from the British Library

Library of Congress Cataloging-in-Publication Data
Westra, Richard, 1954–
  Exit from globalization / Richard Westra. — 1 Edition.
    pages cm. — (Routledge frontiers of political economy ; 193)
  1. Globalization—Economic aspects. 2. Economic policy.
  3. Sustainable development. I. Title.
  HF1359.W47 2015
  337—dc23
  2014023145

ISBN: 978-0-415-83534-3 (hbk)
ISBN: 978-1-138-19509-7 (pbk)
ISBN: 978-1-315-73858-1 (ebk)

Typeset in Goudy
by Apex CoVantage, LLC

Contents

List of figures   xvi
Preface and acknowledgements   xvii
List of abbreviations   xviii

1 Introduction: from the Merchant of Venice economy   1

2 The zero of social change   27

3 Weighs like a nightmare on the brains of the living   63

4 Green dawn   82

5 Neoclassical rapture in *Jurassic Park*   108

6 The institutional matrix of heterogeneous economic life   135

7 Conclusion: a road to the eco-kingdom of freedom   177

Index   199

List of figures

1.1	US as a "global" economy	18
2.1	Levels of analysis in Marxian political economy	53
2.2	The cognitive sequence in Marxism	56
3.1	Historical societies and forms of economic compulsion	78
6.1	Karl Polanyi on economic principles	139
6.2	Karl Marx – Polanyi correspondence	141
6.3	David Graeber on "moral principles" upon which economic principles founded	143
6.4	The Karl Marx/David Graeber correspondence	146
6.5	Directional flow chart of political power in tri-sector community socialist economy	169
6.6	Economic coordination across heterogeneous use value sectors	173

Preface and acknowledgements

Fifteen years and several books later, the present volume brings to life ideas first toyed with rudimentarily in my PhD dissertation supervised by Grant Amyot at Queen's University, Canada. This book in one form or another had always been on my to-do list. Now, however, was the time to write it! The book is about progressive eco-sustainable social change and the possibility of it in the here and now.

In drawing upon the work of Karl Marx, with all the sectarian passion Marxism evokes, I want to say something about my approach to knowledge. Karl Marx in my esteem is certainly one of the greatest economists of all time. However, though this book draws from Marx's corpus, I make no claim to precisely follow Marx's every word. Nor do I present myself as a "Marxist" that "represents" the "true" Marx. Rather, I believe I have taken what is most valuable in Marx's economic theorizing of capital and applied it in creative future directed thinking.

I approach knowledge in terms of what may be understood as "standing on the shoulders of giants". Marx is such a giant. And there are others in that category from whom I have learned some lessons well. But in standing on the shoulders of such intellectual giants I have also gained my own vista. One to be sure I could never have gained without standing on their shoulders. But once up there, well . . . this is how knowledge in small, not necessarily giant ways, moves forward.

In developing the key economic ideas of Karl Marx, I am indebted to Japanese Marxian economist Thomas T. Sekine and Canadian political economist Robert Albritton. I have also had many discussions of late, electronically, with John R. Bell that I have benefitted from. His e-posts regularly turn up interesting source material.

I am extremely grateful to my commissioning editor at Routledge Singapore, Yongling Lam, for her efforts in seeing this volume to press.

As always, over the past 10 years, my wife Ann has been supportive of my work.

I also want to thank two students from the Global 30 international program at Nagoya University, Ann Narukawa and Stormy Kim, for their very professional assistance in producing the lists and index for this book.

Part of the research for this book received support from the National Research Foundation of Korea Grant NRF-2013S1A5B8A01055117

Finally, the usual disclaimers apply . . .

List of abbreviations

ACWI	All Country World Index
ADHD	attention-deficit/hyperactivity disorder
ALBA	Bolivarian Alliance for the Americas
AUM	assets under management
BIS	bank for international settlements
CDR	carbon dioxide removal
CO_2	carbon dioxide
CR	critical realism
CSP	concentrating solar power
DNA	deoxyribonucleic acid
DoD	Department of Defense
EROI	energy return on investment
EU	European Union
FDI	foreign direct investment
FED	Federal Reserve Bank
FIRE	finance, insurance and real estate sector
GHG	greenhouse gas
GPCs	Great People's communes
GRO	grassroots organization
HM	historical materialism
ICT	information and computer technology
IdleM	idle money
IMF	International Monetary Fund
IOU	I owe you
IPCC	Intergovernmental Panel on Climate Change
LETS	local exchange/employment and trading systems
MNB	multinational bank
MNC	multinational corporation
MST	Landless Workers' Movement
NASA	National Aeronautics and Space Administration
NEM	non-equity modes (of control)
NEP	new economic policy
NGO	non-governmental organization

NIEO	new international economic order
OECD	Organization for Economic Cooperation and Development
OTD	originate-to-distribute banking
PFIs	private financial intermediaries
POPs	persistent organic pollutants
PV	photovoltaic
R&D	research and development
RCP	representative concentration pathways
SEZ	special economic zone
SRM	solar radiation management
T-bill	treasury bill
TINA	there is no alternative
TMSA	transformational model of social activity
TPES	total primary energy supply
TPP	Trans-Pacific Partnership
T-TIP	Transatlantic Trade and Investment Partnership
TVEs	town and village enterprises
UNFCCC	United Nations Framework Convention on Climate Change
US	United States
WB	World Bank
WTO	World Trade Organization
WWI	World War I
WWII	World War II
ZIRP	zero interest rate policy

1 Introduction
From the Merchant of Venice economy

As fallout from the 2008–2009 global meltdown radiated across the planet a feeling that society-wide support for political economic change could now be forged welled up among progressive groups and activists the world over. This sense was reinforced when, commencing December 2010, mass demonstrations set in motion processes that by early 2011 would topple Middle East tyrants in Tunisia and Egypt from their once seemingly impregnable perches. By September 2011, what began with scattered protests in major United States (US) cities, coalesced in the Occupy Wall Street movement that brought tens of thousands of people, from all walks of life, out into the streets; activists groups even setting up makeshift "Occupy" encampments in parks from Toronto to Tokyo.

Trending Left gurus captured the times with provocative statements. Slavoj Žižek put it this way:

> As the old proverb says: there is only one thing worse than not getting what one wants – namely, actually getting it. Leftist academics are now approaching such a moment of truth: you wanted real change – now you can have it![1]

Veteran intellectual of 1960s European radical student and worker movements, Alain Badiou, proclaimed:

> The present moment is in fact that of the first stirrings of a global popular uprising . . . As yet . . . lacking a powerful concept or durable organization, it naturally resembles the first working-class insurrections of the nineteenth century . . . [W]e find ourselves in a *time of riots* wherein a rebirth of History . . . is signaled . . . Our masters know this better than us: they are secretly trembling and building up their weaponry, in the form both of their judicial arsenal and the armed taskforces charged with planetary order. There is an urgent need . . . to create our own.[2]

But, how much change is the "real change" purportedly being thrust upon us? Are we talking about thoroughgoing reform, revolution? What does this all really mean? And when can we "have it"? New bosses, much the same as the old bosses, have acceded to power in the Middle East. The Occupy protest encampments are gone. If "a global popular uprising" does occur, and even yields its own "armed taskforce", then what? Karl Marx and Friedrich Engels claim that ruling classes would "tremble" as the "forcible overthrow" of their order by Communist revolution loomed was directed against moribund autocracies of the mid-nineteenth century. Marx and Engels thought it "madness" to frontally assault a modern, professionally militarized bourgeois state as existed in England by the late 1860s, particularly when social transformation could be brought about by other means.[3] Fast forward to April 2013, the US city of Boston was summarily locked down by no less than 30 different "law enforcement" agencies, sporting Hollywood style high-tech paramilitary arsenals, to scour streets for a single teenage bombing suspect![4] Does Badiou, with his "armed task force", really want to go toe to toe with this monster?

As we peer past the radical chic and brouhaha, instructively spewing from a mix of mutually back scratching self-styled Marxist (and sprinkling of anarchist) figures, it is the visage of déjà vu that immediately strikes us, decorated in new, often titillating language to be sure, yet déjà vu nevertheless. That "History", is now being "reborn", for example, has a familiar teleological ring to it. After all, the revolution that brought the Soviet Union into being was based precisely on the view that historical tendencies would unleash heroic working-class struggles. And guided by a "powerful concept" (socialism) as well as led by a "durable organization" (the Leninist vanguard Party) the revolution would take us to a promised land "History" bequeathed.

To be sure, the agency issue has been tweaked. New terms such as the "multitude",[5] the "precariat",[6] have been entered into the lexicon of radical analyses in the twenty-first century. And, the erstwhile end of history, "Mr. Socialism", has been bid "goodbye" to, now replaced by the big step for humankind directly to "Communism".[7] Yet the storyline is familiar if not banal: "It is not that capitalist development is creating communism", Michael Hardt tells us. "Instead, through the increasing centrality of the common in capitalist production . . . are emerging the conditions . . . for a communist project. Capital, in other words, is creating its own gravediggers".[8]

We will have occasion in this book to revisit the foregoing, particularly the issue of transformatory constituencies. Though there is no intention to dwell on the aforementioned literature. Much is simply gibberish: which is extremely disconcerting given that a generation of progressively minded youth across the globe, desperate for genuine answers to the dire predicament humanity faces, and disenchanted with the mainstream policy discourse, lurch from conference to speaking engagement to imbibe it.

Rather this book fills an intellectual gap at a time when not only youth with their stolen future but academics, progressive policy makers and mass publics need hard-headed answers to the Himalayan question: How is an era of human flourishing to be brought about? And, how do we build feasible, progressive, redistributive, environmentally sustainable economies in the here and now to the above end?

It is telling, that from the thousand or so pages of trending Left gurus I have read, rife with revolutionary exhortations, spiced with lengthy quotations from Marx, and chock full of philosophical excursus, there is complete oblivion regarding the morning after question. That is, what happens when we wake up following Badiou's so-called global popular uprising? Do the Left gurus really believe that in today's "pumped-up" psycho-social milieu, gang-ridden urban decay, with a generation of neoliberal ideological savaging of any semblance of human community and neoliberal fostered racism and misogyny, that if "times of riots" vaporize current structures of government (as odious as most of these are) à la Christopher Hill's *The World Turned Upside Down*, oblique notions of reborn "History" can be counted on to forestall a descent into barbarism?[9] Indeed, the studied disconnect between armchair glorifying of "riots" along with philosophical speculation over revolutionary agents *and* discussion of the political economic and institutional contours of a future society that will purportedly be ushered in the morning after the revolution is stunning.

At the other end of the spectrum there are certainly models of future societies on offer for humanity to turn to as it exits from globalization. And debate enjoining traditions among Greens, democratic participatory socialist planning, ecosocialism, "de-growth" environmentalists, and so-called "market socialism" has been engendered. It is that work, and questions the debates raise, which are the proper concern of this book. But even here, the present volume goes where the aforementioned have not dared to tread. For what I will demonstrate in no uncertain terms is the whole enterprise of future directed political economic thinking currently in play is marked by gaping lacunae.

The most debilitating of these, for which the present book is offered as the corrective, is the fact that progressive thinking about the human economic future has proceeded in the virtual absence of any clear idea of from where basic understanding of human *economic* or material life derives in the first place. Mainstream neoclassical economics claims economic life can be studied *directly* in terms of human behavior (see Box 1.1). And the fact that human beings only came to realize this in the eighteenth and nineteenth centuries, is ascribed to simple historical fortuitousness. The absurdity of this approach, labeled "economics", flows from the fact that prior to the eighteenth-century rise of capitalism it was inconceivable to even begin to think about such a thing as an "economy" separate from religion, politics, ideology, culture, and so on. Economic life was always enmeshed with these social practices and indistinguishable in itself from them. Neoclassical economics and the classical economic theories it builds on could *only* have formulated its arguments (bracketing here questions of its veracity and ideological slant) through study of the *capitalist* economy because it is *only* in the capitalist era that economic life appears "transparently" for theory to explore. Yet no mainstream economic approaches problematize this fact. Therefore, until questions of the very historicity of economics as a discipline are sorted out, and subsequent steps required for economic theory to produce knowledge of *capitalism* and *precapitalist* societies grasped, it is impossible to move forward toward creative thinking about how human economic life may be desirably and feasibly organized in future societies.

Box 1.1

The view that we have economic or material interests in human provisioning is hardly profound. Are we humans self-aggrandizing benefit maximizers? Maybe yes, maybe not in the exaggerated, largely spurious sense neoclassical theory claims. But so what if some of us are? What we really want *economic theory* to tell us is something about the *kind* of economy that exists, or existed in the past. And the way that economy and *form* human economic relations take in it both shape our material interests and sets parameters for their articulation. After all, the greediest, precapitalist ruler, let us take, for example, evil "King John" of "Robin Hood" fame, had concrete economic bounds placed on his self-aggrandizing behavior by the fact that social wealth was rooted squarely in inalienable, hereditary landed property. Where, moreover, what wealth landed property generated was tied to work rhythmus of a peasant class over which precapitalist rulers exercised political and military authority but *no* entrepreneurial power. Such precapitalist arrangements persisting for over a millennium embodied concrete social goals that were as much about maintaining hierarchical interpersonal relations of domination and subordination as they were about anything we would describe as "economic" today.

As will be discussed at length in this book, capitalism "frees" human beings from these interpersonal relations of domination and subordination. Its material or economic relations are *impersonal* and *abstract*. Karl Marx demonstrates how such "freed" individuals are then connected or brought into order through the *cash nexus* of the capitalist market. In turn, Marx links the way individuals are brought into order in the capitalist market with the historical emergence of a society where human material affairs are organized for a new abstract, *quantitative* goal of augmenting mercantile wealth or profit-making. Under such economic conditions our material interests are *infinitized*. That is, our individual human need for provisioning, notwithstanding the extent of our individual self-aggrandizing behavior, is tethered to an overriding social goal that transcends whichever individual need we may have. As an impersonal, abstract, quantitative social goal, profit-making has *no* material limit. Therefore, as we human beings "freely" pursue our individual self-seeking proclivities in society-wide markets these are wielded in capitalist economies for a social goal beyond *us*. And to the benefit of a social class that personifies infinite agglomeration of abstract mercantile wealth as that social goal.

Narcotized by neoclassical ideological opium we are driven to see the eviscerating of all semblance of social, communal, material, natural bounds in terms of unchangeable human propensities. And the possibility of genuine economic change rendered dependent upon discovering nuances in our psychology, for example. Whichever side of the psychological, sociological and anthropological research divide over "human nature" one falls, however, what we do know with certainty is that this "nature" has *not* in any way prevented human beings from organizing their economic lives in radically different ways across the sweep of human history. We might have expected, of course, that as the historical conditions of possibility for economic theory crystallized in the eighteenth and nineteenth centuries, the proper concern of the discipline would become precisely the questioning of what we are doing in our economic lives, whether we should keep doing this, and, if not, how we humans can better craft economic institutions to realize our chosen social and economic goals. But sadly, this was not to be.

Marxian traditions, with minor exception, have fared no better on this question. Marx's work has been largely codified in terms of historical materialism (HM), a master theory of historical directionality. Marx's magisterial economic studies in *Capital* are fit into this framework, when they are considered at all, as a *subtheory*. Much of the debate within Marxism swirls around such questions as the extent to which "the economic" determines the course of history and the degree of its privileging with respect to other social practices like "the political". Nevertheless, through these debates that built upon the distinction between "orthodox" Marxism and "neo-Marxism", the fundamental view of Marxism qua HM as a theory of historical directionality, initially elaborated by orthodox figures such as Karl Kautsky, is never challenged.[10] This conflating of Marxism with HM is precisely what channels its revolutionary force into a kind of astrology charting whether stars are aligned for things like "History's rebirth" and sending activists scurrying hither and thither after each new mass demonstration as the harbinger of the final so-called global popular uprising.

The conflation most deleteriously infects Marxian economic studies. The title of the work that consumed Marx's life is clear – *Capital*. Yet, with minor exception, major schools of Marxian political economy have approached *Capital* as if it was a study of the life and times of capital*ism* in its teleological-historical progression. Marx's arguments in the opening pages of *Capital* that it constitutes a self-subsistent economic treatise with an ontologically unique subject-matter are ignored. Instead, *Capital* is apprehended as a long drawn-out example operating in a given context of purported historical "contradictions" or "laws" Marx loosely hypothesized in a few-paragraph pithy statement of HM published as preface to a minor work. This predominating but wrongheaded view completely distorts Marxian economics. As we shall see, *Capital* most certainly *does* interrogate the historicity of its discipline, the *economic* theory of *capital*, which in turn constitutes the foundation for the political economic study of capitalism and comparative exploration of economic life in other historical societies. *Capital* in that way places economic knowledge at the disposal of both exposing the deep causal structures of the present and creative thinking about substantive economic potentialities for the future. Yet, in the hands of self-styled Marxist gurus, *Capital* becomes little more than a repository of revolutionary quotations and the basis of speculation over things like capitalism's "gravediggers": Which still takes us back to the abiding pre-Soviet era question. If the "diggers" rise, dig the "grave", and bury capitalism, then what?

The second major lacuna hamstringing creative thinking about future possible economic worlds is the failure to adequately grasp seismic transformations of capitalism that spawned the current predicament of rotating economic meltdowns and human-life-throttling global austerity. We need to get this issue off the table now, before proceeding to the main concern of the book.

Entitling this volume *Exit from Globalization* plays upon the faddish way "globalization" has emerged as a euphemism in both popular parlance and academic discourse for the world economic sea change commencing in the 1980s. Other more hot-button terms often used interchangeably with globalization are: neoliberalism, financialization, new imperialism, and global capitalism. This volume is a sequel, if you will, to my earlier *Political Economy and Globalization*.[11] In that volume, written as the 2008–2009 global meltdown unfolded, I offered an extended treatment and critique of what I viewed as the single most analytically impoverishing theme that tied disparate so-called globalization writings together. And that prevented the literature as a whole from grasping the true world economic significance of the meltdown.

Marx, I emphasize, always viewed capitalism as a historically delimited society. That is, capitalism arises in history to satisfy a given constellation of human material wants and as the technologies for furnishing these become available. Like the forms of economic organization that preceded it, capitalism passes from history as its ability to manage human material affairs is exhausted and new human wants along with productive techniques and forms of economic organization for satisfying them loom on the horizon. To be sure, Marx's optimism over stirrings of working-class revolt did lead him to advance the position that interruption of capitalism's march in world history by socialist revolution was nigh. But it goes against the grain of Marx's systematic economic studies of capital to leap from his scattered comments on impending socialism to the fallacious view (which Marx himself *never* propounds) that capitalism maintains some kind of supra-historic power to persist until overthrown by a great cataclysm akin to Badiou's so-called global popular uprising.

Yet it is precisely this view, that capitalism is, if not exactly forever as neoclassical economics has it, ever-adaptable, ever-mutable, ever-resilient, which unites otherwise divergent perspectives on globalization emanating from Right and Left sides of the political spectrum. Take Marxist doyen David Harvey, for example:

> . . . Can capitalism survive the present trauma [the global meltdown of 2008–2009]? Yes, of course [sic!] . . . Can the capitalist class reproduce its power in face of the raft of economic, social, political, and geographical and environmental difficulties? Again, the answer is a resounding 'Yes it can' . . . Capital . . . never solves its crisis tendencies, it merely moves them around . . . from one part of the world to another and from one kind of problem to another.[12]

Globalization, in this sense, has become the centerpiece of debate over "freeing" of "the market" and reinvigorated "commodification" following the crisis and demise of post-World War II (WWII) "golden age" in which state macroeconomic policies along with multinational corporate (MNC) organization suppressed market forces and commodification was turned back by state-provided "public goods" and social welfare policies. For neoliberals on the Right, globalization only confirms the truth of neoclassical axioms, that *there is no alternative* (TINA) to capitalism and its teleology is human destiny. The demise of the golden age and unraveling of the Soviet Union is testament to this. Accordingly, society will be all the more prosperous if we "privatize" government investments, shrink government itself, "deregulate" and "liberalize" capitalist wealth augmenting activities, and allow a world of "emerging markets" to bloom. For the Left, which holds with neoliberals to the axiom of globalization as capitalism and "the market" reloaded, the litany of ills besetting the world economy from the 1980s, including increasingly asymmetric wealth distribution and erratic behavior of private capital investment culminating in the 2008–2009 global meltdown, unbridled capitalism qua globalization *is* the problem.

But what is the ideological investment of the Left here? Why does the Left cling as tenaciously as neoliberals to the view of globalization as capitalism reloaded? The Left is surely aware that this cedes the ideological high ground to neoliberals who have been trumpeting capitalism forever all along. There are three reasons for this investment.

The first involves deep-seated theoretical questions relating to the equation of Marxism with HM as a master theory of historical directionality alluded to above. Full treatment of these questions is reserved for Chapter 2. For purposes of the present discussion it can simply be pointed out that it is certainly true that Marx is capitalism's fiercest critic. And there exists no rival to Marx's exposure of capital's logical inner economic workings in *Capital*. Marx's economic theory in *Capital* has a timeless relevance to our thinking about human material life that extends well beyond vicissitudes of capitalism or even the existence of capitalism itself. Yet, in equating Marxism with HM as a master theory of historical directionality, self-styled Marxists mistakenly tie the applicability of Marx's economic studies to the perceived fortunes and historical transformations of capitalism. The most glaring example of this tendency is the fact that when capitalism appeared to be doing "well", as in the triumphal decades of neoliberalism, Marxists laid low. As Eric Hobsbawm notes: "Silence greeted the last instalment of the fifty-volume English translation of the *Collected Works* of Marx and Engels, in progress since the 1970s, when it was finally published in 2004".[13] Yet when there is a major economic cataclysm as occurred with the 2008–2009 meltdown, chants of "Marx was right" abound. It follows that if capitalism changed in a way not allegedly "predicted" by Marx, or in fact ceased to exist while the socialist future had still not arrived, the self-styled Marxists would feel left without moorings.

The second reason is that since the unceremonious collapse of the Soviet Union a significant swath of the Left have tacitly acceded to the belief that capitalism is the only game in town. This swath includes a range of perspectives from in-the-closet Keynesian "Marxists" through "deglobalization" writers. All yearn for a seat at the policy table. With those seats they hope to resurrect a golden age-like "national" social democratic economy with its social welfare policies and robust labor organizations as the next best thing to fallen "real" socialism. What writers in this cohort dub "decommodification" is the call for governments to reverse neoliberal privatizations and reinstate the golden age "commons" of public goods and services. Deglobalization in this discourse entails rolling back neoliberal liberalizations and supports government power to reregulate capital. For this reason much of globalization debate has swirled around the binaries of *state* and *market* and hopes of a progressive future tied to Left policy makers attaining command over the state so as to attenuate ravages of the market. Take long time deglobalization advocate Walden Bello:

> deglobalization does not call for the abolition of the market and its replacement by central planning . . . The market's role in exchange and allocation of resources is important [sic!] . . . Acting to balance and guide the market must not only be the state but also civil society, and in place of the invisible hand as the agent of the common good must come the visible hand of democratic choice.[14]

The third reason follows up on preaching from the other major stream of Left writers' quotations from which opened this chapter. For them, capitalism *must* persist at all costs because this fits with their eschatology of the heroic "global popular uprising" that finally abolishes it. "Communism" here, let us once more defer to Žižek, means "breaking out of the market-and-state frame". Žižek parrots Lenin:

> the goal of revolutionary violence is not to take over State power, but to transform it, radically changing its functioning in relation to its base . . . the "dictatorship of the proletariat" is a kind of (necessary) oxymoron . . . We effectively have the 'dictatorship of the proletariat' only when the state itself is radically transformed, relying on new forms of popular participation.[15]

Of course, again, the eliding of questions of the *kind* of economy or "base" this new "dictatorship of the proletariat" will lord over should make us all very suspicious of what at bottom is really being peddled on the globalized Left conference circuit. We will return to this, but let us now get back to capitalism.

For Marx, economic forms like money, wages, profits, even "markets" of various sorts, existed in human history in what he famously described as the *interstices* of ancient worlds. That is, these forms always remained external to the basic modalities of material reproduction of precapitalist communities whatever the scale and scope of the latter. The historical specificity of capitalism resides in the way it draws these categories into a unique symbiosis predicated upon maintaining human labor power, the very wellspring of human material reproduction and sustenance, as a commodity. In the historical emergence of capitalism, spreading marketization of economic life internalizes as the material reproductive core of human communities that which had been external. The "community", referred to here, is the historically constituted nation-state. It is the Absolutist state that first hones the political instruments of "national" economic intercourse. And it is this state that embodies the concentrated power the bourgeois draws upon to wrest or "dispossess" property and wealth from precapitalist classes. While there is no logical imperative for capital to colonize human material life in the particular geospatial configuration of nation-states, the existence of the latter as a ready-made container was extremely convenient for capital to manage the commodification of labor power and resource asymmetries necessary for accumulation.

The constellation of human material wants capitalism arises in history to satisfy are standardized manufactured "material" goods. The technologies and power sources for furnishing such goods emerged in the eighteenth century. Standardized material goods production commenced with "light" manufacturing of textiles that formed the basis of the factory system. The generalization and modernization of the factory system fostered demand for "heavy" steel and industrial chemicals industries. The latter constitute the foundation for late nineteenth-century/early twentieth-century railway and shipping transportation networks that circumnavigated the globe. Finally, mass production of automobiles and related infrastructure along with consumer durable production generally offers renewed demand for steel and a dynamic sector of mass consumption and capital accumulation. Notwithstanding changes in the complex of goods and manufacturing systems, the satisfying of human economic want for standardized material goods marks capitalism in its historical role as a *production-centered society*.

The historical role of capitalism as a production-centered society synchronizes with the abstract, quantitative social goal of capitalism – the augmentation of mercantile wealth or profit-making. That is, the production of standardized material goods lends itself to the suppression of qualitative considerations in economic life in favor of quantitative ones. The commodification of human labor power is integral to this social goal. Because in divesting precapitalist classes of means of production in land and crafts, labor power is made available on the market to be applied by capital to the production of *any* good in line with shifting patterns of social demand and opportunities for profit-making. The commodification of labor power is thus the primary source of capitalist "efficiency"; meaning, of course, efficiency in augmenting mercantile wealth. And, as Marxists have emphasized, it is the exploitation of commodified labor power that is the root of capitalist profit-making. That is, while all "factors of production" – land, labor, and capital – operate in "concrete useful" ways to produce particular goods according to the specificities of each (tropical soils grow mangoes, carpenters work wood, and precision lathes fashion metal objects), *only* human labor power has the *capacity* for "abstract-general" application to the production of *any* good as the vehicle for creating and augmenting *value* or abstract mercantile wealth.

However, while considerable attention has been devoted to Marx's exposing the exploitative, alienating, asymmetric wealth distributive bents of capitalism that flow from the commodification of labor power, Marxists have paid scant attention to a more fundamental question Marxian economic theory answers. That is, how is it possible for an economy manifesting such an array of ills, and effectively wielding an entire human society for the abstract purpose of value augmentation, to reproduce human material life as a byproduct of this chrematistic?

While in-depth treatment of Marxian economics on this question is preserve of Chapter 2, for purposes of the present discussion we can note the following: Within the parameters of capitalist social class relations of production and division of labor the formation of prices on the capitalist market manifests a certain "coherence" or objectivity that yields the requisite allocation of social resources enabling capital to reproduce the economic life of a human society. The "objective" pricing of commodities that achieves such an allocation of social resources derives from the commodification of human labor power and its deployment by capital as but another input alongside the material inputs capital applies to the production of standardized manufactured commodities. Returning to Marx's view of capitalism as a historically delimited social order, the point here is that the capitalist economy with its architecture of impersonal self-regulating markets and quantitative determinations is "viable" (if at all) as a way of organizing human material life *only* when human society is largely occupied with provision of the relatively narrow range of material goods amenable to standardized production methods.

Before moving on it is important we answer two questions. First, does capitalism operate as an international economy or "world system"? Of course, capitalism from its inception has had an international or global dimension. However the degree of capitalism's internationalization and the forms the global dimension of capital accumulation assumed has varied significantly across the sweep of capitalist history. But the historical specificity of capitalism as a human society is the bourgeois class projects of agglomerating abstract mercantile wealth, predicated upon exploitation of commodified labor power, in production-centered settings of historically constituted nation-state containers. These are the base camps from which patterns of capital's global dimension have been configured across the capitalist era.

Second, how are we to understand the relationship between state and market in the study of capitalism? Bracketing for treatment in Chapter 2 the ontological question of what it is about capital that foregrounds the analytical separation of the two categories in the first place, all "really existing" capitalism has required extra economic support to some degree. Let us take the neoliberal maxim: "[that] demand and supply for goods and services are allowed to adjust to each other through the price mechanism, without interference by government or other forces".[16] The closest historical approximation to such a situation would be the laissez faire capitalist economy of mid-nineteenth-century Britain. Marx was clear however, demand and supply price mechanism adjustments do not take place in a vacuum, but operate in the dynamic context of business cycles that oscillate around prosperity and depression phases. In the decennial cycles of laissez faire capital, the aggravating factor was absorption of what Marx dubbed the *industrial reserve army* that compels capital to revolutionize the *forces of production*. Contra Marxist David Harvey, laissez faire capital did not need to "move its crisis around". Rather it maintained an in-built mechanism in falling prices and devaluation of capital in the depression phase of the business cycle to solve it (Box 1.2).

Box 1.2

We will have several occasions to revisit this important question across the pages of this book. Preliminarily, it can be stated that in a capitalist economy the fact that human labor power is available on the market for a certain price renders it like other commodities – an input to be converted to a particular given output. Yet, labor power is in a very fundamental fashion not just another commodity. Unlike other inputs in the production process, labor power cannot be capitalistically produced. Unlike other commodity inputs, it is impossible to automatically adjust its supply to fit demand. Under conditions of ongoing accumulation, capital tends to absorb the industrial reserve army, precipitating a superabundance or overaccumulation of capital in relation to the size of the working population. As wages rise and profits fall, businesses close while capital turns to speculative endeavors. In the ensuing depression and devaluation of capital, surviving capitalists introduce new technologies, raising the *organic composition of capital* and reconstituting the *industrial reserve army* to spur but another bout of capital accumulation. Marx explained this as capital's struggle to maintain its *relations of production* – the capital/labor relation – by revolutionizing the *forces of production*.

But, as the nineteenth century drew to a close, government was called upon to do more than provide a legal framework for property rights or maintain limited outlays for education, public order, and external defense, which were its tasks under laissez faire. The shift of industry in advanced capitalist states to the production complex of heavy steel and chemicals saw entrepreneurial business give way to monopoly firms. And states already deemed the giant monopolies of this period "too big to fail" given the repercussions of a monopoly firm collapsing on the wider economy. The recruitment of government in ratcheting up levels of extra economic support for capital thus dates from this era. Governments promulgated protectionist policies and superintended their administration in the domestic market. And states engaged in imperialist policies of territorial aggrandizement internationally. The goal of state extra economic support was to insulate monopoly firms from "cleansing" effects of competition and devaluation of capital in business cycle troughs. The "excess capital" that necessarily built up in economies of the period populated by monopoly firms was then exported to imperialist territories. In fact, if there ever exists a time when capital does "move its problems around" as Harvey observed, it is the imperialist era.

12 *From the Merchant of Venice economy*

By the post-WWII golden age, with commanding heights industry of advanced capitalist states dominated by giant MNCs operating sophisticated semiautomatic assembly line technologies of automobile and consumer durable production, the extra economic exertions required of states to maintain production-centered capitalist societies reached Herculean proportions. The high throughput demands of profit-making in semiautomatic assembly line production along with mammoth fixed costs of capital investment in the consumer durable industries put the question of maintaining aggregate demand at the forefront of policymaking. Government provision of so-called public goods and the accouterment of the welfare state that partially decommodified labor power formed one prong of the response. The other prong was state macroeconomic fiscal policy where government invested heavily in everything from militarization through transportation infrastructure in attempts to coordinate the business cycle itself. Of course, notwithstanding state macroeconomic policy, production decisions in the golden age economy were still vested in the hands of private businesses, each pursuing their own profit oriented interests. And, with profitable production based upon high throughput of consumer durables and the economy dominated by oligopolistic MNCs, a trend toward burgeoning overcapacity crystallized. That is, with falling aggregate demand it was always the *output* of automobiles and other durables that fell during the golden age, *not* their *prices*.[17] Indeed, so pervasive were golden age government "interferences" in the market that if it were not for the fact that state extra economic programming operated *ex post*, in response to macroeconomic indications in the course of business cycles, we would have cause to question whether the golden age was even capitalist.

Thus the view held implicit in much neoliberal ranting that a policy choice always existed in advanced capitalist economies from the imperialist era through the golden age to hit the "big government" *off* switch and thereby resurrect laissez faire market principles is, of course, nonsense. But that is not the real import of neoliberal ideology. Rather, neoliberal ideology and shrill chants of globalization as epiphany of "the market" arise precisely at that point in history where the ability of capital to manage human material affairs has been incontrovertibly exhausted.

The making of a "Merchant of Venice" economy

The most obvious sign of the historical exhaustion of capitalism is the disintegration of production-centered society itself. Among advanced capitalist states, the historical period 1950–1980 saw the percent of the total labor force (civilian) employed in manufacturing peak at between 35 and 50 percent. As the twentieth century came to a close, the average percent of working populations among advanced capitalist states employed in industry had fallen below levels existing in 1900. States like the US saw civilian industrial employment plummet to around 20 percent and service sector employment leap to near 70 percent of total employment by 1998.[18] Underlying this shift was MNC disintegration and ultimate disinternalization of the production-centered activities they were built upon;

remaking themselves as "branded" companies that do not actually make anything. Production of material goods was then sliced and diced into component parts with these "value chains" disarticulated across the globe. The information and computer technology (ICT) revolution nevertheless enabled branded MNCs to maintain global suzerainty through non-equity modes (NEM) of control over a group of new "contract manufactures" (often MNCs in their own right) that in turn manage the outsourcing of global material goods production.[19] By 2010, as this dynamic played out, a mere 11 percent of the US labor force remained engaged in manufacturing.[20]

As MNCs relocated the business of making things largely to low wage often proto-capitalist production relations in the third world, they simultaneously restructured their operations in advanced economies by extensive fixed investment in ICTs. In the US, the heartland of neoliberalism, investment in ICTs from the early 1980s into the twenty-first century exceeded that in every other equipment category including transportation, airplanes, and so forth.[21] As industry became increasingly knowledge intensive MNC productivity, in the doldrums since the demise of the golden age, experienced renewed gains.[22] And the fleeting GDP growth this stimulated fed neoliberal triumphalism over its "new economy" of "brain work". The problem here, however, is that the capitalist market to which neoliberals believed they could return the job of economic coordination is attuned to measurement of *direct costs* of standardized material inputs and commodified labor power applied to production-centered activities. It is these direct costs that underpin the objective pricing of commodities enabling capital to allocate resources in a way that reproduces a human society as a byproduct of augmenting mercantile wealth. But as industry became more knowledge intensive it saddled both individual MNCs and the economy at large with necessarily "subjective" or haphazard pricing of goods as a result of the enlarging proportion of *indirect costs* involved in their production and marketing.[23] And with the increasingly arbitrary pricing of goods, the ability of the market to perform its historic role in allocating resources was subverted to an even greater extent than under golden age "big government" social wage and fiscal policy intervention.

The chronic resource misallocation that commences in the neoliberal era rapidly impacted income distribution. The zapping of blue collar jobs and making of a third-world Gini in the US from the 1980s is a story that has been told and retold.[24] Of course, wealth asymmetries have marked capitalism as a class society from its inception. But tendencies unleashed in the 1980s involved far more than can be grasped simply in terms of the fostering of "inequality". In the heady decades of US neoliberalism, very little of MNC total earnings was retained as profit and channeled into productive investment. From 1980 to the years preceding the 2008–2009 meltdown the evidence for the US shows a marked trend of disaccumulation such that US total stock of fixed capital was 32 percent lower than it would have been had the golden age accumulation trajectory been maintained.[25] Instead, much of MNC earnings were siphoned off by a host of *unproductive* knowledge workers – ICT hardware and software patent owners along with software developers and engineers, advertizing firms, fashion designers, and so forth – in the form of *rent*, technological and otherwise. It is telling to see even *Citigroup*, in its infamous "Plutonomy report", touting precisely the foregoing dynamic of rent seeking and opportunistic skewing of social wealth to the überrich.[26] Of course, with complete oblivion to what Japanese economist Thomas Sekine reminds us even classical economists like David Ricardo well knew. That, to the extent revenues flow to rent rather than profits for reinvestment, the economy will trend toward a "stationary state".[27]

A second far more sinister aspect of the exhaustion of capitalism is the predatory ravages of what I refer to in my recent book, *The Evil Axis of Finance: The US-Japan-China Stranglehold on the Global Future*,[28] as idle money or *idle M*. Capitalist efficiency derives from "shape shifting" of capital through its "circuit" of value augmentation where it successively assumes forms of money, means of production and labor power, and commodities. Modern banking plays a crucial role in this circuit. In the course of business cycles, it is always the case that money in the form of profit is drawn from the circuit and set aside as depreciation funds, contingency funds, and potential new investment funds. From the standpoint of capitalist efficiency, such monies deposited in the banking system are rendered temporarily *idle*. But, idle M pooled from individual businesses and held in the banking system is the way capitalism "socializes" funds so that money not immediately in use by this or that capitalist is made available to all. Idle M is then lent or "traded" in the money market at the rate of interest, or price of borrowing, established in the relation between supply of funds and existing demand for their use. The socially redeeming value in capitalist utilization of idle M resides in the fact that credit to businesses engaged in production is offered in anticipation of income created by its determinate use. Similarly, idle M socialized in the banking system is advanced to businesses engaged in buying and selling. If commercial capitalist activity more rapidly discounts bills in sale of commodities it can speed up infusion of profits back into productive investment. The socially redeeming value of bank credit advance here is the income generating potential of buying and selling commodities as part of the capitalist circuit. Nevertheless, in a capitalist economy the accumulation of idle M is to be kept within bounds as the time funds remain idle, minimized.

The central attribute of modern banking in capitalist society is "relationship banking". The operative word here is *relationship*. Modern banks, Levy Economics Institute scholar Jan Kregel reminds us, are not money lenders as they do *not* lend their *own* money.[29] Rather, in capitalist economies banks perform the task of financial intermediation. That is, the social role of banking is to evaluate the creditworthiness of borrowers. This demands banks have foreknowledge of what the borrower intends to do with the funds. The relationship is crucial here because it is to banks that loan plus interest is paid. As long as capitalist commodity production exists, some form of relationship banking is vital for the efficiency of its circuit of mercantile wealth augmentation or profit-making.

During the golden age the potential for pooling idle M was high. Earnings of MNCs in consumer durable industries were such that capital accumulation was largely self-financed, lessening need for recourse to banks or even equity markets for that matter. The partial decommodification of labor power saw worker personal and benefit scheme savings grow. Through to the mid 1970s, however, MNC foreign direct investment (FDI) as adjunct to the domestic production-centered activities of capital offered ample scope for multinational banks (MNB) utilization of pooled funds. Thus the US remained a net creditor nation to that point. The welfare/warfare state mopped up another portion of pooling idle M through macroeconomic countercyclical fiscal spending.

With the demise of the golden age and US abdication of its production-centered economy idle M, with absolutely no possibility of investment in the real economy of production and trade, initially began to bloat aimlessly, but then metastasized into a predatory force. A major element in the bloating of idle M was swelling financial assets of various funds – pension funds, insurance funds, mutual funds, money market funds, hedge funds – referred to en bloc as "institutional investors". Already by 1995, funds resident in Organization for Economic Cooperation and Development (OECD) 17 major economies amassed holdings worth $21.9 trillion equal to 103 percent of OECD 17 GDP. By 2007, institutional investor assets under management (AUM) near tripled to $62. 8 trillion equal to 181.7 percent of OECD GDP; with US investors accounting for around half of all OECD institutional AUM.[30] Institutional investors (particularly pension and insurance funds in the early going) and the private financial intermediaries (PFIs) that "managed" their assets both impelled and became major cheerleaders for neoliberal ideological policy initiatives to "free" capital from its golden age tethers.

This "freeing" of capital, or deregulation and liberalization in neoliberal speak, set off a tsunami of change in rules and practices of financial and corporate governance. The whittling away at the US Glass-Steagall or Banking Act of 1933, and its ultimate replacement by the Gramm-Leach-Bliley or Financial Services Modernization Act of 1999, which demolished firewalls separating commercial and investment banking and insurance is, of course, the signature transformation here. However, paralleling that process, but unfolding even further below the political/public radar, was a concatenating of deregulatory initiatives designed to smooth the flow of institutional funds into riskier, high return, short-term, easily exited, "investments". This in turn drove the engineering of arcane securitization instruments like derivatives to not only "hedge" risk and volatility but speculate on it. It also acted as a surreptitious industrial policy hastening the disinternalizing of MNC production-centered activities touched on above. MNCs then morphed into arch arbitragers in their own right issuing and buying back their own shares in pure speculative gambits.[31] By end 2013 the value of publicly traded companies worldwide had exploded by 524 percent over what it was in 1990 (though with a brief cascade back to reality in 2008–2009).[32] Such activity only compounded the aforementioned siphoning of earnings away from profit reinvestment to unproductive interests that exacerbated deflationary tendencies in the real economy. With the real economy becoming ever more "jobless and wageless", [33] what neoliberals refer to as "growth" could only be spurred by a surrogate economy based on casino play whereby finance simply finances itself. And in financing itself "casino capital" embarked upon orgies of debt and leverage with idle M, even operating a "shadow banking system" that conjured up "collateral" to extend its own money games.[34]

Shadow banking then became the template for a new economy-wide banking model catering to idle M – so-called *originate-to-distribute* (OTD) banking – which replaces the relationship banking at the center of the capitalist, production-centered circuit of profit-making. In the OTD model banks engage in financial disintermediation – originating loans only to package them as marketable securities and sell them off, collecting fat fees as the moves are endlessly repeated.[35] Under OTD banks have little concern for the creditworthiness of borrowers or to what purpose the loans will be applied given that interest payments along with the principal are paid to end buyers of securities, *not* banks. The preferred customers of OTD banking are finance, insurance, real estate, the so-called FIRE sector. And the game is asset inflation through debt.[36] From the late 1980s even the capitalist business cycle is superseded by rotating asset bubbles and meltdowns driven by the casino play with oceans of idle M. Yet, only recently have mainstream economic analysts, such as Bank for International Settlements (BIS) chief economist Claudio Borio (an outlier in the mainstream economics community for his views to be sure), actually taken steps to begin to understand the peculiar phenomenon of the neoliberal decades where finance became unhinged from *real* economy business activity (Borio produces a telling graph here).[37]

In a widely reviewed book, Colin Crouch questions the "strange non-death of neoliberalism" in the wake of the global meltdown despite the fact of neoliberal policies fomenting it?[38] Well, the answer is simple. Neoliberal ideology of "the market" epiphany is *all* that remains. Every last drop of capitalist rationality has been leeched out of the current economy. Neoliberal "freeing" of idle M spawned a modern incarnation of antediluvian usury or "loan capital" as Marx analyzed it. Money lending as such was inveighed against in precapitalist societies precisely because of the paucity of socially redeeming value it held for then human communities. As tragically captured in Shakespeare's work, usury or "loan capital" like OTD finance today is *indifferent* to use of funds and to *how* loan plus interest will be repaid. As such, loan repayment may be arbitrarily set to exact such an exorbitant cost that debtors are destroyed, or must strive for ruin of others to meet debt obligations. The demand of perfidious Shylock to settle a debt with a "pound of flesh" captures this condition. Only now that "pound of flesh" is literally being scraped off bones of humanity from the austerity suffered by Greeks to non-developed-country children perishing from preventable and/or treatable diseases because loan "conditionalities" divert government spending from dealing with these.

Two final points: First, the metastasizing of idle M into a predatory force is intimately bound up with US reorientation as an excrescence I have referred to as a *global* economy. That is, an economy dependent upon the world for the consumer goods its population demands as tantamount to their freedom or "way of life", dependent upon the world to finance its yawning trade, government, capital account deficits along with the world's largest gross national debt, yet parlaying the role of the dollar as hub currency into its position in the global driver seat as if the US was still workshop and creditor of the "free world". The domestic implications of the new US orientation are clear: with the dollar as international reserve currency backed only by Treasury (T-Bill) IOUs (following the demise of the Bretton Woods monetary system), the US was handed an auto-borrowing mechanism. Thus financing its deficit, US government spending expanded without crowding out private sector borrowing. And even as domestic savings plummeted in the neoliberal years there was little sustained upward pressure on US interest rates. And US spending in excess of domestic savings and tax collection proceeded without instigating price inflation.

The international implications are that states must externally orient their economies to gain means of dollar payment by either selling more for dollars than they buy or borrowing dollars (the so-called Washington Consensus became the neoliberal enforcer here). And with increasing global financial volatility states are obliged to hold ever greater volumes of largely dollar reserves. These two compulsions have seen international reserve holdings multiply. This process commenced, to be sure, with the demise of Bretton Woods. But it ramps up exponentially at the dawn of the neoliberal era in tandem with exploding US deficits and debt.[39] And it reverses the golden age pattern where advanced OECD economies held the bulk of global reserves. Today the third world or emerging markets in neoliberal speak hold around 70 percent of global reserves. Following the Asian Crisis when China got into the game, international reserves grew from around $1.6 trillion in 1998 to over $11 trillion by Q1 2013. The "unallocated" portion of this is approximately $5 trillion. Of the "allocated" portion, around 62 percent is held in dollars. But, because China does not report the currency composition of its reserves, hence the swollen "unallocated" figure, we can surmise that given its spiking trade surplus with the US, its holdings if reported would boost the dollar proportion of international reserves to approximately 75 percent of the total.[40]

The upshot of the foregoing is that with such gargantuan sums of global idle M sloshing around international financial markets, much of it drawn to the US as increases in foreign financing of US burgeoning debt shows,[41] Wall Street became the vortex for "casino capital" access to low interest rate idle M funds. And it emerged as the global command center for idle M operations as it impels the funds around the world, under the guise of neoliberal so-called deregulation and liberalization, to engage in predatory games that only further expropriate wealth from *real* economic activities wherever these continue to be plied (see Figure 1.1).

Second, neoliberal ideological policy initiatives have *only* been possible for their three decade run by ratcheting up the role of "big government" from the golden age period to now galactic proportions. The figures in themselves are instructive: on the eve of World War I (WWI), as a percent of GDP government

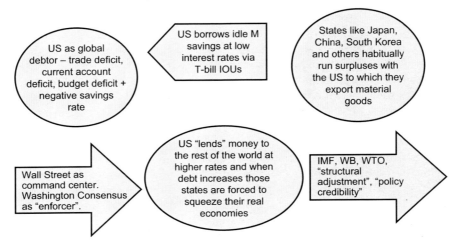

Figure 1.1 US as a "global" economy

spending by Britain (UK) reached only 13.3 percent, that of France 8.9 percent, and the US 8 percent of GDP. By 1973 government spending as a percent of GDP in the UK, France, and US was 41.5 percent, 38.8 percent, and 31.1 percent respectively.[42] In 2009, the OECD 32 country average was near 48 percent with US government spending as a percent of GDP hitting around 43 percent. UK and France government spending now sits comfortably at well above 50 percent of GDP alongside heavy social democratic Scandinavian state spending.[43]

According to economist Richard Duncan, it is not simply a matter here of large state subsidies received by major businesses in each US economic sector or the 50 percent or so of US population receiving government support of one kind or another given the fallout from what I refer to above as the neoliberal "surrogate economy".[44] Rather, for Duncan, the hand of "big government" is bolstered by severing of the link between dollars and gold with the demise of Bretton Woods. What remains is simply *fiat money*, claims upon which are backed by the ability of government to issue (by print or digitally) more fiat money. Thus the power of "big government" now resides in money creation by governments' "big bank" and the manipulation of its value. It is this power that facilitated the expansion of total US credit market debt to over $52 trillion, including US household debt to over $13 trillion in 2010 and 140 percent of household disposable income at the time of the meltdown. That credit, then, underwrites the bloating asset bubbles of neoliberal "growth" (along with securitization games played around them), which in turn engenders the consumption fete amongst those plugged into the bubble upside. Duncan argues this is all a far cry from the capitalist economy on a gold standard economic textbooks study. Duncan calls this new economic system "creditism";[45] or, quite simply, "a government-directed system on a paper money standard".[46]

For Duncan, then, the global meltdown of 2008–2009 and its lingering recessionary aftermath is *not* a crisis of *capitalism* as mainstream economists on the Right along with self-styled Marxists maintain. It is a crisis of his "creditism". Duncan further recognizes that it is simply not possible for the private sector to extricate itself from the debt it has incurred. This leaves "big government" with the task, which it has met heretofore, of bailing out commanding heights financial institutions and arbitraging MNCs *plus* remaining on a robust stimulus footing to avert what would certainly be deep, destructive depression.[47] For Duncan, however, there is a limit to how long "big government" can continue piling on debt (though the US is accorded some wiggle room with debt at just over 100 percent of GDP as compared to the 240 percent of GDP constituted by Japan's debt today). Yet a limit will ultimately be arrived at and debilitating deflation set in unless "big government" pairs its actions with trillions in fiscal spending to remake the US economy with twenty-first-century eco-sustainable infrastructure and technologies, according to Duncan.[48]

But, as prescient as Duncan is compared to much Left brouhaha peddled on the international Left conference circuit, this strategy still leaves us with a several problems. First, to the extent twenty-first-century technologies increase the knowledge intensity of production, in the absence of substantive change in the broader property and social relations of production the skewing of income distribution toward a caste of über-rich will only be exacerbated. As I have argued at length elsewhere, the seismic shift in employment to the service sector in states like the US in particular, has seen a bifurcated structure emerge of low wage McJobs and the high flying managerial, ICT developers and technologists, designers, financial services "1 percent" plugged in to the surrogate economy of rent seeking and asset inflation. The dark underbelly of this is a division of labor that routes manufacturing abdicated by countries like the US through low wage, proto-capitalist production and assembly locales such as China.[49] Without exiting from this side of what is euphemized as globalization paired with significant income redistribution and remaking of the employment landscape (which demands the dramatic shift in property and social relations of production adverted to above) it is not clear how massive fiscal spending alone will get us out of the current morass.

Second, and related to the above, is the elephant in the room. This is the US transubstantiation into a global economy. A "knowledge" or "service economy" is an oxymoron. Medieval "city states" survived only by parasitism on the surrounding community ability to provision them. The US dependence upon the world for the consumer goods its population demands as tantamount to their freedom, furnished by severe repression of labor costs, subtended the aforementioned proto-capitalist if not medieval or modern slave modes of labor control across the third world (though increasingly even in the bowels of US and other advanced economy cities). US commandeering of global wealth to finance its quadruple deficits (trade, government, capital account, saving) and over $17 trillion debt through the role of the dollar as world money has further fomented the most monstrous misallocation of global resources imaginable. There is thus *no* international business as usual for the US in anything remotely resembling a progressive future for humanity.

Third, the sustainable twenty-first-century technologies and infrastructure Duncan has in mind tend to involve a significant move away from the petroleum energy complex and transportation infrastructure it fuels. Whether we are talking about sustainable public transportation grids, redoing the urban/suburban/rural residential divides along with the ways activities of production and agriculture are geospatially related to these; and, of course, remaking the energy matrix, this entails once-and-for-all type installation that defies the sort of "treadmill" characteristic of the age of capital where quantitative considerations in economic life associated with repetitive standardized mass production of goods trumped all.[50] While we will delve deeper into what is fundamentally at stake here later in this book, especially the necessity of factoring environmental considerations into our each and every move into a progressive future, it is worth pointing out how Marx conceptualized this roadblock human material life faces today in terms of the *forces of production* beckoning humanity on the horizon outpacing social *relations of production*, demanding revolutionary social change for human society to move forward.

Then there is the "Merchant of Venice" economic dynamic neoliberal, "state directed" so-called creditism spawned and continues to fuel. As I emphasize in my book the *Evil Axis of Finance*, during its century and a half or so march through human history, production-centered capitalist societies translated industrialization into development and development into growth bringing about rising living standards and wealth tied to capitalist satisfying human wants for standardized material goods. Of course, this process unfolded as a byproduct of capitalist abstract wealth augmentation or profit-making and under wealth asymmetries of capitalist social class relations. Yet, with the abdication of production-centered activities by major advanced states commencing with the US, which rapidly disintegrated and disarticulated production activities across the globe from the 1980s, growth worldwide is decoupled from both development and industrialization as profit-making is supplanted by rent seeking and money games based on debt leverage. The problem our capitalists *without* capitalism face here is that with little in the way of profit from *real* production-centered economic activity to be reinvested in same, there is no way to pay off debt except through deductions from current incomes (private or government), dubbed "austerity" in mainstream parlance, or more debt.[51] On the more debt side of the equation the problem is that the plague each bubble/burst cycle visits upon humanity becomes ever more life throttling each time around. This is because achieving the desired faux growth bang demands ever greater leverage with more debt generated bucks. Governments will then ultimately saddle the backs of taxpayers with the swelling casino markers (at least those taxpayers, unlike über-rich or MNCs, that maintain their economic wherewithal onshore) as it bails out *much* too big to fail financial institutions.[52] On the deductions from current incomes side of the equation, numbing austerity has already befallen much of humanity to service debt from previous meltdowns. There is precious little left in the way of "pounds of flesh" on the bones of humanity. Yet our capitalists *without* capitalism on Wall Street are determined to scrape if off to the end. This is precisely what the surrogate casino economy is all about – expropriation of wealth that will destroy society.

As Edward Fullbrook shows in no uncertain terms, government policymaking in the US is so thoroughly infiltrated with consummate Wall Street casino operatives that no sooner had the last pieces of the bursting bubble from the 2008–2009 meltdown been mopped up by bailout liquidity than the global casino had sprung to life once more.[53] The new bubble flavor of the first post-meltdown decade is what has been explained as the "global government finance bubble". Notwithstanding the recent "deleveraging" discourse, total credit market debt in the US thus leaped from meltdown days by around $6.2 trillion to over $57 trillion as of March 2013. Even more instructive here, given my thesis on the "axis" of finance that lassos Japan and then with a vengeance China into the game to the benefit of the US, is the fact that as China's international reserves spiked around $2.3 trillion from 2008 to end 2013, US Federal Reserve Bank (FED) credit expanded over $3.1 trillion during the same period. Near zero interest rate policy (ZIRP) in seeming perpetuity has also impelled "investor" funds into speculative gambits across third world so-called emerging markets as they have pushed "mom and pop" savers once again into the eager hands of Wall Street, which has been busy devising ever more esoteric speculative vehicles for them. These trends in turn have driven the giddy reinflation of equity prices from 2008–2009.[54]

And atop this house of cards sits a looming Armageddon of $693 trillion (notional value) of derivative contracts according to BIS as of end Q2 2013.[55] Up from $632 trillion, as of Q4 2012.[56] Though there are those that see BIS figures as truncated and the total notional amount of these unregulated contracts coming in closer to a quadrillion. Which is approximately 14 times the world's annual GDP. And given that what we are talking about here is between $10 trillion to $20 trillion *actual* monies invested the leverage is simply mind boggling.[57] "Big government" is also eagerly continuing to play its part as bubble inflating handmaiden with US FED, European Central Bank, Bank of England, and now Bank of Japan pumping over $5 trillion into their economies between mid 2006 and January 2014.[58] As summarized by Doug Noland of *The Prudent Bear*:

> The world is awash in debt – virtually everywhere. The Fed and fellow central bankers have resorted to previously unimaginable measures to "reflate" global Credit and economies. They have manipulated short-term interest-rates to near zero. They have directly purchased Trillions of bonds and other instruments, in the process injecting Trillions into overheated securities markets . . .
>
> . . . This has ensured the ongoing rapid expansion of global debt, too much of it non-productive. The upshot has been unprecedented price inflation for most securities trading all over the world. Moreover, there has been the ongoing inflation in the already massive pool of speculative finance, derivatives and financial leveraging. Such Bubble Dynamics leave debt, securities market and economic structures acutely vulnerable to any reduction in Credit growth and/or central bank liquidity.[59]

22 *From the Merchant of Venice economy*

In the end, this coincidence of the predatory operations of "casino capital" with needs of people forced to eke out their livelihood in a neoliberal surrogate economy has extrapolated irresponsible "big government" backed speculation into what Colin Crouch dubs a "bizarre collective good".[60]

Humanity is now at its final crossroads. Indeed, so entrenched in our economic fabric is the idle M casino dynamic of "Merchant of Venice" expropriation masquerading as wealth generation that it is not clear whether it is even possible to save humanity as we know it on this point alone. Yet neoclassical economists along with much of the Left continue to talk about the old devil we know, capitalism, and debate policy solutions the choices among which might have given humanity some respite from the deluge up to the mid 1970s but now constitute the equivalent of Nero fiddling as Rome burns. Again, this all has little to do with "the market". Remember, already through the golden age, to maintain accumulation capital enlisted the Herculean extra-market support of the state. The neoliberal era commenced with the view that to reinvigorate capital it was necessary to "free" it from its golden age tethers. However the often surreptitious rule changes under the neoliberal banners of deregulation and liberalization gutted the production-centered capitalist economy and unleashed the predatory ravages of idle M. It cannot be emphasized more, that in the surrogate economy created by neoliberal "freeing" of capital, from the issuance of money itself to the generating and backstopping of the credit tsunami through the casino gaming that has ensnared virtually all economic activities in domestic and international economic spaces, it is "big government", "big bank", and "big MNCs" that are politically orchestrating current goings-on. Neoliberalism and the ideology of "the market" is simply the façade. But the policy magical mystery tour has now come to an end. Following the 2008–2009 meltdown, with "big government" madly printing money under ZIRP conditions, and so-called austerity expropriating what meager pickings are left on the bones of humanity, there is simply nowhere left to go except fundamental, thoroughgoing social change. And if we add in to our dire predicament issues of climate change, biospheric despoilment, and the corruption of global food provisioning systems then the discussion this book calls for becomes desperately more urgent.

Outline of the book

This book offers a roadmap to the exit from globalization. Our starting point in the following chapters is *theory*. The endpoint in the last chapters is the *practice* for making not only a livable future, but one of human flourishing.

Chapter 2 as advertised treats questions of the very theoretical foundations for thinking about substantive economic life and the possibilities that exist to transform it. Without the grasp of this *zero* of social change there is no passing *go* to *any* human future.

Chapter 3 clears the historical air around Soviet-style socialism.

Chapter 4 critically examines the most recent evidence on climate change and biospheric despoilment and explores the Green case for eco-sustainable social change and the framing of Green socio-economic alternatives.

Chapter 5 puts abiding questions of "the market" vs. "the state" along with motivation and innovation, as these have formed the centerpiece of debate over constraints on future directed economic designs, to long awaited, rest.

Chapter 6 advances a model for a successor society the building of which is realizable in the here and now. It demonstrates the material economic reproducibility of the future society, its eco-sanctity, progressive and wealth redistributive pedigree, and the way it eviscerates ills associated with capitalism.

Chapter 7 brings the book to conclusion with discussion of questions of social constituencies for change, and also examines the shrinking political options, and narrowing strategic roads, for progressive socio-economic transformation into the human future.

Notes

1 Slavoj Žižek, *Living in End Times* (London: Verso, 2011) p. 404.
2 Alain Badiou, *The Rebirth of History: Times of Riots and Uprisings* (London: Verso, 2012) pp. 5–6.
3 Richard N. Hunt, *The Political Ideas of Marx and Engels II: Classical Marxism 1850–1895* (Basingstoke: Macmillan, 1984) p. 326ff.
4 Phil Rockstroh, "Within the National (In)Security State", *Counterpunch*, http://www.counterpunch.org/2013/04/26/within-the-national-insecurity-state/.
5 Michael Hardt and Antonio Negri, *Empire* (Cambridge, MA: Harvard University Press, 2001).
6 Guy Standing, *The Precariat: The New Dangerous Class* (New York: Bloomsbury Academic, 2011).
7 Antonio Negri and Raf Valvola Scelsi, *Goodbye Mr. Socialism* (New York: Seven Stories Press, 2008).
8 Michael Hardt, "The Common in Communism", in Costas Douzinas and Slavoj Žižek, *The Idea of Communism* (London: Verso, 2010) p. 143.
9 Christopher Hill, *The World Turned Upside Down: Radical Ideas During the English Revolution* (Harmondsworth: Penguin Books, 1975) captures precisely such a social situation where political authority is vaporized following the execution of Charles I in 1649.
10 See Richard Westra, "Kautsky, Lukacs, Althusser and the Retreat from the Economic in Marxism – with the Return in Uno", *Political Economy Quarterly*, 44, 2 (2007) pp. 77–87.
11 Richard Westra, *Political Economy and Globalization* (London: Routledge, 2009).
12 David Harvey, *The Enigma of Capital and the Crises of Capitalism* (Oxford: Oxford University Press, 2011) pp. 215–16, 262.
13 Eric Hobsbawm, *How to Change The World: Reflections on Marx and Marxism* (New Haven: Yale University Press, 2011) p. 385.
14 Walden Bello, *Capitalism's Last Stand? Deglobalization in the Age of Austerity* (London: Zed Books, 2013) pp. 272–3.
15 Slavoj Žižek, "How to Begin from the Beginning", in Costas Douzinas and Slavoj Žižek, *The Idea of Communism* (London: Verso, 2010) p. 220.

24 *From the Merchant of Venice economy*

16 Colin Crouch, *The Strange Non-Death of Neoliberalism* (Cambridge: Polity Press, 2011) p. 17.
17 Thomas Sekine, "A Thought on Recent Trends in the World Economy", The Uno Newsletter: Rejuvenating Marxian Economics through Uno Theory, Vol. II, No. 9, November 2012, http://www.unotheory.org/en/news_II_9.
18 Charles Feinstein, "Structural Change in the Developed Countries during the Twentieth Century", *Oxford Review of Economic Policy*, 15, 4 (1999).
19 Martin Hart-Landsberg, *Capitalist Globalization: Consequences, Resistance, and Alternatives* (New York: Monthly Review Press, 2013) pp. 18–19.
20 Suzanne Berger, "How Finance Gutted Manufacturing", *Boston Review*, 1 April 2014, http://www.bostonreview.net/forum/suzanne-berger-how-finance-gutted-manufacturing.
21 Gérard Duménil and Dominique Lévy, *Capital Resurgent: The Roots of the Neoliberal Revolution* (Cambridge, MA: Harvard University Press, 2004) pp. 152–3.
22 Indeed evidence points to ICT as the main component of productivity gains in the US. See Berger, "How Finance Gutted Manufacturing".
23 Sekine, "A Thought on Recent Trends in the World Economy".
24 William Lazonick, "Financialization of the U.S. Corporation: What Has Been Lost, and How It Can Be Regained", Munich Personal RePEc Archive (MPRA) Paper N. 42307, 29 October 2012, http://mpra.ub.uni-muenchen.de/42307/, p. 6.
25 Gérard Duménil and Dominique Lévy, *The Crisis of Neoliberalism* (Cambridge, MA: Harvard University Press, 2011) pp. 151–2.
26 *Citigroup*, "Plutonomy: Buying Luxury, Explaining Global Imbalances", 16 October 2005, http://pissedoffwoman.wordpress.com/2012/04/12/the-plutonomy-reports-download/, accessed 22 April 2014.
27 Sekine, "A Thought on Recent Trends in the World Economy".
28 Richard Westra, *The Evil Axis of Finance: The US-Japan-China Stranglehold on the Global Future* (Atlanta, GA: Clarity, 2012).
29 See, for example, the discussion in Jan Kregel, "Minsky and the Narrow Banking Proposal: No Solution for Financial Reform", *Public Policy Brief*, no. 125, Levy Economics Institute of Bard College, 2012, http://www.levyinstitute.org/pubs/ppb_125.pdf.
30 International Monetary Fund, *Global Financial Stability Report: Grappling with Crisis Legacies*, September 2011, http://www.imf.org/external/pubs/ft/gfsr/2011/02/pdf/text.pdf, accessed June 20 2013.
31 Lazonick, "Financialization of the U.S. Corporation"; Berger, "How Finance Gutted Manufacturing".
32 Martin Hesse and Anne Seith, "Feeding the Bubble: Is the Next Crash Brewing?" *Spiegel Online*, 3 December 2013, http://www.spiegel.de/international/business/cheap-central-bank-money-contributes-to-dangerous-bubbles-a-936823.html.
33 United Nations Conference on Trade and Development (UNCTAD), *Trade and Development Report 2011*, http://unctad.org/en/docs/tdr2011_en.pdf, p. 3, accessed 20 June 2013.
34 On this see, for example, Erik F. Gerding, "The Shadow Banking System and its Legal Origins", 23 August 2011. Available at SSRN: http://papers.ssrn.com/sol3/papers.cfm?abstract_id=1990816, accessed 26 June 2013.
35 Global investment banking fees in 2007 were $103 billion. In 2012 they were still a significant $75 billion. See Martin Hesse, Thomas Schulz, Christoph Scheuermann, and Anne Seith, "Snakes and Ladders: Investment Banking on the Brink", *Spiegel Online*, 18 January 2013, http://www.spiegel.de/international/business/investment-banking-faces-massive-layoffs-and-identity-crisis-a-877710.html.

36 Michael Hudson, "Banking Wasn't Meant to Be Like This", 27 January 2012, http://michael-hudson.com/2012/01/banking-wasnt-meant-to-be-like-this/.
37 Michael Sauga and Ann Seith, "Out of Ammo? The Eroding Power of Central Banks", *Spiegel Online*, 16 April 2014, http://www.spiegel.de/international/business/central-banks-ability-to-influence-markets-waning-a-964757.html.
38 Crouch, *The Strange Non-Death of Neoliberalism*.
39 Richard Duncan, "A New Global Depression?" *New Left Review*, 77 (2012) pp. 7–9.
40 International Monetary Fund, Currency Composition of Official Foreign Exchange Reserves (COFER), http://www.imf.org/external/np/sta/cofer/eng/cofer.pdf, accessed 10 July 2013.
41 Justin Murray and Marc Labonte, "Foreign Holdings of Federal Debt", Congressional Research Service, 3 July 2012, http://www.fas.org/sgp/crs/misc/RS22331.pdf, accessed 17 April 2013.
42 Angus Maddison, *The World Economy: A Millennial Perspective* (Paris: OECD, 2006) p. 135, table 3–9.
43 OECD iLibrary, *Government at a Glance 2011*, http://dx.doi.org/10.1787/888932389873, accessed 4 July 2013.
44 See, for example, Philip Mattera, "Subsidizing the Corporate One Percent: Subsidy Tracker 2.0 Reveals Big-Business Dominance of State and Local Development Incentives", February 2014, http://www.goodjobsfirst.org/sites/default/files/docs/pdf/subsidizingthecorporateonepercent.pdf, on the sheer extent the top US MNCs are subsidized by various layers of government expenditure.
45 Duncan, "A New Global Depression?" p. 14ff.
46 Richard Duncan, *The New Depression: The Breakdown of the Paper Money Economy* (Singapore: John Wiley & Sons, 2012) p. 160.
47 Ibid., p. 149ff.
48 Duncan, "A New Global Depression?" pp. 26–9.
49 Westra, *Political Economy and Globalization*, Chapter 4.
50 The term "treadmill" is used by Moishe Postone, *Time, Labor and Social Domination* (Cambridge: Cambridge University Press, 1996) to denote the chrematistic of value augmentation characteristic of capital.
51 The notion of "capitalists without capitalism" follows usage by John R. Bell, *Capitalism and the Dialectic: The Uno-Sekine Approach to Marxian Political Economy* (London: Pluto Press, 2009).
52 Tyler Durdan, "Geithner's Legacy: The '0.2%' Hold $7.8 Trillion, Or 69% Of All Assets; And $212 Trillion Of Derivative Liabilities", Zero Hedge, 26 January 2013, http://www.zerohedge.com/news/2013-01-26/02-hold-78-trillion-assets.
53 Edward Fullbrook, "The Political Economy of Bubbles", *Real World Economics Review*, 59 (2012), http://www.paecon.net/PAEReview/issue59/Fullbrook59.pdf.
54 Doug Noland, "Latent Market Bubble Risks", *The Prudent Bear*, 21 June 2013, http://www.prudentbear.com/2013/06/latent-market-bubble-risks.html#.UedPMj-QjN4; idem, "April/May/June Dynamic?", *The Prudent Bear*, 21 March 2014, http://www.prudentbear.com/2014/03/aprilmayjune-dynamic.html#.U1dxFShpe_J.
55 Bank for International Settlements (BIS), "Statistical Release: OTC Derivatives Statistics at End-June 2013", November 2013, http://www.bis.org/publ/otc_hy1311.pdf, accessed 23 April 2014.
56 Bank for International Settlements (BIS), *BIS Quarterly Review*, June 2014, http://www.bis.org/statistics/dt1920a.pdf, accessed 20 July 2013.

57 Michael Sivy, *Time*, 27 March 2013, http://business.time.com/2013/03/27/why-derivatives-may-be-the-biggest-risk-for-the-global-economy/.
58 *Economist Intelligence Unit*, "The End Isn't Nigh: Central Bank Challenges as the Era of Cheap Money Enters a New Phase", 2013, http://www.eiuresources.com/EndOfCheapMoney/.
59 Noland, "Latent Market Bubble Risks".
60 Crouch, *The Strange Non-Death of Neoliberalism*, p. 117.

2 The zero of social change

As socio-economic orders putrefy, nowhere does the war waged by moribund ruling classes to maintain their stranglehold on power become more intense than in the world of ideas. In the dying days of the Middle Ages the ideology of divine right of kings was asserted with ever increasing ferocity to extend feudal rule. Today, the ideological battleground has shifted from hereditary rights of monarchs to economics. Neoclassical economists, particularly the cult of neoliberalism, are the new apostolate – and globalization as epiphany of "the market", the new creed. Yet, like the ideology of divine right of kings, the insidiousness of neoclassical economics resides precisely in the way it naturalizes an order that has long exhausted its capacity to manage human material economic affairs; and in the fashion by which it brooks no dissent. Yes, Divine inquisitions no longer exist. But beginning in the US and spreading across the world – Britain, Australia, Japan, to name a few states – all alternatives to neoclassical dogma are being exorcized from university economics curriculum by academic authorities, surely on advice from the neoliberal apostolate. Both the challenge to neoclassical ideological hubris, as well as the key to remaking human material existence for the pursuit of human flourishing into the future, this chapter argues, is to be found in Marxian *economic theory*.

It is fruitful to begin our explorations here through the prism of a recent two volume study by Ben Fine and Dimitris Milonakis.[1] In their opus, widely reviewed in heterodox economics and Marxist political economy circles, Fine and Milonakis assail the extirpating of all historical and social content from the field of economics by neoclassical "imperialism". In their own words:

> The efforts of Adam Smith, Karl Marx and the German Historical School for a unified social science based on the mutual intermingling of the social and the historical with the economic in a multidimensional political economy . . . gives way to a unified social science based on the colonisation of the social, the historical and the political by the economic. This colonisation takes place on the basis of a dehydrated set of (economic) principles following the ultimately desocialising and dehistoricisation effects of the marginalist revolution.[2]

Leaving to one side Fine and Milonakis's nuanced treatment of individual theoretical contributions to this trajectory we can set out several of the key steps as follows: First, Fine and Milonakis emphasize in both volumes the fact that economics "forgot history" in a dual sense. On the one hand, the historical origins of economics in political economy: on the other, historical change itself; within capitalism and in terms of comparing capitalism with other kinds of economy. Second, economics elides cutting-edge debate in epistemology or methodology of science/social science seeking on the one hand to emulate purportedly "value free" natural science yet, on the other hand, clinging to a long discredited methodology of that science, according to Fine and Milonakis.[3] Third, economics leeches the social from the discipline through a layered reductionism. Agency questions are reduced to those of individuals. The individual is reduced to optimizing, utility maximizing behavior. And economic theory is reduced in the neoclassical tradition to the quantification and "value free" rigorous analytic of such "rational" individual calculus.[4]

What is then to be done, ask Fine and Milonakis? The authors conclude the second volume of their work with a series of questions; most, in fact, long central to debate in Marxist political economy and heterodox economics circles. Their queries include that of "the appropriate value theory" for grappling with "issues of power and conflict" in capital accumulation, the role of classes and the state in capitalism, relations between the economic and political/cultural, relations between the capitalist and pre/non-capitalist, prospects for development under conditions of "globalization", and so forth. In their own words: "A new and truly interdisciplinary political economy, then, is necessary, focusing on the economic but fully and consciously incorporating the social and the historical from the outset".[5]

But given the vanishing or at best dystopian future humanity faces as it stands at the crossroads of its existence, is this really *all* the Left can muster to counter the ideology that enslaves the world? And what foundation does this self-styled "interdisciplinary political economy" provide for creative future directed economic thinking? It is astounding that from over 500 pages thematically focused on abandonment of the historical and social by mainstream economics Fine and Milonakis never tackle the abiding question of the very historicity of systematic thinking about economic life in the first place!

To recapitulate, it is *only* in the age of capital that it is possible to even speak of such a thing as an "economy" separate from religion, ideology, politics, culture, and so on, with which the economic had always been enmeshed. Bourgeois economics, which has its origins in what Marx referred to as "classical political economy" (commencing with the likes of William Petty, Adam Smith, and culminating in David Ricardo to be followed only by what Marx dubs "vulgar" economics) *never* problematizes capitalism as such. Rather, classical political economists commence their theorizations as mouthpieces of the ascendant bourgeois class touting the superiority of capitalism over precapitalist societies and proclaiming it as an "ideal" or natural order. Indeed, from the earliest days of capitalism, the view of "the market" operating unobstructed yielding an "optimal" outcome was established by bourgeois political economy. Sekine puts it thus: "Adam Smith already had talked of the *Invisible Hand of Providence*, which coordinated and reconciled all disparate and conflicting interests of human beings (like 'monads') into a world of the Leibnizian Pre-established Harmony".[6]

Fine and Milonakis, in laying emphasis upon purported general affinities of Marx and classical political economy – "Marx . . . conceives the object of political economy in the *broadest terms* [emphasis mine] to include both social and historical elements" they assert – elide the fundamental and revolutionary divergence of Marx from both classical political economy and the German Historical School, which Fine and Milonakis go on to discuss as the last bastion of "economic history" preceding the neoclassical deluge.[7] It is certainly true that Marx engaged in extensive philosophical, historical, and socio-legal studies before delving into analysis of the capitalist commodity economy. And that Marx's efforts here yielded his pithy statement of HM in the famous preface to *A Contribution to the Critique of Political Economy*.[8] But Marx's pronouncement in the preface that HM constituted the "guiding principle" of his further in-depth studies of capitalism was never intended to support the subsequent codification of HM as a "science" or even as a *theory* of history in any strong sense (we will discuss the proper status of HM in the Marxian research agenda below). Rather, the ideological hypothesis of HM that human history unfolded through a series of modes of production, with capitalism as the last class society that is then supplanted by socialism, ingrained in Marx the view of *capitalism as a historically delimited society*. And this firming of his socialist ideological world view immunized Marx, as he turned to in-depth study of capitalism, against infection by bourgeois ideology imbibed and strengthened by classical political economy, which upheld capitalism as a natural order.[9] With no grasp of what so clearly differentiates Marx's approach to economic theory from that of classical political economy as well as forms of vulgar economics, including neoclassical economics, which litter the field, Fine and Milonakis's huffing and puffing amounts to little more than comprador critique.

Indeed, Fine and Milonakis decry neoclassical economics clinging to discredited methodology of science. Yet, their work, similarly, takes little account of cutting edge developments in the philosophy science (for example, Fine and Milonakis belabor the "schism" between deductivism and "inductive/historical" method as if these are the only research strategies on the scientific menu).[10] Much of the debate action here, with particular relevance for grasping the approach to economic thinking of Marxian economic theory, swirls around Critical Realism (CR).[11] With the work of Roy Bhaskar going furthest "to provide a comprehensive alternative to the positivism that has usurped the title of science".[12]

CR's opening salvo entails the simultaneous confuting of positivist claims of empirical observation as the root of scientific discovery and billiard ball model of causal laws derived from that. According to CR, neither inductive research strategies that generalize from empirical cases to produce a rule nor axiomatic/deductive research strategies that proceed from rules established by inductive methods can produce *new* knowledge. Such knowledge, as manifested in major scientific discoveries, emerges from elimination of the "puzzlement" that crops up over phenomena deemed surprising in terms of both observation and limitations of current theories. Whether scientists avowedly conceptualize their endeavors in the following fashion or not, the fact of the matter is that acquiring new scientific knowledge proceeds through a *retroductive* mode of inference. Retroduction, that is, proposes something that cannot be directly observed other than in its "surface" manifestations and offers a hypothesis that it is believed if explored will lead to explanation of the phenomenon in question.[13]

Put differently, the process of scientific discovery cannot be reduced to empirical observation. Nor can scientific knowledge of the world be equated with empirical regularities or constant conjunctions of events as positivism would have it. As Bhaskar makes clear, observation manages only a limited grasp of events that, further, are often "out of phase" with such experiences. However, though the totality of events are never captured by empirical observation, even if they were, we would still be left with questions of what caused this or that event and why it occurred when it did. For Bhaskar, the very intelligibility of experiment in the natural sciences relates precisely to operations in "closed systems" designed to search for and identify in "open systems", causally efficacious structures or "generative mechanisms" that produce "the flux of phenomena that constitute the actual states and happenings of the world".[14]

CR's contradistinguishing a world of "deep" ontological structures and causally efficacious mechanisms with the "flat" ontology of positivism further challenges positivist argument over "value free" science that in turn has been used to foster a sharp divide between social science purportedly rooted in hermeneutics and a natural science defined in terms of making claims about empirical regularities for purposes of prediction. It is this divide that neoclassical economics upholds to assert its spurious physics-like qualities against other more (from its perspective) interpretive social sciences. As CR maintains, however, the business of both natural and social science is necessarily plied with a socially and historically constituted set of cognitive resources such that even the simplest empirics or observations are always theory laden. And, because in a world of ontological depth causal powers rarely if ever reveal themselves directly, discovery and explanation in both natural and social science is necessarily two-pronged: that is, it operates in two *dimensions*. The *transitive* dimension of science entails work on and through existing theories of the world. These theories are the "raw material" of science. On the other hand, the *intransitive object* of science is the causally efficacious structures of the mind independent world that science seeks to deepen knowledge of.[15]

Ultimately, CR forges links between what things do and what they are and what sort of knowledge about them we are able to produce. This in turn mandates existence of a correspondence, as put succinctly by Christopher Norris, "between the *causal structure* of those objects or events to be explained and the *logical structure* of the theory that purports to explain them".[16] On this account, what divide does exist demarcating natural from social science has nothing to do with facts vs. values opposition. Rather it relates firstly to the role physical experiment plays in natural science. Physical experiments in natural science create "closed systems" as previously noted, where a given mechanism is isolated and "decisively" tested.

It is this possibility that renders natural scientific theory predictive as well as explanatory. Social sciences cannot reproduce such physical experimental closure. Thus, for Bhaskar, social science is more "theoretical" and dependent upon conceptualization as well as "exclusively explanatory".[17] But stating this in no way detracts from the scientificity of social science. Whether we are talking about natural or social science as Andrew Collier declares:

> Theories which relegate mechanisms to a lower ontological league, as "theoretical entities", "logical constructs", etc., are refusing to allow causal criteria for reality – i.e. they will only let something through the ontological customs office if it is a possible object of experience.[18]

Though it may be pointed out here, and we will return to the implications of this for social science further on, Bhaskar ignored the role of *thought experiments* in the natural sciences. Thought experiments, however, are *real* experiments, and vary in their configuring and possibility of application as do physical experiments with the particular object and field of scientific enquiry.[19]

Second, as we previously maintain, both natural and social science commence their work in the transitive dimension with the socially and historically constituted cognitive resources and theories of the world that exist as the raw material of science. The shared approach here is what allows us to talk about social science in the same sense as natural science as capital-S science. But when we turn to the ontological or intransitive dimension of science the theoretical objects of natural and social science are altogether different. The difference, to be crisply clear, does *not* relate to questions of deep structural powers or causal mechanisms of intransitive objects in the natural and social worlds. Rather the difference is that causally efficacious structures of the social world are socially and historically constituted. That is, the social world *is a human creation*. It is made, transformed, and remade by us from the "inside". Nature, on the other hand, is *not* a human creation. Of course, we are part of nature in the sense of being natural objects, but this does not change the fact of the natural world being "outside" us; something that we humans can at best learn to "adapt", or "conform" to.

For example, though it is not possible to prevent earthquakes, science will aid us in predicting them and experiments assure us that structures we build withstand their predicted force. Neoclassical economics sleight of hand here, hence, is not simply methodological, to be then remedied by a "multidimensional" and/or "interdisciplinary political economy", as Fine and Milonakis would have it. Rather, it is ontological. That is, neoclassical economics along with its classical precursor upholds capitalism as a natural order, "irrevocably given to us" as Sekine puts it.[20] And, as such, it circumscribes human action to implementing policies that aid us in conforming or adapting to the force of "the economy". In fact, the focus of the "unified social science" of the German Historical School touted by Fine and Milonakis was precisely such "policy science" as it drew upon anti-Marxist intellectual currents.[21] The fundamental issue is not that economics "forgot history" or reduced the social to market optimizing behavior (we will return

32 *The zero of social change*

to this last point), but that bourgeois economics in toto along with Fine and Milonakis "forgot" the subject matter of economic theory is socially and historically constituted. And all are oblivious to the ramifications this carries for producing economic knowledge.

Capitalist reification and the upside-down world

In his widely referenced contribution to addressing questions of the historicity of economic theory, economic historian Karl Polanyi refers to the peculiarity of capitalism in terms of the way the economic appears to "disembed" from the social (religion, ideology, culture, politics, and so forth) with which it had always been enmeshed prior to the capitalist era.[22] But Polanyi was never clear on what is behind this phenomenon of the economic levitating, if you will, from the social.[23] Writing over a half century before Polanyi, Marx, working through a broad spectrum of socially and historically constituted cognitive resources – philosophy, history, socio-legal studies, classical political economy – also grasped the ontological peculiarity of capital as an object of scientific study in the social world. I thus agree with Richard Marsden that Marx would have followed a retroductive mode of scientific inference to reach his conclusion that to produce deep structural knowledge of capital beyond its empirical manifestations, as Marx ultimately did in *Capital*, required the highest level of epistemological sensitivity to its discrete social ontology.[24]

It is important at this point to interject into the discussion that for CR mind independent reality is marked not only by a deep structural "layering" of causally efficacious mechanisms but by ontological "strata". In the words of Andrew Collier,

> [The] differentiation and stratification of the sciences is not due to any historical accidents such as which emerged first or how university departments are organized . . . [Rather] there are also intrinsic divisions based on real stratification of the aspects of nature of which these sciences speak.[25]

Ontological stratification in this sense has a "vertical" dimension involving operation of causal mechanisms of a particular stratum as well as a "horizontal" dimension in that explanation of a specific phenomenon may demand understanding the confluence of varying causally efficacious powers and recourse to different sciences. The concept of "emergence" is then deployed by CR to deal with the way new things happen in the world that may be linked to other phenomena in an "ordered" fashion – entailing both vertical and horizontal lines of explanation in their apprehension by science – but are not simply reducible to them.[26]

Unfortunately, while CR has treated at length questions of ontological stratification in the natural world, far less has been done with regards to ontological stratification in the *social world*. As noted above, if we take CR criteria for scientific enquiry as causal/explanatory movement from observable phenomena to generative mechanisms, then the relational or structured ontological properties of society make it a fitting object of capital-S science. But Bhaskar does not take us substantively beyond this. Though this is not the place to exhaustively explore these issues, the agency/structure debate that animates his analysis of social ontology is certainly an abiding problematic in the social sciences. There is also nothing "wrong" with his elaboration of a transformational model of social activity (TMSA) as a general resolution for this. Human beings do act purposively. And the purposive action of human beings unfolds in encountered social or "relational" circumstances not of their own choosing (see Box 2.1). The characterizing of psychological and social science in terms of different generative mechanisms of each as discrete strata also constitutes an original contribution to bridging the social action social structure divide for social explanation in a non-reductionist fashion.[27]

Box 2.1

Danermark et al. define structure as being composed "of a set of internally related objects". They then argue that in both major competing paradigms of the structure/agency debate – methodological collectivism and methodological individualism – there exists a "conflation" of structure and agent. In methodological collectivism the conflation operates "downwards" in rendering individuals epiphenomena of social structures. In methodological individualism the conflation operates "upwards" in that structures become epiphenomena of self-seeking individual behavior. In a third paradigm advanced to resolve the debate – so-called "structuration" theory – there is a "central conflation" in that structure and agency are seen to "only exist by virtue of each other". Bhaskar's TMSA, on the other hand Danermark et al. maintain, offers a fourth model consistent with arguments made in defense of the other models but which moves beyond them utilizing CR's concepts of emergence and strata to that effect. They conclude: "The most productive contribution to social practice that social science can make . . . is the examination of social structures, their powers and liabilities, mechanisms and tendencies, so that people, groups and organizations may consider them in their interaction and so – if they wish – strive to change or eliminate existing social structures and to establish new ones".

See Berth Danermark, Mats Ekström, Liselotte Jakobsen, and Jan Ch. Karlsson, *Explaining Society: Critical Realism in the Social Sciences* (London: Routledge, 2002) pp. 178–82.

It is telling that Fine and Milonakis in *From Economics Imperialism to Freakonomics* (pp. 153–58) hang their hat on structuration theory for their "interdisciplinary and multidimensional political economy". This follows from their inability to grasp the ontological peculiarity of capital as an object of study in the social world that calls for an approach to questions of structure and agency divergent from those that are founded on transhistorical categories such as "individual" and "society".

Returning to Marx, it was his genius combined with a socialist ideological world view to question that which sailed over the head of classical political economy with its bourgeois ideological inclinations. As well as that which astute economic historian Karl Polanyi never asks. That is, what *caused* the economy in the capitalist era to suddenly appear to levitate from the social and why, if "the economy" has always been present, have we only now become aware of this and attempted disciplined study of it?

Marx's retroduction posited how under specific historical conditions, as marketization increasingly penetrated internal life of human communities, a *subset* of human activity, the purposive economic activity of material production in *capitalist* society, came to manifest unique ontological properties of a discrete generative mechanism marking it off as an emergent strata of the social world. Marx described these properties variously as the "alien", "upside-down", "fetishistic" bent of capital that converted *concrete* interpersonal social relations of production into *abstract* impersonal "relations among things"; these "things" – commodities, money, capital – then taking on a "life of their own". It is therefore not simply a question of the economic "disembedding" from the social à la Polanyi, but capital as a historically constituted object of the social world turning the tables if you will on the very subjects of its social and historical constitution to objectify them as it wields the social for its own self-aggrandizement, the augmentation of value. And it is this unique ontological propensity toward *reification* that is the very condition of possibility for economic theory. Put differently, the historicity of "economics" is the age of capital precisely because economic life – something without which human society would be an impossibility – appears *transparently* therein for the very first time in human history. Of course deploying the term "transparent" here is not to suggest that the deep structural or generative mechanisms of capital reveal themselves directly, or that knowledge of capitalism may be attained without theoretical effort in the transitive dimension of science. Rather, it is intended to capture what in fact is a fundamental tenet of CR bringing ontology back in to natural and social science: the relationship between what capital *is* as an emergent strata and theoretical object in the social world, and the sort of knowledge of it we are able to produce.

Which brings us to the next question: If the upside-down reified world of capital is the very condition of possibility for economic theory, then what kind of social scientific theory must economic theory be?

Marx left us with few direct remarks on the role of the ontology of capital for theory construction. And no part of the Marxian research agenda has been as befuddling as Marx's avowal of his debt to G.W.F. Hegel and his affirmation of the dialectical epistemology of *Capital*.[28] But let us build on what Marx did say. In the preface to the first German edition of *Capital* Marx declares how in every science "beginning[s are] difficult . . . In the analysis of economic forms . . . neither microscopes nor chemical reagents are of use. The force of abstraction must replace both".[29] At first glance, this is a rather unremarkable claim that conceptual abstractions regularly made by scientists assist them in better understanding their world. However, when Marx's words here are placed within the context of his retroduction of capital as an ontologically peculiar self-reifying social science object their significance becomes clearer. That is, the conversion of concrete interpersonal economic relations into abstract relations among things adverts to the ontologically significant fact that as the products of human labor are subsumed by the commodity and money forms their qualitative differences are suppressed as the differentiation of commodities in the capitalist market proceeds in quantitative terms. In this way, the resultant abstraction (from the sensuous qualities of things to relate them in quantitative terms) is grounded in action of a particular kind, not in thought. And it is this ontologically unique "force of abstraction" characteristic of capital that constitutes a necessary condition of dialectical theorizing. As succinctly summarized by Robert Albritton:

> . . . The basis for Marxian political economy is real abstraction, but real abstractions are not always recognisable without a theoretical effort that gets to the necessary inner connections of their deep structure. "Real abstraction" implies that it is fundamentally capital itself that does the abstracting, and it is we who discover its inner logic, a logic that it certainly does not wear on its sleeve.[30]

But there exists another issue in apprehending the role of dialectics in economic theory. Marx's cryptic remarks on Hegel's dialectic – that for Hegel, "the real world is only the external, phenomenal form of 'the Idea'. With me, on the contrary, the ideal is nothing else than the material world reflected by the human mind, and translated into forms of thought". And that "materialism" turns Hegel "right side up"[31] – led to the exciting but erroneous view that it was possible to graft the dialectic onto "matter" (nature) or "materialism" manifested in human history. However, as Stefanos Kourkoulakos explains, while formal or axiomatic logic is operable in varied methodological contexts and may be directed toward explanation of a multiplicity of phenomena across the sciences, the dialectic is a "special purpose" or "content specific" method demanding a theoretical object with unique ontological properties for its operation. These properties being, that the object is self-abstracting, self-reifying, self-infintizing, self-purifying, and self-revealing (this latter in the sense of the subject matter "telling its own story" from the inside). Hegel's quest was for philosophy (which was the science of his day) to arrive at "objective" knowledge or capital-T truth of the universe by defeating epistemological scepticism in all its forms.[32] The possibility of this for Hegel resided in the belief that such knowledge or capital-T truth had a "storyteller". This was God or the Absolute Idea. Truth of the universe was accessible to philosophy because it is bound up in a schema of logical interconnections determined by the Absolute. Hegel believed he could reach that truth by tracing out links to it in categories of philosophy that the Absolute had been revealing, piecemeal through the ages, across the history of philosophy. The dialectic, then, was the special purpose method for this task. To translate this into the language of CR, Hegel's generative mechanism is the revelatory procedure of the Absolute. And the dialectical structure of Hegel's theory purportedly corresponds to the causal structure of the Subject writ large (God).[33]

Hegel's dialectic earns the appellation *idealism* here not because Hegel in any way denied the existence of the material world (he did not). But because consummating the dialectic was predicated not upon taking soundings from a mind independent reality; rather it involved the self-abstracting or self-purifying of thought *itself*. That is, thought becomes *pure* and objective as it divests itself of its materiality in terms of the one-sided, subjective views, prejudices, and so on that mark it to reach Absolute capital-T truth.

Therefore, to turn Hegel "right side up" by deploying the special purpose dialectical methodology in the material world requires a theoretical object that is either an Absolute, or evidences Absolute-like characteristics.[34] It was Marx's great acumen to discern that *one* such object exists in the material world – capital. That legions of Marxists overlooked this, Sekine suggests, most likely relates to their grand pretensions that saw in Hegel's dialectic the attempt to arrive at capital-T truth of the universe; and disappointment that instead of a theory that detailed everything on the large canvas of either the natural world or human history in toto, Marx's dialectic grasped the reification of but a subset of human activity, the purposive economic activity of material production in capitalist society.[35]

Marx, it is too often forgotten, never completed *Capital* in his lifetime. And he bemoaned pressures to publish it before the intricacies of the dialectic of capital were better worked out. In an 1865 letter to Engels, Marx declares:

> But I cannot bring myself to send anything off until I have the whole thing in front of me. Whatever shortcomings they may have, the advantage of my writings is that they are an artistic whole, and this can only be achieved through my practice of never having things printed until I have them in front of me *in their entirety*. This is impossible with Jacob Grimm's method which is in general better with writings that have no dialectical structure.[36]

Thus, while *Capital* could never have been written without Marx's grasp of dialectical reasoning, it would fall into the hands of Japanese Marxian economists Kozo Uno and Thomas Sekine to more fully capture the dialectical inner logic of capital and elaborate it in economic theory that consummates Marx's project in *Capital*.[37] It is Uno and Sekine's refinement and completion of Marx's project in *Capital* that I follow when explicating lacunae in what Marx left us at his passing.

Let us however get back to the question of "beginnings". The operationalizing of the special purpose dialectical epistemology on its self-reifying, self-revealing object of knowledge necessarily commences with a primary category containing the fundamental "contradiction" or categorical opposition that drives the dialectical synthesis forward. For Hegel, as Sekine explains, the categorical opposition is between *being* and *naught* (nothing), where being indicates the presence of the Absolute, naught the absence. However, because naught offers scant resistance to being, thus assuring the ultimate triumph of the Absolute Idea (and subjugation of naught in perpetuity), Hegel's idealist dialectic is rendered "lopsided" and his dialectical reasoning often "forced and unnatural".[38]

As touched on above, the unfolding of categories in the materialist dialectic of capital is "reality assisted" in the sense that the "force of abstraction" propelling the dialectical synthesis is a *real* contradiction. That is, Marx commences the dialectic in *Capital* with the most elemental indicator of capitalism – the *commodity*. It is within the commodity that the contradiction between *value* and *use value*, the fundamental contradiction of capital, as well as driving material force of capitalist reification and the dialectic, first appears. Given the recent overflow in Marxist writing bandying the term "contradiction" about, we cannot emphasize more that to the extent contradictions of capital exist, they are all fundamentally bound to that between value and use value, which is why Marx begins *Capital* with this contradiction. Use value, then, is the material foundation of human existence, and the qualitative, transhistorical side of the contradiction. Value is the historically specific, capitalist, quantitative side. But *Capital* is *not* a genetic theory of capitalism: the *commodity* Marx is theorizing is that which exists in a *capitalist* economy. As elegantly captured by Robert Albritton:

> ... [A] much misunderstood and sometimes maligned category of dialectics is "contradiction". The use of "contradiction" in dialectical reasoning does not violate the law of non-contradiction in formal logic. To say that within the commodity form there is a contradiction between value and use-value is to say that they are mutually dependent and mutually opposed semi-autonomies. Mutual dependency implies that a value must always be attached to use-value, and mutual opposition implies that as pure quantity, self-expanding value must overcome difficulties posed by incorporating use-value as pure quality. Value must incorporate use-value without compromising its self-expanding quantitativeness, which it does by producing a sequence of categories that overcome and subsume successive use-value obstacles.[39]

The claim by Fine and Milonakis that Marx adopts a "logico-historical mode of presentation" recapitulating "the sequence in which . . . categories appeared historically" is one of the most hackneyed and debilitating impositions Marxian economic theory has faced.[40] Its Marxist lineage can be traced to the work of Second International doyen Karl Kautsky who maintained the existence of a "petty commodity" society as historical precursor to capitalism.[41] The phantasmagoria of Kautsky's petty commodity precursor is paralleled by neoclassical economics conceptualizing of capitalist "exchange" as nothing more than a simple extension of barter for which humans, à la Adam Smith, are naturally programmed (we will pursue this further in Chapter 4 discussion of Green alternatives). This is the ideological concomitant to neoclassical naturalizing of capitalism through its positivist methodology because it places the focus upon the transhistorical: *use value* in *consumption*. Whether we are talking about Smith's mythical meeting between beaver trapper and deer hunter or the benefit maximizing individual/household consumer today the historical specificity of capitalism is lost. And Fine and Milonakis's critical call to "rehydrate" neoclassical economics "rational" self-seeking agent of consumption with social and historical attributes is really no remedy here.

Marx, on the other hand, rightly approaches the commodity in *capitalist* society from the perspective of the *seller*. A commodity is a commodity precisely because its owner is *not* interested in its use value but in its *value*. Remember, capitalism is a society in which the overarching social goal is the augmentation of value or abstract mercantile wealth. The direct producers in capitalist society have been "freed" from the means of production and land that confronts them as capital and private property. What they have to sell on the market is their labor power that capital then buys and sets in motion producing *any* good for which there exists social demand and opportunities for profit-making. Put differently, capital is *indifferent* to use value except as a byproduct of value augmentation. Marx conceptualizes the commodity (from the perspective of the seller) as the "cell form" of capitalism because he wants to expose the idiosyncratic operation of capitalist profit-making. And the commodity *already* contains within it the basis for the logical unfolding of all the economic categories of capital to that end.[42] As Albritton puts it:

> Just as simple cells divide and differentiate in the formation of biological organisms, so does the commodity form divide and differentiate in the formation of capital as an integrated system of self-valorizing value . . . . The theoretical starting point for Marx . . . is the . . . commodity form, through whose development and differentiation the necessary inner connections of the basic categories of capital can be derived.[43]

The mode of dialectical exposition, therefore, proceeds from the abstract to the concrete. But "concrete" does *not* mean empirical concrete. It refers to the *concrete-synthetic* or concrete-in-thought where we begin with the most abstract least specified concept and generate more specified concepts until the dialectical circle is consummated.[44]

The dialectic of capital that reconstructs and completes Marx's three volume *Capital* consists of three *doctrines* that correspond to the organizational pattern of Hegel's *The Science of Logic* (see Box 2.3) and roughly with the construction of *Capital* as Marx left it at his passing. The *doctrine of circulation* and *doctrine of production* are commensurate to materials in Volumes 1 and 2 of *Capital*: the *doctrine of distribution* to material in Volume 3.[45]

In the *doctrine of circulation* the contradiction inhering in the commodity that commences *Capital* and propels the dialectic forward involves value seeking to escape its use value encumbrance by expressing itself in terms of "price". That is, as a definite quantity of the use value of other commodities. The further specification of this expression leads the dialectic to *money*. Money is the commodity, such as gold for example, the use value of which the world of commodities express themselves in. Thus, the first function of money is as a *measure of value*. That is, money becomes the social connector or social nexus in capitalist society because it can purchase *any* commodity without qualitative restriction. The second function of money is its role as *active money* or means of exchange. The third function of money is as a store of value – idle money or idle M, as referred to in Chapter 1 – subsisting outside the process of commodity circulation awaiting the opportunity for conversion into capital. The doctrine of circulation concludes with the understanding of capital as money that makes more money or M – M`. The dynamic of M – M`, in the form of antediluvian usurers or "loan capital", as noted above, is expropriation. M – M` restated as M – C – M` (where C denotes the commodity) is the characteristic form of *merchant capital*. Merchant capital, however, finds itself wholly encumbered by use value because the merchant is simply the middleman who intervenes between producer and consumer. It is only *industrial capital* that is freed from use value encumbrances under the specific historical conditions where human labor power is commodified. For then it can purchase that labor power on the market and set it in motion producing *any* good for its abstract purpose of mercantile wealth augmentation.

The *doctrine of production* further specifies the contradiction between value and use value in terms of its "new" categorical opposition; that being the contradiction between the chrematistic operation of capital as self-augmenting, self-valorizing value and the production of use values in general. Expressing the contradiction between value and use value in this fashion drives the dialectic into the inner sanctum of capital where the dialectical ordering of categories necessitates introduction of the labor theory of value and exploration of how the validity of the law of value and fundamental material economic reproducibility of capitalism as an historical society imply each other. That is, use value constitutes the transhistorical foundation of human existence. However, capital produces commodities not for their use value but for the production of surplus value that the commodities contain. The production of surplus value necessitates the specifically capitalist mode of production characterized by the material accouterment of industrial capital – manufacturing and factory production along with the commodification of labor power (see Box 2.2).

Put differently, as capital subsumes the real economic life of human societies to wield it for its abstract purpose of surplus value production or value augmentation it must nevertheless meet what Japanese Marxian economist Kozo Uno refers to as *general norms of human material existence* as a byproduct.[46] Otherwise capitalism could never exist as a form of human society. Approached from but another angle, the labor and production process entails the metabolic interchange between human beings and nature. And it furnishes the use values without which human society would not be possible. While the chrematistic operation of capital is hellbent upon augmentation of abstract mercantile wealth, it must nevertheless viably reproduce human material life along the way. The *doctrine of production* therefore moves from the study of capital as a production-process "inside" its manufacturing/factory system, to the circulation-process of capital "outside" the factory that entails coordination and non-interruption of operations across all separate units of capital, to the reproduction-process of capital that captures the self-expansion of aggregate social capital to confirm the possibility of capitalism as an historical society. The material of Volume 2 of Marx's *Capital*, including the famous *reproduction schemes*, is devoted to the latter two ends.

> **Box 2.2**
>
> All factors of production – land, labor, and capital – contribute to the production of use values. However, the historical distinctiveness of capitalism as an economic order is that use value life, the transhistorical foundation of all human existence, is subsumed by the motion of value and wielded by capital for its own self-aggrandizement. The historical possibility of a capitalist economy therefore is predicated upon a factor of production with the inherent dual property of being use value *and* value productive. To be value productive the factor must be both abstract-general (for it is in the form of abstract constituents, money, and capital, that wealth in capitalist society is measured) and concrete-useful (for the furnishing of concrete use values to sustain human life, as in all human societies, must necessarily remain the byproduct of augmenting value). Of all the factors, it is only productive labor that is simultaneously abstract-human and concrete-useful. The other factors of production – land and capital – are use value specific or concrete-useful alone.
>
> It is *only* in capitalist society, a society where accumulation of abstract wealth is the fundamental social goal, where the emphasis is paradigmatically placed upon the abstract-human attribute of labor. That is, to produce value, capital must render productive labor *indifferent* to the production of particular use values. Rather, capital requires labor power available to apply to the production of *any* use value in response to the changing patterns of social demand and opportunities for profit-making. The historical prerequisite for this is the divesting of labor of means of production including land to "free" labor, converting it into a commodity available in the market for capital to deploy for its abstract purpose. In this sense, *the condition of possibility or sine qua non of capitalism as an historical society is the commodification of labor power*. Restating this in the language of the dialectic, capital manages to solve the contradiction between value and use value by surmounting the impediments to value augmentation faced by merchant capital through its internalization of material reproductions' very wellspring.
>
> Proving the validity of the labor theory of value confirms that capitalism, a society where the product of labor assumes the form of a commodity, is materially reproducible as an historical mode of organizing human economic affairs.
>
> To grasp how capital produces surplus value requires understanding of the concept, *necessary labor*. Necessary labor quite simply is the work direct producers must perform to reproduce their livelihood. This, as Marx made clear with the well known example from *Capital* of Robinson Crusoe on his island, may even entail working to stock up on things for a rainy day. What Marx refers to as *surplus labor* is performed by direct producers *only* in class societies. In capitalist society the price the capitalist pays to deploy

commodified labor power, or the *wage* the free laborer is remunerated with must, at minimum, be equivalent to the cost of those commodities in the market necessary for the survival of the worker (which includes also the reproduction of workers as a class). Put differently, the prices of all commodities, including labor power and the necessities of human sustenance, are set in the capitalist market. Wages, or the value of labor power, must be equal to the product of the workers' necessary labor, both measured in money terms.

Thus, to offer a microcosmic illustration of capitalist production, let us picture a capitalist textile business that invests $100 in machinery or means of production, $50 in raw materials, and $50 in wages for commodified labor power. If in four hours of working for the capitalist our laborer can produce commodities equal in value to the $50 in wages that is the money measure of the laborer's necessary labor then, supposing means of production are depreciated and raw materials exhausted in a day, factoring in the $150 of value these transfer to the product and the $50 worth of value added by the laborer as equivalent to his/her necessary labor, we end up with the $200 with which we began. In other words, following our assumption – labor power purchased in the market for its abstract quality of being amenable to indifferent application in producing any use value in demand, then set into motion by capital to produce one such good – *value* has been created but not *surplus value* or profit. For surplus value to be created, and the augmenting of value characteristic of the capitalist economy to be realized, workers must toil for more time than is simply required to produce the equivalent of their necessary labor; which is precisely what occurs in capitalist society where the capitalist owners of the social means of production set the time of the *working day*. So, in fact, with an eight-hour working day, where in four hours the worker produces $50 of value equivalent to his/her necessary labor, in four further hours of surplus labor, the worker produces $50 of surplus value or profit for the capitalist as $250 dollars ultimately emerges, like magic, from the capitalist production process.

In the *doctrine of distribution*, which builds on the incomplete and often fragmentary material of Volume 3 of Marx's *Capital*, the contradiction between value and use value manifests itself in but another form. That is, on establishing the material economic reproducibility or "viability" of capital "in general", as a society in which use value life is wielded for the abstract social goal of value augmentation, the dialectic is propelled to treat the more concrete-in-thought operations of the historically specific *capitalist market*. It is in the capitalist market that capital must reconcile its fundamental indifference to use value in its chrematistic of surplus value production and value augmentation with the heterogeneity of use value that demands capital adopts varying techniques to produce divergent use values. Thus the contradiction between value and use value is expressed in the *doctrine of distribution* in terms of the contradiction between the capitalist indifference to use value and the unavoidability of technical variations in use value production. To surmount this use value encumbrance the surplus value produced by capital "in general", or as a whole, is distributed to each individual capital in proportion to the magnitude of their initial investment. It is in this context that the dialectic deals with exigencies of capitalist competition, the formation of an average rate of profit, the divergence of production-prices from values in the capitalist market, and the oscillations of capitalist business cycles through prosperity and depression phases.[47]

However, in treating the distribution of surplus value among individual sectors and units of industrial capital the dialectic is driven to confront other claimants on surplus value. The first of these is landed property. Land is not directly involved in the production of value. Yet it is a crucial factor in the production of use values as landlords rent land to capitalist farmers who hire wage labor to produce commodities for sale on the capitalist market. Landed property also plays a role in maintaining capitalist relations of production in that its modern existence coincides with the debarring of peasantries from the land. Thus capital surrenders a portion of surplus value to landed property in the form of *ground rent* to tie landed property owners into the capitalist market. But in ceding a portion of surplus value to an entity *external* to it, capital establishes the principle of property ownership as entitlement to an income.

On establishing this principle with landed property capital demonstrates its characteristic cunning by seeking to "reconceptualize" itself as simply an asset or property that is automatically entitled to an income stream – in this case *interest*. The specification of the category interest first involves the delegation by industrial capital of its circulation functions to modern loan capital that is composed of industrial capital's own funds socialized in the banking system that in turn makes the funds available to industrial capital as commercial credit to accelerate value augmentation. *Commercial capital* similarly avails itself of funds socialized in the banking system that it puts to use contributing indirectly to surplus value production through hastening the sale of commodities that decreases the turnover time of capital as profits are rapidly plowed back into manufacturing activity of industrial capital. Interest is therefore the most fetishized category of capital exposed by dialectical economic theory because of the way it operates to efface all traces of the subsumption by capital of use value life in the labor and production process to service value augmentation.

This is the case because commercial labor as in age old merchant activity of buying and selling commodities appears as the only "work" capitalists perform. The profit accruing to commercial capital similarly appears not as a portion of surplus value ceded to it by industrial capital but as merchant or *entrepreneurial profit*. With the dividing of commercial profit into interest and entrepreneurial profit, in that our entrepreneurs must pay for the money they borrowed to pursue their buying and selling operations, the idea is crystallized "of capital *as an automatically interest-bearing force*" such that even industrial capital "begins to view its own capital as 'funds' lent to it by itself" and *its* profits springing from the activity of wily entrepreneurs.[48]

Hence the dialectic of capital is consummated with the commodity with which it began. Only now it is capital presenting itself as a commodity or asset entitled to an income stream that, like Hegel's Absolute, has divested itself of all qualitative use value materiality to become pure and objective "quantity" or value bent upon self-expansion.

> **Box 2.3**
>
> On the question of the intriguing homology of Marx's *Capital* and Hegel's *Logic* with respect to the dialectical structure of both it is worth quoting Albritton in *Dialectics and Deconstruction in Marxist Theory* (p. 78) at length. Albritton declares:
>
>> I find myself unable to fully assess Hegel's success in theorising the deep structure of thought in *The Science of Logic*. And yet it is clear to me that Hegel's development of the structure of dialectical logic is without parallel . . . Why is it that the basic structures of the dialectic of the deep structure of thought and of the deep structures of capital are so similar? Was Hegel's *The Science of Logic* a giant displacement of the logic of capital or of the deep structure of capitalist rationality onto thought in general? Or is it simply that capital as an object of knowledge is, like thought, a highly "organic" object, such that the structure of the necessary inner connections is similar in the two objects? What is certain is that the structure of the dialectic in Hegel's *The Science of Logic* provides the basis for establishing the objectivity of the dialectic of capital.

To sum up, the dialectic of capital that refines and completes Marx's project in *Capital* unfolds each and every category of capital to produce the definitive economic theory of an "economic society" par excellence. Unlike the phantasmagoric world of neoclassical economics, neither the economic theory nor the commodity economic society is a model invented according to this or that ideological whim. Capital dialectically constructs its commodity economy by purging or "purifying" human material life of all extra-economic, extra-capitalist encumbrances. Dialectical economic theory extrapolates this process of "real abstraction" to conclusion in what Uno and Sekine dub the *theory of a purely capitalist society*.

Restating this in the language of CR, the deep causal or generative mechanism of capital is its self-reifying, self-abstracting inner logic. The dialectical structure of the theory corresponds to the self-reifying, self-abstracting ontology of its object – capital. But dialectical economic theory provides more than *explanation* of the causal power of the inner logic of capital. Uniquely in the social sciences the ontological structure of capital undergirds theoretical closure akin to a closed system created by experiment in the natural science. In this sense, we can talk about dialectical economic theory of capital as thought experiment, the possibility for which is tied to the peculiar nature of the object.[49] And, as a thought experiment, where we listen to capital "tell its own story" through an objective process of logical self-synthesis, exposing each and every one of its inner secrets, dialectical economic theory gives us a timeless *definition* of what capital *is* in its most fundamental incarnation. It is this definition, therefore, that constitutes the touchstone for elaboration of Marxian political economy, the research agenda of HM, and the Marxian theorizing of socialism.

Concretizing the logic of capital in Marxian political economy

One is struck reading *Capital* by the way Marx seems to "mix" dialectical exposition as in his discussion of the commodity form with examination of cotton manufacturing as the representative *type* of capital existing in mid-nineteenth-century century Britain and extended historical excursus of this and that political economic aspect of the society of his day. But as Albritton makes so abundantly clear in his meticulously documented book, Marx well understood that even during his lifetime because economic phenomena in capitalist history appeared with predictable distortions they could not be addressed in terms of the inner logic of capital alone. And that Marx strongly inveighed against the so-called "logico-historical" method Fine and Milonakis attribute to him.[50] It is true that *Capital* and other writings of Marx such as the *Communist Manifesto* are rife with remarks to the effect that capital was tending toward the subsumption of the totality human use value life in actual history; its marketizing logic soon to be "battering down all Chinese walls" in Marx's words. But this is because from Marx's historical vantage point in mid-nineteenth-century Britain it did appear that capital was "purifying" its environment of non-economic, non-capitalist encumbrances. Marx, on the other hand, also believed the march of capital in history would be crushed by socialist revolution before such a horror came to be. Further, Marx passed away in advance of the momentous economic transformations of the late nineteenth, early twentieth centuries that brought to an end the historical tendency of capital to purge its environment of the non-economic and non-capitalist. However, the fact that a purely capitalist society does not materialize in history *in no way vitiates* the methodological correctness of Marx's dialectical theorization of the inner logic of capital. It simply saddles Marxian political economy with a theoretical problem Marx was not pressed to solve; though one for which Marx left a suggestive outline in *Capital*.

The resolution to that theoretical problem requires, on the one hand, consummating the deep reificatory inner logical tendencies of capital as dialectical economic theory or thought experiment of a purely capitalist society to provide a timeless definition of what capital in its most fundamental incarnation *is*. Again, the epistemological warrant for such a procedure is the actual historical tendency for capital to reify human material life. If capital did not exhibit such a tendency economic theory would be impossible. On the other hand, Marxian political economy is tasked with bridging the theoretical divide between the logical tendencies of capital and their historical manifestations. Indeed, Fine and Milonakis adverting to the "colonization" of the social, historical, political by neoclassical economics in the quote at the beginning of this chapter is in fact a far too deferent reference to conceptualizations of a vacuous discipline laden with bourgeois ideological presuppositions of capitalism as an ideal or natural order. In other words, it is capitalist reification that is doing the "colonizing". Neoclassical economics is just the messenger boy. But Fine and Milonakis's solution of simply pouring the social, historical, and political back into this "economics" in an ad hoc fashion is a recipe for a muddled conceptual soup.

A more robust scientific procedure that builds upon the unique ontology of capital, Marx's layered emphasis in *Capital,* and the contribution of Kozo Uno to debate on *periodizing* capitalism sparked by theories of imperialism, is to approach the matter in terms of *levels of analysis* predicated upon levels of logical *necessity*.[51] Going back to Sekine's point about the lopsidedness of Hegel's dialectic due to the fact that naught puts up scant resistance to being and its ultimate dialectical synthesizing the end of the matter as the Absolute Idea then reigns in perpetuity. In the synthesizing of capitalism by dialectical economic theory, abstract, quantitative value prevails over use value *only* to the extent that it is permitted to do so by use value. And, in the end, because capitalism is a historically transient society, it is use value as the embodiment of concrete material wealth for human beings that wins out when capitalism, a society that reproduces human economic life as a byproduct of value augmentation, is cast into the dustbin of history. This, however, puts the spotlight on use value and the way Marx permitted value to subsume the totality of use value life by assuming an *ideal* use value space.

In dialectical economic theory all inputs and outputs of society's material production and reproduction process are specified in terms of the fact that they are all subsumable under the commodity form. Even the productive technology of industrial capitalist manufacturing is materially specified only as a capitalistically operable industrial technology complex. Subject positions are personifications of economic categories as human agency is ordered according to commodity economic logic. And laws of capital work themselves out with "iron necessity". As captured by Collier: "For a law to be true, it must hold when the mechanism it designates works unimpeded – i.e. in a closed system".[52] Dialectical economic theory is one such system where to truly grasp what capital *is* and what it *does*, theory synthesizes capitalism as if capital had its way with the world.

However, as Collier notes regarding the natural world, mechanisms discovered by experiment, though "affect[ing] outcomes in open systems, don't get it all their own way".[53] The challenge for Marxian political economy is therefore how to move from dialectical economic theory to the vast open system of capitalist history where capital does not get it all its own way? There, questions of the historical emergence of capitalism and its historical passing must be treated: those of manifest capitalist varieties and differences and concatenation of the capitalist and non-capitalist as well. Then there are questions of human agency. Whether we are talking about individuals or collectivities human agency not only resists or interferes with the logic of capital in multifarious ways but may act to suspend that logic completely. Also, outside the rarified environment of dialectical economic theory, the way capital is both supported by the political and ideological superstructure and opposed by political and ideological practices must be taken fully into account. After all, as already alluded to earlier in this book, to the extent the contingent course of history renders human economic life increasingly unmanageable by capital, it may well be that remnants of bourgeois society are sustained *only* by the superstructure. Further, considering modern human history, capitalist history is but one "history". Other historical forces such as religion, patriarchy, gender, or race, for example, could potentially act to affect historical outcomes in ways that intersect, channel, or conflict with the causally efficacious mechanisms of capital. Then there is the paramount question of the *heterogeneity of use value*. I say paramount because, as we may recall from discussion in the previous chapter, capitalism itself *only* comes into historical being around a particular constellation of human use value wants the satisfaction of which are amenable to its chrematistic operation and as the technologies for furnishing those goods become available. And, capitalism, like historical societies preceding it, is destined to vanish from human history as human use value wants along with the means for satisfying these arise that cannot be managed according to its economic principles.

Marx deals sketchily with the amenability for value augmentation of a particular type of use value production in the manuscript fragment "Results of the Direct Production Process".[54] He refers to the "putting-out" system of wool production in Britain, where merchant capital exerts a limited force in transforming the labor process, in terms of the "formal subsumption" by capital of production. However the "real subsumption" by capital of the labor and production process of society, for Marx, only occurs under the auspices of industrial capital as exemplified by the paradigmatic capitalist industry of mid-nineteenth-century Britain, textile production. And it was the structure of capital accumulation during this period – the capitalist owner operated entrepreneurial nature of the firm, straightforwardly financed "light' industrial technological base innovated in the context of business cycle oscillations, arms length market transactions of businesses, standardized light use value output, factory organization of the labor process, proletarianizing of the working population, commodity based monetary system, minimalist state, and so on – which Marx saw as closely approximating the image of capital unfolded by dialectical economic theory.

The "heavy" steel and chemical technologies of the second industrial revolution, however, were not so easily managed according to the reifying commodity economic logic of capital. The empirics of this – the vastly expanded financing requirements of the new industries compelling either the reorganizing of industrial capital in the joint-stock company form and/or placing of it at the behest of "finance capital", the eschewing of market competition by commanding heights monopoly business, the expanded policy role of the state (externally in imperialist territorial aggrandizement and internally with increased protections for home markets and in mounting ideological offensives against the growing resistances of the working class), and so forth – were treated by theorists of imperialism. Notwithstanding their internecine disputes, major players in debates of the era largely concurred that these transmutations forced on capital could not be dealt with in terms of a simple divergence in the trajectory of nineteenth-century accumulation. Hence they made references to the notion of a new "stage" or phase of capitalism, a practice in Marxist writings that expanded into its own cottage industry following new developments of WWII capitalism and continues today with regards to so-called globalization.[55] But this "stages/phases" discourse has largely unfolded as an extremely fuzzy enterprise with little to no connection made to Marx's theorizing in *Capital* of what in its most fundamental incarnation capital *is*. Nor has there been careful attention devoted to thorny epistemological issues involved.

What levels of analysis accomplish in Marxian political economy is the concretizing of the inner logic of capital in theory with a mediating step. This step theorizes capital in its management of the contradiction between value and use value in terms of the specification of key forms of use value production marking leading capitalist sectors in world historic stages of capitalist development. Marxian political economy in this framework, therefore, includes *dialectical economic theory*, *stage theory*, and *historical analysis* of capitalism. Stage theory as a level of analysis of Marxian political economy shows how the logic of capital is refracted into distinct types or *structures* of accumulation as it confronts the recalcitrance of stage specific use values. Theorizing these structures of accumulation, as guided by dialectical economic theory, thus begins by identifying the paradigmatic form of capital required to manage production of the stage specific use values. From the stage specific form of capital stage theoretic analysis delves into stage specific types of monetary/finance/credit system, form and degree of the commodification of labor power in the capital/labor relation, characteristic type of capitalist business cycle/crises, and so forth. Dropping the assumption of logical necessity stage theory must also consider that which was held implicit in dialectical economic theory – the superstructure. In particular, stage theory is called upon to theorize characteristic state policies that support capital accumulation in a stage. In fact, Uno follows Austrian Marxian economist Rudolf Hilferding in naming capitalist stages according to stage specific state economic policies pursued on behalf of the dominant form of capital (for Hilferding the policy of *finance capital* was *imperialism*). Stage theoretic analysis further explores stage specific forms of politics, ideology, and law. Stage theory must also theorize a stage specific international dimension of capital. In the closed system of dialectical economic theory the geospatial is specified like other dimensions of use value life as operable according abstract commodity economic logic, a "global" commodity economy if you will. Finally, stage theory also sets out stage specific forms of class struggle and social resistances to capital.

Stage theory as a level of analysis in Marxian political economy is *not* an "ideal", "stylized", or "average" type produced by systematizing empirical history. If we were to give a name to the structures of accumulation it theorizes that would be *material types*. Again, it was Marx's puzzlement in the face of manifest phenomena of his world and the inadequacy of existing theories in the transitive dimension of science that drove his retroduction of capital as a discrete generative mechanism and intransitive object of science. It is the unique ontology of capital as an intransitive object of science that grounds Marx's deployment of a dialectical epistemology to theorize capital as a self-contained thought experiment. It is only on the basis of knowing precisely what capital *is* in its most fundamental incarnation that we are able to draw upon historical analysis to theorize the material types of capital in stage theory. And, as the course of history cannot be read off the logic of capital, so history also cannot be grasped as a function of stage theory. Rather the levels of analysis work in concert to produce the most complete knowledge of capitalism – from the earliest empirical indications that a reifying force has subsumed human material existence to evidence of the last residues of capital being wiped from the slate of human history.

The stages of capitalism are *mercantilism*, *liberalism*, *imperialism*, and *consumerism* (see Box 2.4).

Box 2.4

For Uno himself, and among select scholars active in the approach to Marxian political economy initially developed by him, in particular Uno's student Thomas Sekine and Canadian Unoist John R. Bell, only mercantilism, liberalism, and imperialism are claimed as *stages* of capitalism. Uno had argued from his historical vantage point that imperialism was the final stage of capitalism and that following WWI capital entered an indeterminate phase of "ex-capitalist" transition. Uno was certainly influenced in this prognosis by the cataclysm of WWI and the rise of socialism as an historical force with the revolutionary emergence of the Soviet Union in 1917. Uno, however, never dealt directly with the post-WWII economy in his writings. In fact, a cardinal tenet of his approach is that theory rises to the occasion only when history becomes "grey" as per Hegel's "owl of Minerva" metaphor; that is, theory captures processes only *after* their complete development is manifest. That Uno himself never enjoyed this vista with respect to the post-WWII golden age economy is thus significant in my view.

In any case, the work of Sekine offers the most sophisticated defense of Uno's position. Sekine maintains that while monopolization characterizing the imperialist era "warped" the periodicity of prosperity and depression phase business cycle oscillations through which the law of value manages the commodification of labor power, "stage-theoretic determinations" demonstrate how the law as captured in the theory of the dialectical inner logic of capital is nevertheless maintained as a force up to a point in imperialist history. In the aftermath of the war the law no longer operates in its "pure" form as demonstrated by the inability of capital to recover "automatically" from the Great Depression according to Sekine. Ergo, capitalism sensu stricto no longer exists (see Sekine, "Towards a Critique of Bourgeois Economics", pp. 252–5). Sekine argues that the period following WWI including the post-WWII "golden age" is to be examined at the level of analysis of *historical analysis* of capitalism in its process of disintegration: and that this history can be divided into eras of historical disintegration of which the golden age and current neoliberal trajectory of US financial dominance of the world constitute two (idem, p. 256ff.).

My concern here is with Sekine and Bell's inclination to theorize the stage of *imperialism* too close to the theory of capital's inner logic. Stage theoretic material types are constructed on the basis of idiosyncratic operations of capital in a stage; and on the basis of the clearest, most developed paradigmatic expression of these. Not upon the actual historical trajectory of a stage. As well, comparative historical analysis of intervening periods between the consolidation of stages shows such periods to be punctuated by extended times of crises and/or war. And that even with regards to technological change the transition between stages entails factors exogenous to the logic of capital as Sekine himself has explained. That capital did not recover automatically from the Great Depression should in no way be surprising. Following the breakdown of accumulation in a stage capital might be faced with extraordinary historical exertions to consolidate its renewal, which besides sea changes in its economic organization wholesale transformation of the superstructure is also to be expected. Because Uno never theorized a stage of capitalism following *imperialism* I can certainly understand Sekine's interest in maintaining the argument of *imperialism* as the final stage.

Robert Albritton, on the other hand, in his *A Japanese Approach to Stages of Capitalist Development* (Basingstoke: Macmillan Press, 1991), develops the insights of stage theory but set in the context of extensive historical analysis. In each of the stages Uno did theorize, Albritton compellingly confirms the power of stage theory (undergirded by dialectical economic theory) in producing knowledge of the actual course of capitalist history in a stage. Yet his efforts also elucidate ways stage dynamics differ from the image of capital synthesized by dialectical economic theory and draw more on extra-economic, extra-capitalist support than Uno recognized in his published work on stage theory. In particular, Albritton explores the great distance between the theory of a purely capitalist society and the stage structure of *mercantilism* where commodification of economic life is tenuous at best. Yet *mercantilism* still deserves to be studied as a stage of capitalism rather than in terms of historical analysis of an era where the real subsumption of human economic life by the logic of capital is only immanent. Albritton then carefully considers the period following WWII. His efforts are aided in the transitive dimension of science by important writings of the French Marxist "Regulation School" and that of the US

Marxist "Social Structures of Accumulation School", work that was not available to Uno. Albritton thus formulates a stage theoretic analysis in the Unoist tradition of the post-WWII stage of *consumerism* (following in that tradition by naming a stage based on the paradigmatic state economic policy supportive of capital accumulation).

My own work in *Political Economy and Globalization* develops the Uno approach in following Albritton's theorizing of *consumerism* as a stage of capitalism. My reading of the so-called "Great Transformation" treated by economic historian Karl Polanyi (that guides Sekine's historical perspective), is that there was certainly no guarantee that capital or even viable human economic life could reconstitute itself following the seismic shifts in the world economy that led to WWII. But a materially reproducible economy did take shape. And this economy developed the potential of a cluster of technologies that had come into being during the Great Transformation, the promise of which however was never realized in the economic, political, and ideological milieu of the era.

My emphasis in theorizing *consumerism* as a stage is placed upon the amenability of standardized mass production of consumer durables, the automobile being the representative type of use value production, for value augmentation. I note also that automobile production in particular and consumer durable production in general deeply entrenches standardized material goods production – production-centered societies being the hallmark of the capitalist era – in the economic reproduction process of society. In fact, in terms of human labor power involved in manufacturing activity as a percent of the total workforce activity across three major economic sectors in the US and other advanced national capital accumulators, the stage of *consumerism* is the capitalist apex. I further consider the type of capital characteristic of the stage, *corporate capital*, in terms of a qualitative transformation of finance capital and monopoly form of enterprise of imperialism. I certainly recognize the exigencies of corporate capital managing the capitalist production of a complex standardized consumer durable use value as the automobile. The massive fixed capital investment, economies of scale, and high throughput/mass consumption/profitability nexus of automobile production renders price competition anathema to capital. I thus accept Sekine's historical analysis of the fact that the foregoing not just "warps" but dampens capitalist business cycle oscillations through which the law of value regulates the value of labor power and hence its commodification as per the deep dialectical inner logic of capital. But a scientific law is a law because it holds in a closed system. In open systems laws, including those of capital, do not get it all their own way.

The question, then, is whether "stage-theoretic determinations" as Sekine puts it, which includes the determinant support of the superstructure, sustain the force of the logic of capital (capital in this sense at least getting enough of it its own way) in the historical trajectory of *consumerism*? As Sekine and Bell well know there is no "objective" answer here. It is a judgment call predicated upon what we know about the deep inner logic of capital as a generative mechanism and historical analysis and/or stage theorizing of the era. Sekine's position draws upon what the logic of capital in the *doctrine of distribution* tells us about the way the value of labor power is determined in the course of the business cycle. In the stage of *consumerism* or history of the golden age (as Sekine sees it) this determination is left ambiguous because, instead of cycles of "normal" or equilibrium prices in the prosperity phase and plummeting prices during the depression phase (around which the absorption and reconstituting of the industrial reserve army occurs), in an economy dominated by oligopolistic MNCs producing expensive consumer durables like automobiles, the cycles instead oscillate around expansions to full capacity utilization followed by contractions of output with maintenance of overcapacity where price levels of key consumer durables fluctuate minimally.

What I argue on this point firstly, is that golden age social wages along with acceding of capital and state to unionized collective bargaining over wage/benefit packages partially decommodify labor power. Yet, when we set this within the context of macroeconomic countercyclical fiscal policymaking of the state we can see how, paradoxically, partial decommodification of labor power serves to maintain labor power as a commodity. That is, production decisions in the golden age are still "anarchic" in that they are made by individual firms with their own private profitmaking strategies and horizons at heart. Already from the stage of *imperialism* monopoly power enabled firms to innovate selectively at various junctures in the business cycle. In combining economies of *scope* with those of scale, *corporate capital* of the golden age was further empowered to maintain less productive technologies alongside more productive ones according to competitive conditions it faced. Nevertheless, competition still impelled cycles of overaccumulation of capital and falling profits the cumulative effects of which ultimately led to the demise of the golden age by the mid 1970s. Stage-theoretic determinations thus explain how the role the law of value plays in maintaining labor power as a commodity is mediated on the one hand by falling profits and resultant unemployment/curtailing of production (with resultant overcapacity) at that point above which wages cannot rise. On the other hand by ex post macroeconomic countercyclical policymaking that ensures wages do not fall below that point required under exigencies of corporate capital accumulation.

Secondly, I argue that when we approach the question of a stage of *consumerism* from the perspective of what we learn about capital from the *doctrine of production* (which studies capital not only "inside" the production process but "outside" the factory in the circulation process of capital entailing the coordination and non-interruption of operations across all separate units of capital and reproduction-process of capital that captures the self-expansion of aggregate social capital), what we see is an economy heavily based on material goods production with determinable direct costs or production prices that feed into the capitalistically rational pricing underpinning an allocation of resources ensuring the reproducibility of *consumerist* capitalism as an historical society. Could "the market" guarantee such an allocation in the period without mediation of the superstructure? No. But, if we take account of the major existing economic principles by which the general norms of human economic life can be met (more on this below and in Chapter 6), the planning principle of the state (what Polanyi refers to as *redistribution*) though significant is *not* preponderant. And, to repeat, it kicks in ex post in the course of business cycle oscillations: which leaves enough of market operations (capital getting enough of it its own way) to guide us in building the material type of *consumerism* at the stage level of analysis. And, ergo, refer to *consumerism* as a stage of capitalism.

Does this debate within the Unoist temple over whether the post-WWII capitalist golden age is addressed by stage theory and/or historical analysis in any way detract from the power of the approach for the study of human material life? Of course not! The major point of agreement among all above mentioned players in the Uno approach to Marxian political economy is that from the stage of *mercantilism* to *liberalism*, capital accumulation increasingly approaches its ideal image. But, from the stage of *imperialism* capital accumulation moves asymptotically away from its ideal image such that debate over a stage of *consumerism* simply boils down to how far? The next major point of agreement is that given what we learn about capital from dialectical economic theory, it is more than evident that the current excrescence or "economy", which gestated from the 1980s, cannot be theorized as *capitalist*, but as a period where capitalism is disintegrating with *no* possibility of resurrection. And, unfortunately for humanity, neither does the current "economy" have at its core an economic principle or principles with sufficient force to ensure the material viability of human society. It is simply a beast bent upon expropriation and rent seeking that will devour humanity if collectivities do not rise to make change. Though the ideology that capitalism secretes continues to hold humanity in thrall to the view of "the economy" as a natural force to which we humans can only but conform.

Let us look diagrammatically at how levels of analysis in Marxian political economy surmount the impoverishing choices imposed by the faux-Marxist "logico-historical" method or simple ad hoc "rehydration" of neoclassical models with the "social" as advanced by Fine and Milonakis (see Figure 2.1). The flow of

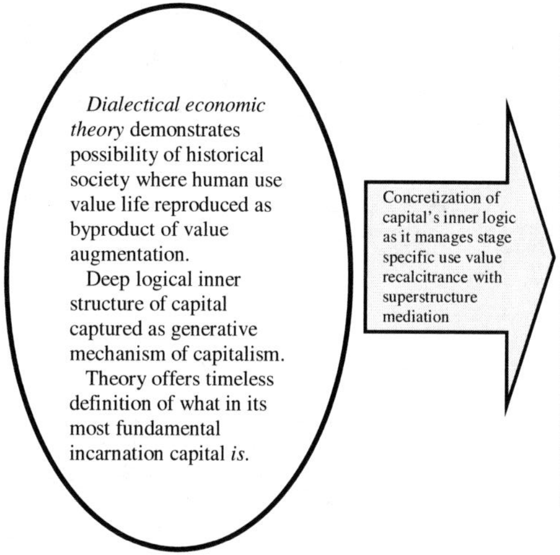

Dialectical economic theory demonstrates possibility of historical society where human use value life reproduced as byproduct of value augmentation.
  Deep logical inner structure of capital captured as generative mechanism of capitalism. Theory offers timeless definition of what in its most fundamental incarnation capital *is*.

Concretization of capital's inner logic as it manages stage specific use value recalcitrance with superstructure mediation

Stage and key state policy	Dominant capital accumulator(s)	Representative use value	Type of capital	Industry structure
Mercantilism (key era: 1700–50)	Britain	Wool	Merchant capital	putting-out (cottage-industry)
Liberalism (key era: 1850–73)	Britain	Cotton	Industrial capital	factory system (owner-operated)
Imperialism (key era: 1890–1914)	Germany/USA/ Britain	Steel/heavy chemicals	Finance capital	monopoly/ joint-stock company
Consumerism (key era: 1950–73)	USA	Automobile/ consumer durables	Corporate capital	oligopoly/ MNC

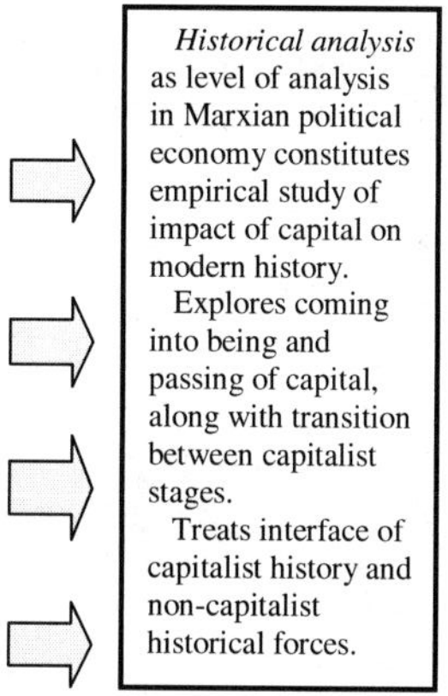

Historical analysis as level of analysis in Marxian political economy constitutes empirical study of impact of capital on modern history.
  Explores coming into being and passing of capital, along with transition between capitalist stages.
  Treats interface of capitalist history and non-capitalist historical forces.

Figure 2.1 Levels of analysis in Marxian political economy

54 *The zero of social change*

the figure traces the concretization of the inner logic of capital through levels of theory that in the end all work in concert to produce knowledge of capital with explanatory power for our understanding of the course of history and the "meeting" of capitalist history with other "histories".

Historical materialism and the cognitive sequence in Marxist theory

It has truly been one of the tragedies of Marxism that the subtlety of the *cognitive sequence* in Marx's work has so rarely been appreciated. The ramifications of this misapprehension in the field of Marxist studies, as alluded to in Chapter 1, is the codification of Marxism in terms of HM, a master theory of historical directionality. This then slotted Marx's economic writings in *Capital* as but a *subtheory* of HM. That is, when it is considered at all. Again, Marxists were surely misled by Marx's comments in the iconic preface to the effect that his pithy outline of HM constituted the "guiding principle" for his studies. The fact is however, Marx had already completed the manuscript of the *Grundrisse*, his "workbook" from which *Capital* took shape, itself reflecting at least a decade in-depth analysis of the capitalist economy, prior to penning those words. And, no sooner were the words penned, Marx immediately dove into what would be his life work, *Capital*. What debt *Capital* owes to HM is simply as stated above. Hypothesizing HM immunized Marx from infection by bourgeois ideology that had rooted itself so deeply in classical political economy.

What debt does HM owe the study of capital? Everything! Indeed it is inconceivable that HM could have been formulated in any way other than in the light of Marx's economic theorizing of capitalism. Let us show this unequivocally with each of its propositions. Marx's claim of an economic substructure as the "real foundation" of the political, ideological, legal superstructure is only possible to sustain under the historical conditions of capitalist reification where the economic tends to separate or "disembed" from these other social practices. Even the notion of a *mode of production* can only but be based on the theorizing of capital as an economic society par excellence or purely capitalist society that reproduces human material existence by commodity economic means alone. Its subconcepts, forces of production and relations of production, also have determinate economic meanings solely in the study of capitalism. What is the distinction between the two concepts, for example, in the context of seminomadic "primitive communistic" native societies or slave orders of antiquity? In dialectical economic theory the forces of production refer to the technical category of the technology complex operated by industrial capital. The relations of production constitute the objective value relation that exists between technically specified capital and labor. Marx's statement that at a certain point the development of the productive forces "comes into conflict" with the relations of production is scientifically proven, as touched on preliminarily in Box 1.2 (and treated in Chapter 5 at length), in analysis by dialectical economic theory of the course of capitalist business cycles (at a given level of technological development overaccumulation in the prosperity phase of each cycle absorbs the industrial reserve army only to impel capital into a depression phase from which it recovers by renewing fixed capital at a higher technological level to maintain labor power as a commodity).[56] And we can go on with concepts such as exploitation or the appropriation of surplus labor that can be objectively shown only in capitalist appropriation of surplus value.

The locus of scientificity in Marx's writing is dialectical economic theory. Again, the ontological foundation of this claim is the capitalist reification of human social relations. It is the social scientific or objective knowledge of human social relations produced by Marxian economic theory that informs HM, the Marxian approach to precapitalist societies and human history in toto. In other words, the cognitive sequence in Marxism runs from Marxian economics and political economy to HM. Not vice versa.

Approached from another angle, we can say that the very condition of possibility of *social* science itself is the historical existence of capitalism. The "zero" of social science in this sense is the objectifying of that subset of human social relations, the social relations of material production in capitalist society. It is this peculiar ontology of capital that calls forth dialectical economic theory as the science of the substructure of capitalism. The deep inner logic or generative mechanism of capital, however, never appears directly in capitalist history. Rather, the casual force of capital is mediated by the superstructure and manifested as a material type of capital as captured in stage theory. Marxian political economy hence encompasses the three levels of analysis – dialectical economic theory, stage theory, and historical analysis. It is the role of the superstructure in mediating the causal force of capital that constitutes the basis in turn for integrating other social sciences such as political science, law, sociology into the study of capitalism.[57] Of course, in contrast with Fine and Milonakis's afore stated fuzzy notion of "focusing on the economic but . . . consciously incorporating the social . . . from the outset", it should be abundantly clear that the very task of bringing the social back in makes sense *only* on the basis of our settling the ontological question of what it is about capital that foregrounds the analytical separation of base and superstructure or economic and sociopolitical in the first place! And, it is therefore *only* in the light of this integrated knowledge of capitalism founded on political economy that it is possible for us to study non-economic aspects of precapitalist societies in the research agenda of HM. Marxian political economic study of capitalism and HM, in other words, constitute two distinct projects with divergent subject foci. It is simply the case that HM develops in the *comparative* light of the study of capitalism (see Figure 2.2).

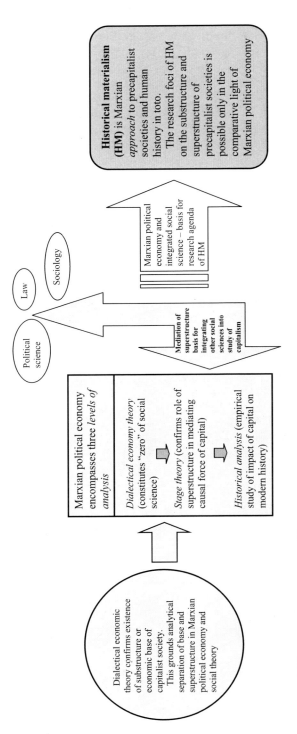

Figure 2.2 The cognitive sequence in Marxism

Marxian economic theory and the possibility of socialism

We will deal throughout the following pages of this book with the more practice oriented issues of materially reproducible, progressive, redistributive, eco-sustainable societies of the future. The name Marx gave to such societies is socialism. While collectivities rising to make progressive change in the human exit from globalization may decide to give the future world other names, for purposes of this book, I will retain socialism. Names, however, are not important. What is important, are the ideas behind the names. And, as is the case with HM, the Marxian approach to socialism necessarily commences with ideas that spring from the kernel of Marxian scientificity, dialectical economic theory. Marxian economic theory is the zero of social change because it is the only incorrigible vista we have into human material life. Marx himself did not leave us with much in the way of systematic theory of socialism. Though, in several important writings, he did give us a glimpse of what he had in mind for the progressive future. We will have numerous opportunities in this book to refer to what Marx actually said about socialism in this regard. But to bring this chapter to conclusion, I would like to point out what *Capital* reconstructed and completed as dialectical economic theory contributes to future directed thinking about socialism.

In a recent book devoted to Marx's understanding of socialism, Peter Hudis takes up the question of Marx's vision of socialism as articulated in *Capital*.[58] While those interested in Marx's views on socialism will certainly appreciate Hudis's effort in painstakingly picking through Marx's corpus as a whole to capture what Marx actually said in this or that context about socialism, it is on the place of Marxian economic studies in future directed thinking that Hudis's book evinces its most glaring lacuna. Hudis mines *Capital* for passages "amenable to immediate application on behalf of political or social causes".[59] For Hudis, much of this is to be found in Volume 1 of *Capital*, the only volume as we have noted that Marx saw off to the printer in his lifetime. In my earlier work, I referred to the propensity among Marxists to use the first volume of *Capital* as a grab bag for revolutionary quotations, to the dearth of dealing with three volumes as the founding work of a new science, as "Volume One Marxism".[60] Hudis, to be fair, does not fall directly into this trap, but in his seeking to draw upon *Capital* for its political implications he unwittingly reproduces it.

Hudis is unequivocal with his view on Marxian economic theory: "Marx is . . . the founder of a distinctive approach to the understanding of capitalism that retains its historical relevance so long as capitalism remains in existence".[61] This position essentially completes the trifecta of debilitating and revolutionary edge blunting conceptions of the Marxian contribution to future directed thinking – the first two being the conflating of Marxism with HM as a master theory of historical directionality and that of Marx's purported deployment of a "logico-historical" method in *Capital*. The very need for a *social* science, as argued above, is that human economic relations *cannot* be studied directly. Human economic or social relations of material life *only* reveal themselves, disentangled from other social relations or practices, in the reified form they assume in the capitalist era. The social *science* of Marxian dialectical economic theory captures the reified social relations of production of the capitalist commodity economy in their *totality*, leaving no economic category unearthed and none of the cunning or logical inner secrets of capital unexposed. Thus Marx's refined and completed project in *Capital* firstly constitutes the definitive economic theory of an economic society or "bourgeois utopia" par excellence. The objective knowledge of capital the dialectic establishes secondly offers a critique of bourgeois political economy and vulgar "economics" in their one-sided, subjective, ideologically laden enterprise. Finally, in demonstrating how capital satisfies the general norms of economic life to reproduce a human society as a byproduct of its abstract chrematistic of value augmentation, *Capital* scientifically confirms the possibility of those very same general norms being satisfied for the concrete designs of free associations of free human beings.

Put differently, the project of *Capital* is *timeless* because it constitutes the theory of the economic substructure of society. The very condition of possibility for theorizing the economic substructure of human society is when human material relations appear transparently as a result of capitalist reification. Of course material or economic life is the foundation of all human societies – precapitalist, capitalist, and postcapitalist. But to the extent there exists transhistorical aspects of human economic life common to *all* societies it is *only* possible to scientifically confirm what precisely these are in dialectical economic theory. The transhistorical aspects of human economic life are the general norms. The cardinal general norms of economic life are:

1 No human society could survive for long if the direct producers do not at minimum receive the product of their necessary labor (though any substantive social reproduction demands productive labor produce *more* than is required to reproduce his/her labor power);
2 No human society could survive for long if social demand for basic goods is not met with a minimum misallocation of social resources, primarily human labor power (this necessitating producing means of production and means of consumption in appropriate proportions);
3 If the productive technology of a society remains constant, its reproduction process cannot expand faster than the natural rate of growth of the working population (this ultimately is the root of conflicts between the forces and relations of production discovered in dialectical economic theory exploration of capitalist business cycle oscillations). This point is treated at length in Chapter 5.

But there is more inhering in the economic theory of capital for progressive future directed thinking. In theorizing the substructure or economic base of human society as the commodity economic management of human material life by capital, dialectic economic theory shows the historical advancement of capitalism over past historical societies. That is, capitalism frees human beings from imbrication in interpersonal social relations of domination and subordination and extra-economic compulsions of material life. Rather subjecting them solely to its impersonal, abstract economic compulsion. Thus, in reconsidering Engels summation in *Anti-Dühring* Part II of Marx's view of the transition from capitalism to socialism as "humanity's leap from the kingdom of necessity to the kingdom of freedom", it is important to grasp the question of "necessity" in terms of the enslavement of human beings in capitalist society to the commodity economic as a natural force to which they must conform, or at best adjust their lives by "policy" measures.[62] Hence, in its substantive ontological sense, the socialist "kingdom of freedom" though certainly constituted upon a material substructure as other historical societies, requires the management of the substructure by superstructure itself organized by free associations of free human beings making their economic lives according to their concrete purposes and needs. And, with these free human beings acting, as we shall discuss in following chapters, on the basis of motivations divergent from the interpersonal extra-economic compulsions of precapitalist societies and economic compulsion of capitalism.

Finally, in theorizing capitalism as an "upside-down", "alien" social order that reproduces human economic life as a byproduct of capital's abstract chrematistic of value augmentation, dialectical economic theory points the way to socialism as the diametrical opposite of capitalism. In this sense capitalism is the limit form of what a human society should not be. And knowledge of capitalism produced by dialectical economic theory is to be marshaled in guiding us as to what must be undone in our economic lives to rid them of capital and its disabling residues. As will be made evident in the following chapter, this is the antithesis to the approach to socialism advanced by Marxism codified as HM that animated so-called socialist experiments of the past.

Notes

1 Dimitris Milonakis and Ben Fine, *From Political Economy to Economics: Method, the Social and the Historical in the Evolution of Economic Theory* (London: Routledge, 2009); Ben Fine and Dimitris Milonakis, *From Economics Imperialism to Freakonomics: The Shifting Boundaries between Economics and Other Social Sciences* (London: Routledge, 2009).
2 Fine and Milonakis, *From Economics Imperialism to Freakonomics*, p. 14.
3 Milonakis and Fine, *From Political Economy to Economics*, pp. 4–5.
4 Fine and Milonakis, *From Economics Imperialism to Freakonomics*, pp. 18ff, 134–5.
5 Ibid., pp. 166–7, 173.
6 Thomas Sekine, "Towards a Critique of Bourgeois Economics", in John R. Bell (ed.), *Towards a Critique of Bourgeois Economics: Essays of Thomas T. Sekine* (Berlin: Owl of Minerva Press, 2013) p. 245.
7 Milonakis and Fine, *From Political Economy to Economics*, pp. 38, 71ff.
8 Karl Marx, *A Contribution to the Critique of Political Economy*, http://www.marxists.org/archive/marx/works/1859/critique-pol-economy/index.htm.
9 Sekine, "Towards a Critique of Bourgeois Economics", pp. 244–5.
10 Milonakis and Fine, *From Political Economy to Economics*.
11 The work of Roy Bhaskar has been pivotal in the development of CR relevance to Marxist theory. On Bhaskar's formative work see Andrew Collier, *Critical Realism: An Introduction to Roy Bhaskar's Philosophy* (London: Verso, 1994). A succinct summary of

CR's central claims by Roy Bhaskar himself is, *Reclaiming Reality: A Critical Introduction to Contemporary Philosophy* (London: Verso, 1989).
12 Roy Bhaskar, *A Realist Theory of Science* (London: Verso, 2008) p. 8.
13 Norman Blaikie, *Approaches to Social Enquiry* (Cambridge, UK: Polity Press, 1993) pp. 161ff.
14 Bhaskar, *A Realist Theory of Science*, p. 47.
15 Collier, *Critical Realism: An Introduction to Roy Bhaskar's Philosophy*, pp. 50–1.
16 Christopher Norris, *Against Relativism: Philosophy of Science, Deconstruction, and Critical Theory* (Hoboken, NJ: Wiley-Blackwell, 1997) p. 102.
17 Bhaskar, *Reclaiming Reality*, pp. 82–4.
18 Collier, *Critical Realism: An Introduction to Roy Bhaskar's Philosophy*, p. 44.
19 See for example James Robert Brown, *The Laboratory of the Mind: Thought Experiments in the Natural Sciences* (London: Routledge, 1991); Roy A. Sorensen, *Thought Experiments* (Oxford: Oxford University Press, 1992).
20 Thomas Sekine, "Uno's Method of Marxian Economics", in Bell (ed.), *Towards a Critique of Bourgeois Economics: Essays of Thomas T. Sekine*, pp. 4–5.
21 Hobsbawm, *How to Change The World: Reflections on Marx and Marxism* (New Haven: Yale University Press, 2011) p. 240.
22 Karl Polanyi, *The Livelihood of Man* (London: Academic Press, 1977).
23 See the discussion in David P. Levine, "Political Economy and the Idea of Development", *Review of Political Economy*, 13, 4 (2001).
24 Richard Marsden, "The Unknown Masterpiece: Marx's Model of Capital", *Cambridge Journal of Economics*, 22, 3 (1998) pp. 297–324.
25 Collier, *Critical Realism: An Introduction to Roy Bhaskar's Philosophy*, p. 107.
26 Ibid., pp. 107ff.
27 Bhaskar, *Reclaiming Reality*, pp. 70–80.
28 Karl Marx, *Capital* V1, Afterword to the Second German Edition, http://www.marxists.org/archive/marx/works/1867-c1/p3.htm.
29 Marx, *Capital* V1, Preface to the First German Edition, http://www.marxists.org/archive/marx/works/1867-c1/p1.htm.
30 Robert Albritton, *Dialectics and Deconstruction in Political Economy* (Basingstoke: Macmillan Press, 1999) pp. 31–2. The "force of abstraction" however is not a one way street: as added by Albritton (p. 184 note 17), "Real abstractions are helped along by theoretical ones in the sense that theorists such as Smith and Ricardo have a real impact on economic practice in the sense of actually fostering policies that make social life more capitalist (or more *laissez faire*)".
31 Marx, *Capital* V1, Afterword to the Second German Edition.
32 Stefanos Kourkoulakos, "The Specificity of Dialectical Reason (for Hegel)", in Robert Albritton and John Simoulidis (eds.), *New Dialectics and Political Economy* (Basingstoke: Palgrave, 2002) pp. 191–4.
33 Ibid. As Kourkoulakos argues (p. 203 note 23), the correspondence theory of truth Hegel deploys differs from conventional accounts of it in empiricist and rationalist epistemology. The correspondence, for Hegel, is between objectivity and its Concept which inverts the subject-object dualism.
34 Ibid.
35 Thomas Sekine, "An Essay on Uno's Dialectic of Capital", in Bell (ed.), *Towards a Critique of Bourgeois Economics: Essays of Thomas T. Sekine*, pp. 44–5, 52.

The zero of social change   61

36 Karl Marx, "Marx to Engels in Manchester", http://www.marxists.org/archive/marx/works/1865/letters/65_07_31.htm.
37 See, Kozo Uno, *Principles of Political Economy* (Sussex: Harvester Press, 1980); Thomas Sekine, *The Dialectic of Capital*, 2 Volumes (Tokyo: Toshindo Press, 1986); idem, *An Outline of the Dialectic of Capital*, 2 Volumes (Basingstoke: Macmillan, 1997). For discussion of the theoretical and historical context for Uno and Sekine's efforts to refine and complete *Capital* when Marxists had largely migrated the discipline of Marx studies away from economics to history and philosophy, see Westra, "Kautsky, Lukacs, Althusser and the Retreat from the Economic in Marxism – with the Return in Uno", *Political Economy Quarterly*, 44, 2 (2007) pp. 77–87.
38 Thomas Sekine, "Dialectic, Logic, Economics", in Bell (ed.), *Towards a Critique of Bourgeois Economics: Essays of Thomas T. Sekine*, pp. 18–9.
39 Robert Albritton, *Economics Transformed: Discovering the Brilliance of Marx* (London: Pluto Press, 2007) pp. 95–6.
40 Milonakis and Fine, *From Political Economy to Economics*, p. 40.
41 For a critique of Kautsky's wrong-headed appropriation of Marx's work see Westra, "Kautsky, Lukacs, Althusser and the Retreat from the Economic in Marxism"; idem, *Political Economy and Globalization*, (London: Routledge, 2009) pp. 46ff.
42 Albritton, *Economics Transformed*, pp. 36–40. In fact Albritton's Chapter 2 in toto contains one of the best commentaries on the commodity form that I have read.
43 Albritton, *Economics Transformed*, p. 24.
44 Thomas Sekine, "The Dialectic of Capital: An Unoist Interpretation", in Bell (ed.), *Towards a Critique of Bourgeois Economics: Essays of Thomas T. Sekine*, pp. 23ff for this and what follows over the next paragraphs.
45 Besides reading the three volumes of Marx's *Capital* there is no real substitute for Sekine's *The Dialectic of Capital*, 2 Volumes or idem, *An Outline of the Dialectic of Capital*, 2 Volumes. However, John R. Bell *Capitalism and the Dialectic: The Uno-Sekine Approach to Marxian Political Economy* (London: Pluto 2009) is a recently crafted summary and elaboration of Sekine's *Dialectic*. Richard Westra, "*Capital* as Dialectical Economic Theory", *Journal of Australian Political Economy*, 70 (2012/13) pp. 233–50, offers an article length summary of Marx's *Capital* reconstructed and completed as dialectical economic theory.
46 Uno, *Principles of Political Economy*, p. xxv.
47 On the importance of theorizing the oft neglected but important question of business cycles in Marxian economics, see Westra, *Political Economy and Globalization*, pp. 27–35.
48 Uno, *Principles of Political Economy*, pp. 115–8.
49 Brown, *The Laboratory of the Mind*, p. 32.
50 Albritton, *Economics Transformed*, pp. 114–26.
51 On the research agenda of periodizing capitalism see the extended discussion in Westra, *Political Economy and Globalization*, Chapter 3.
52 Collier, *Critical Realism: An Introduction to Roy Bhaskar's Philosophy*, p. 43.
53 Ibid., p. 36.
54 Karl Marx, "Results of the Direct Production Process", *Economic Works of Karl Marx 1861–1864*, http://www.marxists.org/archive/marx/works/1864/economic/.
55 See Westra, *Political Economy and Globalization*, pp. 46–53 on imperialism; Chapter 4 on so-called globalization.
56 Marxian crisis theory is treated at length in ibid., pp. 30–4.
57 Sekine, "An Essay on Uno's Dialectic of Capital", pp. 63–4.

58 Peter Hudis, *Marx's Concept of the Alternative to Capitalism* (Chicago, IL: Haymarket Books, 2013) Chapter 3.
59 Ibid., p. 169.
60 Westra, *Political Economy and Globalization*, p. 47.
61 Hudis, *Marx's Concept of the Alternative to Capitalism*, pp. 5–6.
62 Frederick Engels, *Anti-Dühring* Part II, 1877, http://www.marxists.org/archive/marx/works/1877/anti-duhring/ch24.htm.

3 Weighs like a nightmare on the brains of the living

From the *Eighteenth Brumaire of Louis Bonaparte*, Marx's terse phrase entitling this chapter captures ever so well what the experience, and even more so bourgeois ideological representation of Soviet-style socialism (including its purported continuing legacies in places such as North Korea), means for progressive, future directed, transformatory agency.[1] Indeed, the view broadly accepted amongst mass publics in most "Western" democracies that socialism "failed" when the Soviet Union collapsed in 1989, or "does not work" as evidenced by the 1970s onward increasingly dismal economic performance of Soviet-style societies in comparison to "free world" success stories, ranks a close second to neoclassical economics' ideological naturalizing of capitalism as the backstop to the TINA premise. There is also the question of the authoritarian political structure of Soviet-style societies when considered in the comparative light of even actual political practices (which certainly fall short of ideals) in "free world" democracies. Western socialist-minded intellectuals of the day found themselves squirming uncomfortably as they rolled out their apologia for this. I most definitely agree with Peter Hudis that informed readers of Marx would hardly identify his writings on social change with the authoritarian states that were constructed in his name.[2] And we can add to this the fact that all "really existing" socialisms came into being well after Marx's passing. But there still must be something in Marx's writings, unintended to be sure, but nevertheless there, that support interpretations that misled Marx's followers and helped materialize Soviet-style regimes. In this sense I agree with the remark made by Robin Blackburn to the effect that "the anti-capitalist Left will have no credibility unless it can account for the dire experience of Communism since 1917".[3]

That something I argue is, at bottom, Marx's own words, scattered across his corpus, which lend credence to what would become a studied misapprehension of the cognitive sequence in his work. It is this that in turn drove the conflation of Marxism with HM as a master theory of historical directionality. That wrong-headed understanding of Marxism was then bolstered by the claim that the repository of Marxist scientificity is HM rather than *Capital* or Marxian economic theory. In earlier work I have slapped much of the blame for shaping future generations of Marxist scholars' view of Marxism codified as HM on Second International doyen Karl Kautsky.[4] I did this because it was in Kautsky's hands that the very notion of

"Marxism", set out as a body of thought based on writings of Karl Marx, first germinated. However, Kautsky's position as well as that of following generations of Marxists that clung to the conflation despite supplanting Kautsky's "orthodox" interpretation of HM with their "Western" or "neo-Marxist" one, can be traced primarily, though not solely, to Marx's statements in the recondite preface. To this we can also add Frederick Engels's admonition in *Socialism: Utopian and Scientific* that Marxists need not spend time spinning "blueprints" of the future (a point we will definitely return to).[5] Eric Hobsbawm explains it thus:

> The shape of the future and tasks of action could be discerned only by discovering the process of social development which would lead them, and this discovery itself became possible only at a certain stage of development. If this limited the vision of the future to a few rough structural principles ... it gave to socialist hopes the certainty of historical inevitability.[6]

The "rough structural principles", of course, refers to the purported historical "contradiction" between the productive forces and relations of production thematic to HM as set out in the preface. Again, as argued in Chapter 2, the fundamental contradiction of *capital* as Marx makes abundantly clear in *Capital* is that between value and use value. And the contradiction between value and use value that dialectical economic theory demonstrates emerges in the context of the oscillation of prosperity and depression phases across capitalist business cycles is resolved by capital revolutionizing the forces of production (the technology complex) to maintain labor power as a commodity (the capital/labor relation). Marx's pithy statement of HM in the preface, which could *only* have been formulated based upon Marx's study of the capitalist commodity economy, was intended as a suggestive "guide" to thinking about the delimited and transitory nature of capitalism as was the case with precapitalist societies.

Marx's passionate revolutionary summation of Volume 1 of *Capital* further fanned the flames of such inevitability inhering in HM by linking socialism to the purported historical dynamic of capitalism. In Marx's iconic words: "Centralization of the means of production and socialization of labour at last reach a point where they become incompatible with their capitalist integument. This integument is burst asunder ... The expropriators are expropriated".[7] When placed in the context of HM as a master theory of historical directionality within which Marx's economic studies of capitalism are ensconced as a subtheory, Marx's words here further support the hackneyed "logico-historical" method that seeks to read history as a function of capital's logic. For exactly this reason I have long inveighed against Marxist "quotology" and maintain Marx's mission in *Capital* is best fortified by taking the work as an economic whole rather than a grab bag for revolutionary sayings by Marx in this or that context. Again, tracing the logic of capital to conclusion and exposing the inner laws or deep causal program of capital establishes the material reproducibility of capitalism as an historical society. It would be nonsense to claim that such laws simultaneously lead to their own historical denial. And, as we shall see, notwithstanding the revolutionary rhetoric spicing his writings, such was hardly the genius Marx's intention. In any case, it is precisely this perspective of a socialized or "monopolized" capitalism as "the antechamber of the socialist economy" that would ultimately frame the entire future debate over the Soviet-style experience.[8]

In fact it would beg the very question of why revolution in Russia, of all places, in 1917? After all, Russia, early socialists recognized, was hardly an example of the advanced centralizing and socializing tendencies of capitalism from which socialism would supposedly spring. Part of the formative theorizing of imperialism as a new stage of capitalism entailed the addressing of this anomaly.[9] It was argued that in the most advanced capitalist states, which were the dominant imperialist powers, the fruits of imperialism allowed capital to buy off important segments of the working class; in effect creating an "aristocracy" of labor that counteracted the radicalization of labor that was to accompany its socialization under capitalist monopolization. Further, while rival imperialist states struggle with each other over the division of the globe into economic territories slated to become the preserve of "national" monopoly capitalist exploitation, the net impact is to create a "chain" of interests among the imperialist bourgeoisie everywhere in the imperialist international capitalist system. The task of international socialist forces hence was to break the imperialist chain at its weakest link – enter Russia.[10]

But, while the historical inevitability of socialism as inculcated by HM was never substantively questioned, V. I. Lenin and the early Soviet revolutionaries nevertheless were forced to confront a series of tactical and strategic-theoretic nuances. The overriding issue was that of what had to be done under conditions where capitalism had not developed to its "socialized" or monopolized apex. This issue became hypertrophic when reality set in that the Soviet revolution was not going to be the catalyst for world proletarian revolution that drew into the equation advanced productive forces and mass working classes of the most "monopolized" capitalist economies. Lenin maintained "we always said that the victory of the socialist revolution . . . can only be regarded as final when it becomes the victory of the proletariat in at least several advanced countries".[11]

The ramifications of the foregoing reflect on the schema of HM, which saw in the development of the productive forces both the requisite technological advancement as the basis for that modicum of abundance purportedly required to redistribute wealth and aforementioned socialization rendering the forces of production amenable to state economic planning. There also arose the question of the working class – its proportionate size, role, and influence, formation of its class consciousness – in an historical context where a mass socialized, class conscious proletariat had not yet been constituted by the development of capitalism. This all then placed a Herculean burden square on the shoulders of the Marxist-Leninist "vanguard" political party as the sanctum of proletarian class consciousness. It would be the Marxist-Leninist party that was charged with managing the development of the productive forces that capitalist development would "normally" have undertaken. The Marxist-Leninist party was also seen as responsible for inculcating working-class consciousness in the growing proletariat along with fostering solidarity with proletarian goals among other social classes. Finally, the

Marxist-Leninist party had to superintend the socialist pedigree of the whole capitalist "socializing" process now carried forward under socialist auspices.[12] Lenin, for example, once went so far as to suggest how "electrification of Russia" was synonymous with its development of socialism.[13] He further harbored the view as per the dictums of HM of "small production" as the primary locus of the bourgeoisie; such demanding socialist vigilance over its replacement by industrial giganticism.[14]

With the question of socialism framed thus it is hardly surprising to this day to see Western based Marxist commentators stock-taking on what happened to the historically inevitable process place the spotlight on the corrupting of the Marxist-Leninist party and the rise of Stalin. It is true, the discussion puts the rise of Stalin in its context of historical struggles of Soviet socialism against bourgeois adversaries, but it seems to hold implicit that inclinations and political policies of one man were at the root of the Soviet and *socialist* downfall. British Marxist Tariq Ali expresses this sentiment as follows:

> ... Lenin's last struggle, waged from his sick bed ... was against this growing bureaucratization [fostered under Stalin] ... He realized that changes were needed and, in his last political testament, demanded that Stalin be removed from his position as General Secretary of the Party. It was a desperate attempt to reverse the course, but it came too late. Stalin represented the party bureaucracy and the real task was to reverse the institutional trends within party and state.[15]

The victory of Stalinism marked a qualitative break in the continuity of the revolutionary process.[16]

If not the promised land, what?

With "continuity" in the HM mandated revolutionary trajectory supposedly broken by Stalinism, the next question Marxists were pressed to answer was that of what precisely the unpalatable edifice of Soviet-style socialism evolved into? In other words, if "really existing" socialism was not *socialism*, then what was it? Probably the most enduring response to this question is that Soviet-style socialism was in fact not a kind of socialism at all, but a type of capitalism. Let us look briefly at the main international Marxist positions here.

For French Marxist Charles Bettelheim, the riddle of Soviet-style socialism reduces to the point that immediate post-revolutionary nationalizing of the commanding heights of the economy and subsequent instituting of economic planning do not in themselves guarantee a successful transition to socialism. This is because during the early period of transition they are simply superimposed upon capitalist "commodity relations" such as the existence of money, wages, and "separate" enterprises.[17] Consolidating the revolution demands state functionaries foster working-class political and ideological practices that promote *de facto* control by ordinary workers over their conditions of existence. As Bettelheim puts it, "it is only when ... a *growing control* by the laborers over the means of production and products [is ensured] that [we can say]the transition to socialism has effectively taken place".[18] In the Soviet Union, Bettelheim argues, this did not occur. There, both worker representatives in charge of the state and directors of state owned enterprises continued to perpetuate capitalist practices and social relations, eventually transforming themselves into a "state bourgeoisie" and the Soviet Union into a "state capitalist" formation. In sum, for Bettelheim, the ultimate test for socialism during a potentially extended period of transition is "the class character of state power".[19]

American Marxists Stephen Resnick and Richard Wolff take up the Soviet Union is "state capitalist" thesis. However they reject what they understand to be Bettelheim's "power theoretic" approach to the question of what characterizes socialism and distinguishes it from capitalism. Power, they contend, is a vague concept with multifarious meanings, and proves exceedingly difficult to operationalize with respect to its actual distribution and efficacy in complex social environments. For Resnick and Wolff, the crux of Soviet-style "state capitalism" was the form of "surplus appropriation" and specific organization of "social surplus labor". Because the process in fact *did not* in any way involve the direct producers themselves but unfolded through a complex web of appropriation linking enterprise managers, elements of the bureaucracy, and ultimately the Council of Industrial Ministers at the apex of the Soviet economy, it replicated the exploitation endemic to all capitalisms albeit doing so in a "statist" guise.[20] According to Resnick and Wolff, the instating of collective property and economic planning disguised "the continuation of capitalist class processes inside state enterprises", and this misled analysis. As they conclude, "differences *among* kinds of capitalist class structure should not be confused with differences *between* capitalist and communist class structures".[21]

Another US Marxist, Paul Sweezy, leaped into the debate skeptical of characterizing the Soviet Union as capitalist. He accepts how factors such as dearth of control by workers over appropriation and distribution of the social surplus, along with Soviet intergenerational transfer of privilege, render such orders a far cry from Marx's vision of socialism. But he maintains that in the absence of an "autonomously functioning market", competition among separate units of capital and the inherent tendency towards increased accumulation that is impelled by the latter, there is little left in Soviet-style societies of capitalist substance.[22] Indeed, for Sweezy, such societies contain "enough basic differences from both capitalism and socialism to be considered and studied as a new social formation".[23]

Belgian Marxist Ernest Mandel adds a further dimension to this debate. He concurs with Sweezy over the point that the erstwhile Soviet Union was not capitalist but disagrees with suggestions that it constituted some kind of "new social formation". To support that claim, Mandel argues, would require demonstrating things like the "laws of motion" of this "new formation" or the means by which the necessarily "new" ruling class rose to dominance. Mandel maintains, rather, that the revolution was hijacked by a bureaucratic "layer", suspending the Soviet Union in a state of permanent transition; a kind of twilight zone between capitalism and socialism.[24] History according to Mandel ultimately vindicated his position when a segment of the bureaucracy aware of the mounting impediments to prolonging its ambivalent balancing act began maneuvering to break up collective property and reinstate capitalism.[25]

For a final view along the neither capitalism nor socialism line, prominent French Marxist economists Gérard Duménil and Dominique Lévy maintain how beginning in the stage of imperialism capitalism itself evidences a bifurcation in function of the capitalist as personification of capital in terms of ownership *and* control over the value augmentation process. The outcome of this historical trend for Duménil and Lévy is that by the close of the post-WWII golden age the social class relations of capitalism had *already* been transformed into a new class configuration that they dub "managerialism".[26] As Duménil and Lévy see it, this vitiates Marx's prognosis that the "socializing" tendencies of capital would reveal the "parasitic" status of the capitalist persona that in turn underpins the idea of the working class overthrowing capitalists through revolution to manage the "socialized" economic base itself. And that the historical successor to capitalism will be socialism or communism. Duménil and Lévy argue that neither is necessarily the case. Rather, it is the "social order" (this term for them refers to shifts in class patterns of shorter duration than modes of production) of "managerialism" that emerged as the historical successor to capitalism and Soviet-style socialism was an authoritarian variant of that.[27]

To gather the threads of the discussion then, what the foregoing so glaringly displays is the complete bankruptcy of predicating the momentous human enterprise of future directed transformatory social action on HM as a master theory of historical directionality that says as little about the future as it does about the present. It veers close to the surreal to see Marxist debate seeking to differentiate socialism from capitalism in order to make a case against characterizing Soviet-style societies as socialist when the theorizing of socialism commenced with neither a bedrock definition of socialism as per Engels admonition nor one, for that matter, of what precisely capitalism *is*! Rather, it was based on the "rough structural principles" of HM the telos of which in the historical context of capitalism were to materialize socialism. This exercise in historical astrology then finally spruced up with revolutionary quotations culled from Marx's writings.

Let us deal first with the dissonance on the defining of capitalism side of the ledger. The notion of "laws of motion", for example, has applicability in the social world only to capital as a reified object that "takes on a life of its own", as Marx put it, to wield a human society according to its inner logic or laws of value augmentation. In precapitalist societies the economic imbricates with other social practices as human beings find their material lives enmeshed in interpersonal relations of domination and subordination. Capitalism "frees" the material intercourse of human beings from such interpersonal bonds. But it subjects human beings to the economic compulsion of capital that they confront as an "extra-human" force of nature if you will. It is precisely the vanquishing of human servitude to commodity economic "laws of motion" that socialism, if it is to offer an historical advance over capitalism, must guarantee. To assert that even socialism has "laws of motion" irrevocably given to human beings and to which they must kowtow is to perpetually confine humanity to the kingdom of necessity instead of its liberationist advance into the kingdom of freedom that is at the heart of the Marxian revolutionary mission.

Second, the issue of a "state capitalism" is hugely problematic on a number of levels. Dialectical economic theory captures the substructure of capitalist society as a mode of production that reproduces human material life as a byproduct of value augmentation. In synthesizing capitalism in economic theory as such, Marxian economics demonstrates how in its most fundamental incarnation capital disavows the state. Disavowing the state as it may, the historical record shows how capital in its process of becoming harnessed the concentrated force of the state to hone geospatial containers in which it spawned into fertile ground for bourgeois accumulation projects. And, as established by stage theory, it is the superstructure that mediates the causal force of capital as it reproduces human economic life in its distinct world historic stages of accumulation. In fact, it is in the capitalist stage of consumerism, where the capitalist state is called upon to play a promethean role in support of capital accumulation easily opening that stage to the charge of being "state capitalist". Though, because the state plays some role in supporting capital accumulation in each stage of capitalism, applying the concept to the erstwhile Soviet Union as way of distinguishing a particular "kind" of capitalism from socialism, is meaningless.

Then we have the unspecified use of terms such as "surplus appropriation", or appropriation of "social surplus labor": Marx never used these concepts in the study of capitalism. In capitalist economies it is *surplus value* production that feeds the chrematistic augmentation of abstract mercantile wealth. To the extent Marx refers to surplus labor, it is in the doctrine of production of dialectical economic theory in relation to the division of the working day between necessary labor time and surplus labor time. But the objective measurement of this and the incorrigible evidence of the existence of surplus labor as the source of exploitation is its materialization in surplus value. The "social" manifestation of surplus value appropriation is studied in the reproduction-process and self-expansion of aggregate social capital to confirm the possibility of capitalism as an historical society. In HM, the Marxian approach to material life in human history, general notions of "surplus appropriation" may be used only in the comparative light of Marxian political economy. But demarcating historical epochs of slavery, feudalism, and so on by HM in terms of the particular way surplus labor is extracted from the direct producers can never be a scientific enterprise given the extra-economic compulsion involved and enmeshing of economic with other social practices.

In fact the question of compulsion is the crux of this argument. In the Soviet Union and Soviet-style societies *labor power is decommodified*. As put by Valerie Bunce:

> power . . . came from the party's commitment to full employment – a commitment that, along with the labor hunger of enterprises . . . produced the infamous deal wherein workers pretended to work and enterprise directors pretended to pay them. The absence of unemployment was particularly

important in the socialist context.... Thus, in giving workers job security, their political power was necessarily augmented. Moreover, the regime was deprived of one mechanism that capitalist systems have long used to police their publics – elastic labor markets.[28]

Remember, in capitalist economies where the direct producers are paradigmatically "freed" from interpersonal relations of domination and subordination as well as, of course, "freed" from access to the means of production in agriculture and subsidiary activities rooted in it that they had at their disposal prior to the dawn of the capitalist era, the only coercion they face as they make their commodified labor power available for capital to purchase in the market is *economic* coercion. As Bunce's quote illustrates, with enterprise directors only "pretending" to pay workers under conditions where employment is guaranteed, work required another form of compulsion that was *extra-economic* and thus constitutes an historical regression from capitalism. Debates of the era over so-called moral and material incentives for work capture what the stakes here were presumed to be.[29] However, a genuine socialism, to constitute an historical advance over capitalism, *must* decommodify labor power (which extirpates economic compulsion) *but without reinstating extra-economic compulsion*, even of so-called moral incentives that imbricate direct producers in interpersonal relations of domination and subordination as the system of Soviet-style authoritarian rule unequivocally demonstrates. Marx's quote above of socialism as stripping away the "capitalist integument" is hardly helpful in this regard is it lulls transformatory actors into the false understanding that in simply decommodifying economic life one "finds" socialism. Without institutional bulwarks, decommodification easily lends itself to forms of extra-economic coercion. This is a momentous issue that, as we shall see, must be confronted head on in thinking creatively about institutional configuring of future socialist societies.

Treatment in the debate of "commodity relations" further highlights the hazards involved in seeking to differentiate capitalism from other forms of society in the absence of the synthetic definition of what in its fundamental incarnation capital *is* as provided by dialectical economic theory. Marx, after all, was crisply clear on the fact that *forms* of value such as money, wages, even profits, have appeared across various differing precapitalist formations. However their impact has always been exogenous to substantive modalities of precapitalist material reproduction. It is only in capitalist society that such exogenous or "external" economic forms are "internalized" as spreading marketization draws them into a unique symbiosis in the chrematistic of value augmentation. As will be discussed in both Chapter's 5 and 6, given their exogenous origins in human material reproduction across the sweep of human history, they may under certain institutional conditions even persist benignly in socialist economies.[30]

Sweezy's notions of "autonomously functioning markets" or competition among "separate enterprises" (the latter referred to by Bettelheim as well) are also not very helpful. We can speak about the former in the context of dialectical economic theory. However, when we leave its rarified environment, and begin to deal with concretizing of the inner logic of capital in stage theory or historical analysis of capitalism, the operations of integrated systems of self-regulating markets of capitalism must always be understood in terms of varying degrees of state support or superstructure mediation received by the value augmentation process. What the stage theory of imperialism displays is that even in the temporal period of emergence of Soviet-style socialism both state policies of home market protectionism and the commanding heights monopoly enterprises own competition curtailing business practices preclude use of that concept without substantial qualification with regards to really existing capitalism. Nevertheless, Sweezy's basic argument against simple explanations of the Soviet Union as capitalist is not necessarily wrong. Along with the decommodification of labor power touched on above, money in the Soviet Union was also substantially decommodified as prices in Soviet-style economies were not set by market forces but mostly officially "fixed".[31]

On the issue of "separate enterprises", finally, it is really not clear what is being argued. If it is that socialism constitutes an order organized as one big factory, without separation among production units, that would be just as humanly alienating as neoliberal obverse of society as one big market. And, as Hudis's study concludes, Marx himself never made the case for socialism based on contrasting of separate units operating in an anarchic market and the "organization" offered by the factory.[32] On the other hand, the competition among Soviet "separate" enterprises was quite different from that in capitalist economies. With labor power decommodified the competitive process that plays out around the replacement of fixed capital in the course of prosperity and depression phase business cycle oscillations in capitalist economies does not hold. Rather, competition among Soviet "separate" enterprises took a peculiar form of "hunger" for labor, as alluded to by Bunce above, and hunger for shares of social resources allocated by state central planning authorities as enterprises "competed" to fulfill or exceed central plan goals. This dynamic manifested itself in what Hungarian economist János Kornai famously explained as the "economics of shortage".[33]

The dissonance on the "what were Soviet-style societies?" question is similar on the socialism side of the ledger. It is rooted in the approach to socialism of HM as a theory of historical directionality and the subtheory status of Marx's study of capitalism within it – which in turn is the breeding ground for the hackneyed "logico-historical" method. Marxists continue to make much of Marx's revolutionary quotations such as that from *Capital* Volume 1, that "socialization" of capitalism will fulfill the telos of HM. However, when Marx's economic writings are taken as the self-contained whole of dialectical economic theory, what the more concrete-in-thought dialectical elaboration of capital in its market operations from Volume 3 or the doctrine of distribution show, is that the "socialization" of capital in economic theory always refers to *capitalist socialization*. For example, reference earlier in this book to the "socializing" of idle funds in the banking system, which makes monies saved by individual capitals during the course of business cycles available to all capital, is a distinctly capitalist process where the term "socialization" has nothing to do with presaging of a socialist future.

Similarly, centralization of capital, which is another part of the HM "socialization" story, simply refers to usurping of one capital by another or *expropriation of capitalist by capitalist* in the service of the capitalist social goal of value augmentation. Centralizing of capital performed important functions for capital even in Marx's time such as enabling it to complete certain large-scale tasks like railway construction that, like Lenin's "electrification" of Russia, has little, *in itself*, to do with socialism.

Even the multiple references at the close of *Capital* Volume 1 through Volume 2 to the sociality of capital in this or that part of its logic of operation always boil down to the basic point that private labor is *never* directly social. What we are talking about here is general norm of economic life number two, set out in the previous chapter. That in all human societies some economic principle, or set of these, must operate to ensure that supply of basic goods in society is adequate to meet social demand. Otherwise the material economic reproducibility of that human society will be called into question. In precapitalist economies private labor is rendered social *on top* of the backs of direct producers through interpersonal production relations of domination and subordination that ensnare them. In capitalist economies private labor is rendered social *behind* the backs of the direct producers as capital validates that labor ex post as "socially necessary labor" that contributes to its abstract social goal of value augmentation. The whole point of the reproduction schemes in Volume 2, as we note in the previous chapter, is to explain how capital coordinates the flow of its activities across all separate units of capital to guarantee the self-expansion of aggregate social capital as it simultaneously ensures the reproduction of capitalism as an historical society (We will return to this point in the following chapter as the phantasmagorias of Adam Smith's "invisible hand" as Kautsky's "petty commodity society" persist in haunting discussion of future alternatives!).

A recurring theme in the debate over Soviet-style societies is that of the paucity of worker control over their conditions of existence and detachment of workers from control over the "surplus" their labor produces. But *what* precise economic principles are involved in these "conditions of existence" or what *kind* of economy the "surplus appropriation" to be put in workers hands stems from are questions left unaddressed. This again derives from the opacity of HM that lulled transformatory actors into the view (leaving to one side here the debate in the Marxist-Leninist temple of how state power and "dictatorship of the proletariat" achieved) that stripped of capitalists the economic "base" bequeathed by "socialized" capitalism to socialism *was* socialist.

Indeed, Marxist persistence in approaching socialism *not* with any substantive definition but, rather, with HM and its working out of "rough structural principles", as Hobsbawn puts it, can hardly be inspiring for future transformatory actors. And it is not a question, again, of Lenin finally realizing that he had made strategic mistakes, particularly given the material conditions of Russia's pre-revolutionary capitalist underdevelopment.[34] It is true that the pathologies of building socialism according to a purported historical logic of capitalism were exacerbated in the Soviet context. The perfect storm of a socialist revolution to grow capitalism, to build socialism, a peculiar concoction sometimes dubbed "developmental socialism", could hardly be expected to yield anything other than the most unpalatable social outcomes.[35] This is the case in part because undeveloped capitalist "socialist" aspirants were getting varying doses of, well, capitalism. That the bureaucratic "layer" (Mandel), "Council of Industrial Ministers" (Resnick and Wolff), "state functionaries" (Bettelheim) often behaved badly instead of doing what these analysts saw as the right thing (fostering worker control over their material conditions of existence, whatever this meant) should not be surprising as building *capitalism* to socialize the forces of production that workers would then allegedly take control of as per the HM schema was also part of their job description. As well, the coupling of this building of socialism with the most odious authoritarian modes of social control was inevitable given the perceived task of a vanguard group "channeling" capitalist development to develop socialism.

Yet, on the other hand, as Makoto Itoh opines:

> . . . It is also not clear that the powerful ruling-class like position of State and Party bureaucrats was entirely anti-working class. The legitimacy of their rule lay in working for the workers in the name of socialism. This was not merely a propaganda slogan. Education, medical services, child care, general welfare, and real personal income were obviously improved, with some degree of egalitarianism. . . . In exchange for such gradual improvement of social and personal economic life, and for job security, the ruling-class like bureaucrats could claim the support of the majority of working people. Put differently, in exchange for improvements in economic life the majority of working people accepted the de-politicised and regimented social order . . .[36]

The shift of the debate terrain by Duménil and Lévy is even more confounding. They in effect accept the wrongheaded apprehension of Marxism codified as HM itself advanced as a theory of historical directionality, but substitute "managerialism" for its historical telos. It cannot be reemphasized more that the logic of capital builds *capitalism*. And the laws of capital are not self-defeating. Meaningful discussion of the sorts of transformations of capitalism Duménil and Lévy take up is the preserve of stage theory and historical analysis as levels of analysis in Marxian political economy. The changes in capital accumulation Duménil and Lévy identify, for example, do not occur in any economy-wide way. In the stage of *imperialism* the separating of ownership and management is characteristic of the large oligopolistic firms in steel and heavy chemicals. In the stage of *consumerism*, the MNC form is prevalent in automobiles, transportation equipment, agricultural machinery, petroleum, and so forth, yet huge swathes of the economy involve non-MNC types of companies. Moreover, the separating of ownership from management is not as simple a process as the term seems to imply. As giant oligopolies and MNC behemoths capture the commanding heights of capitalist economies it is these organizations that increasingly superintend the reproduction process of society. As part of this shift, the role of the small capitalist entrepreneur is transferred to management specialists. Given the prevalence of the joint-stock form of enterprise, the massive agglomerations of capital make for the division of the capitalist class through shareholding into a large group of shareholders or "owners". But even during the "golden age" studies show that around half of the top 300 MNCs listed in the Fortune 500 were still largely "family owned" with near 50 percent of stockholdings held among founding families and their descendants.[37] Thus, while shareholding disperses ownership it facilitates a level of control by large shareholders of MNCs far greater than their actual capital investment. Whether large shareholders manage the business themselves or delegate the role to a professional management stratum, what we are talking about here is the "concentrating of controlling power" amongst shareholder "owners" *not* the separating of control from ownership.[38]

It is true, as per the debate among theorists working with the Uno approach to Marxian political economy, that much of capitalist substance has been leeched out of the current order. But to make such a determination with a reasonable degree of scientific certainty requires recourse to Marxian economic theory as well as stage theory, not the hackneyed "logico-historical" method that Duménil and Lévy tacitly summon in their contraposition of class they assert Marx erroneously forecast for the nineteenth century and their own self-styled notion of "managerialism" purportedly established by the logic of capital [sic!] in the twentieth century. Returning to our question here, however, their position only reinforces the trend we have identified, which is rooted in the Mariana Trench sized chasm HM leaves in its approach to socialism, in which with no definition of socialism in its basic incarnation at its disposal, determinations of the future, as the above debate shows, reduce to fuzzy questions of things like social class and the behavior, subjective intentions or "class consciousness of "bureaucratic", "managerial", state actors. Remember, HM operates with concepts of class grounded in dialectical economic theory. Once we leave its reified conceptual space where classes are personifications of economic categories the sketching of class maps, even within levels of analysis in Marxian political economy, is a complex endeavor. And there is even less certainty in establishing whether a given social grouping is a social class or not in the empirical milieu of non-capitalist societies. In any case, class and/or class consciousness as such is not a very inspiring metric for determining whether a society is on the road to socialism or communism.

Dialectical economic theory and the ontology of socialism

En route to advancing our alternative Marxian approach to socialism it is vital that we clear a set of nagging issues off the table. First, the inveighing against "blueprints" of the future was intended as a strong caution to all varieties of utopian socialists of Marx and Engels's day over their spinning models of new societies without a clear grasp of what precisely capitalism *is*. The necessity for producing complete knowledge of capitalism is the case for the obvious reason that if the future society is to offer a progressive historical advance over capitalism, without a grasp of what precisely capitalism *is*, transformatory actors would have no way of knowing whether their efforts would genuinely result in the human material betterment they sought. But there is more. When in the *Contribution to the Critique of Political Economy* Marx states "[t]he anatomy of man is a key to the anatomy of the ape", what he adverts to is the fact *only* in capitalist society are human social relations of production reified and thus reveal themselves "transparently" for social science to subject to systematic study.[39] The historical condition of possibility for Marx striving to complete this project of systematic study of capitalism in the social science of dialectical economic theory was the tendency of mid-nineteenth-century capitalism to approximate its "pure" ideal. Dialectical economic theory and Marxian political economy, in turn, constitute the ground for HM as the comparative study of precapitalist societies in the light of the study of capitalism. And, Marxian economic theory, in its exposing the substructure of economic life as subsumed and organized by the commodity economy, also provides the basis for our thinking about a socialist economy of human flourishing that will satisfy the general norms of economic life (revealed in the study of capitalism) through economic management by free associations of human beings. In short, Marx never instructed us *not* to think creatively about economic configuring of a future socialist society. But rather to wait until we had a scientific foundation in dialectical economic theory for doing so.

Second, revolutionary quotations Marxist activists are renowned for bandying about aside, Marx's understanding in the famous preface of the role capitalism plays in bringing the "prehistory of human society [to a] close" has little to do with the HM claim that the productive forces of capitalism "build" socialism. Rather, as touched upon in the previous chapter, the capitalist era constitutes an important step in the advance of human freedom. That is, it liberates human beings from their enmeshment in the interpersonal social production relations of domination and subordination that marked all earlier class societies. However, the capitalist era saddles humanity with one momentous remaining non-freedom. This is the fact that "the economy" – effectively meaning the reified commodity economy of capitalism with its deep causal logic of value self-augmentation – confronts human beings as an "alien" or "extra-human" force, confining them to the "kingdom of necessity" as it compels human beings to conform to its impersonal, abstract chrematistic. The progressive alternative a genuine socialism offers humanity demands capitalist non-freedom be surmounted as free associations of human beings assume the management of their economic lives according to their democratically decided priorities. Put differently, all human societies including socialism have an economic substructure. In capitalism, it is the economic substructure that determines the superstructure. For a socialist society to constitute a progressive advance over capitalism, it is the superstructure that must assume control over the substructure. In this sense, in bringing "the prehistory of human society to a close", socialism obviates HM – which approached human economic history with the presupposition of the economic base as determinant of the superstructure. And our argument in the first chapter that much of the capitalist substance has been leeched from the current economy in no way invalidates the above argument. Still holding human beings in thrall is the ideology of neoliberalism secreted by capital in its death throes. That notwithstanding the fact of the capitalist market being largely superseded by a global network of casinos commanded by Wall Street, or that the casinos along with material reproducibility of human life itself being increasingly dependent upon a raft of state and extra-capitalist supports, that the lot of humanity remains subservience in perpetuity to blind economic forces irrespective of their deleterious outcomes.

What can be drawn from the foregoing on the one hand, therefore, is that for transformatory actors to talk about piggybacking on current economic trends to find "grave-diggers" of capitalism or to "build" socialism amounts to little more than gibberish. In fact, even in the context of erstwhile production-centered societies of Marx's or Lenin's day, *the conceptualizing of socialism in its most fundamental incarnation should always have been about socialism as the diametrical opposite or antithesis of capitalism.* That is, in reproducing human economic life as a byproduct of the extra-human goal of value augmentation, capitalism may be conceived as the limit form of what a human society should *not* be.

On the other hand, if we add to this understanding of socialism as the antithesis of capitalism Marx's view that our formative thinking about socialism is to be based upon knowledge of capital produced by dialectical economic theory, we arrive at a further contribution dialectical economic theory makes to socialism besides robustly confirming its feasibility. As I have argued, it is possible to derive an *ontology of socialism* – a "defining" of what socialism *is* in its most fundamental incarnation as the antithesis of capitalism – from dialectical economic theory.[40] This ontology of socialism is not a "blueprint" in the sense of a precise design of each and every aspect of building a socialist society. Given the variety of potential social transformatory scenarios by which socialist societies will come into being and/or specific geospatial, socio-cultural/socio-historical conditions and contingencies socialist actors will certainly face, it would be sheer folly to set about drawing up a detailed one-size-fits-all "how to" chart. But it is also sheer folly to expect the forging of broad transformatory social constituencies for genuine post-capitalist change in the absence of transformatory social actors' articulation of basic economic and institutional principles that a socialist society must follow. As we shall see in Chapter 7, despite the widespread, seething discontent across the globe in both advanced and non-developed societies over a raft of grave ills marking current socio-economic orders, something that has given rise to varied social movements (the "Occupies") and dramatic social upheavals (the Middle East "Springs"), it is the dearth of an articulation of principles of a viable, materially reproducible, progressive order that has led to movements and upheavals hitting dead ends, or worse.

The following four ontological principles of socialism are therefore offered as foundational guide to creative thinking about a future of human flourishing. That is, the ontological principles of socialism define what socialism *is* in its bedrock conceptualization as the diametrical opposite of capitalism. They provide a touchstone for the configuring of economic forms, institutions, and types of property relations through which the general norms of economic life outlined in the previous chapter are satisfied as progressive socialist goals simultaneously met. We will return to them at points throughout the upcoming chapters of this book in order to show how in more concrete situations of economic and institutional change they are to be operationalized. And how cognizance of them helps us navigate thorny issues for the future of environmental sustainability and mitigating climate change.

Ontological principle one flows from the elaboration in dialectical economic theory of capitalism as not only an exploitative, alienating, class divided, asymmetric wealth distributive society, but an "upside-down", reified order that reproduces human material existence as a byproduct of its abstract goal of value augmentation. The ontological principle of socialism that springs from this understanding of capitalism is that *socialism constitutes a non-reified economy in which the responsibility for organizing human material life is vested in human beings themselves, and that material reproduction is managed for concrete human purposes.* To repeat, it is precisely in this sense that socialism brings "the prehistory of human society to a close" and hence obviates HM. This is the case because with the advent of socialism, for the first time in human history economic life is consciously managed according to the "concrete" democratically determined priorities of communities of freely associated human beings. In Chapter 5 below we will demonstrate the importance of the guidance this principle offers with regards to debate over the state and market in socialism as well as that on purported dynamism and innovativeness of this thing referred to as "the market" (read capitalism) that many on the Left today seem enraptured by and determined to hold fast to in the future.

Ontological principle two derives from the exposure by dialectical economic theory of the commodification of labor power as the sine qua non of capitalism. Bourgeois ideologues, of course, point to capitalism effacing interpersonal relations of domination and subordination marking earlier historical societies as the epitome of human freedom and basis of capitalism as a society that suspends class conflict. But, while it is true that capitalism liberates the direct producers from extra-economic compulsions for work they suffered in precapitalist orders, it nevertheless remains a very peculiar class society that subjects the direct producers (the proletariat) to *economic* compulsion for work. A genuine socialism therefore, demands the decommodification of labor power. But this must not be accompanied by reviving forms of extra-economic coercion as occurred in Soviet-style societies for capitalism already constitutes an historical advance over that. In short, *socialism necessitates the decommodification of human labor power without the reinstatement of extra-economic compulsion.*

Ontological principle three follows from the foregoing. Capitalist reification as dialectical economic theory demonstrates entails the reproducing by capital of the material life of a human society as a byproduct of augmenting abstract mercantile wealth. To fulfill its social goal of augmenting abstract mercantile wealth, capitalism requires the commodification of human labor power that reduces the worker to a commodity economic input available in the market for capital to deploy producing *any* good according to shifting patterns of social demand and opportunities for profit-making. Recruited by capital in the service of value augmentation as such renders labor *indifferent* to *use value* in production as it engenders *disinterest* amongst workers as "consumers" to the wherewithal and modalities of the production process itself (such facilitating the production of use values with the potential to destroy human life itself on the planet). Therefore work, the metabolic interchange between human beings and nature as that elemental human activity upon which the existence of human society rests, is destined to remain for direct producers in capitalist society a *disutility* or *alienated*. That is, no matter how high wages paid to workers are, remuneration is simply a means for workers to secure only *future* sustenance or enjoyment. The subsumption by capital of the metabolic interchange between human beings and nature through the commodification of labor power bequeaths a world that stands above workers as abstract mercantile wealth, *alien* to them. Simply decommodifying human labor power as occurred in Soviet-style societies, however, does not in itself surmount capitalist alienation. What emerges, therefore, as a definitive ontological principle of a genuine socialism, is that *to constitute an advance over capitalism work, even its most arduous forms, must become self-motivated*. That is, the compulsion for work cannot be extra-economic or economic (see Figure 3.1). Work in a genuine socialism, as Marx himself put it in *Critique of the Gotha Program*, must become "life's prime want".[41] The paramount challenge for the socialisms of today is the economic principles, institutional matrix, and forms of property that will enable self-motivation as such as the paradigmatic compulsion for work.

Ontological principle four brings each of the previous three principles into a more concrete relief. What dialectical economic theory so glaringly captures is the stultifying homogeneity the subsumption of human economic life by capital brings. Dialectical economic theory exposes this homogeneity beginning with its formative analysis of the very cell form of capital, the commodity. It demonstrates that as the products of human labor are subsumed by the commodity and money forms their sensuous, qualitative, use value heterogeneities

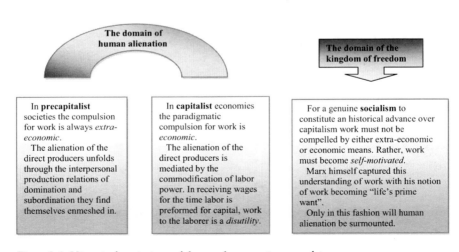

Figure 3.1 Historical societies and forms of economic compulsion

are suppressed given the way commodities are differentiated only *quantitatively*, as value objects, in the capitalist market. Remember, the fundamental contradiction of capital is that between value and use value: use value being the transhistorical qualitative foundation of all human material existence; value the historically specific abstract quantitative principle of capital. The contradiction between value and use value or, what amounts to the same thing, the incongruity or gap between value and the substantive foundation of human economic life, confirms capital as a historically delimited society. Contrary to bourgeois economics, from classical to neoclassical, that upholds capitalism as a natural order. Indeed, dialectical economic theory from its formative analysis of the commodity form through its consummation in the fetishized category of interest, as emphasized in the previous chapter, is a story about how at every turn, capital seeks to neutralize or tame all heterogeneous use value recalcitrance to reproduce the material life of a human society for its abstract, quantitative, homogenizing goal. However the managing by capital of use value recalcitrance is possible only to the extent the use value side allows it. Dialectical economic theory assumes an ideal use value space, allowing capital to have its way with the world, because it wants to give capital all the rope it needs to hang itself, to reveal its innermost secrets. Real, historical use values though, are *not* equally subsumable by capital. Stage theory proves this vividly. Not only do stage specific use values press capital into adopting discrete structures of accumulation to augment value. But capitalist management of heavier more complex use value production in world historic stages of *imperialism* and *consumerism* sees value augmentation draw heavily upon an array of non-economic, extra-market superstructure supports.

The point here then is that socialism must begin with what capital seeks to expunge – the heterogeneity of use value life. The ontological principle that stems from this is that a genuine socialism demands *the entrenchment of the heterogeneous use value dimension of material existence in each and every aspect of socialist economic and institutional configuring*. It is argued in this book that all questions of choice of economic forms or principles (markets, planning, communal reciprocity, and so forth), all questions of economic scale (large scale, small scale), geospatial questions ("local", central, regional, "global"), as well as questions of forms of property (private, public, communal, associational, commons) must be approached through the lens of the heterogeneity of use value life for a genuine socialism that provides a progressive advance over capitalism to take shape. That is, in all the aforementioned distinctions the question for socialists is reversing the capitalist legacy by suppressing quantitative determinants in economic life in favor of qualitative ones. Indeed, it is not clear how self-motivation as the paradigmatic compulsion for work in a socialist society, work as "life's prime want", could ever be instated in lieu of qualitative heterogeneous use value considerations in economic life being brought to the fore. And, as will be addressed in the following chapter, fashioning human material existence in the face of environmental and climate change challenges is a qualitative, heterogeneous use value question writ large!

Notes

1 Karl Marx, *The Eighteenth Brumaire of Louis Bonaparte*, 1852, http://www.marxists.org/archive/marx/works/1852/18th-brumaire/ch01.htm.
2 Hudis, *Marx's Concept of the Alternative to Capitalism*, p. 5.
3 Robin Blackburn, "Fin de Siècle: Socialism after the Crash", *New Left Review*, I/185 (1991) p. 7.
4 Westra, "Kautsky, Lukacs, Althusser and the Retreat from the Economic in Marxism".
5 See Frederick Engels, *Socialism: Utopian and Scientific*, 1880, http://www.marxists.org/archive/marx/works/1880/soc-utop/index.htm.
6 Hobsbawm, *How to Change the World*, p. 86.
7 Marx, *Capital* V1, Chapter 32, http://www.marxists.org/archive/marx/works/1867-c1/ch32.htm.
8 Michael C. Howard and John E. King, *A History of Marxian Economics* Volume 2 (Princeton, NJ: Princeton University Press, 1992) p. 365.
9 Westra, *Political Economy and Globalization*, pp. 46–53. Cf. V. I. Lenin, *Imperialism, the Highest Stage of Capitalism*, 1916, http://www.marxists.org/archive/lenin/works/1916/imp-hsc/index.htm; Rudolf Hilferding, *Finance Capital: A Study of the Latest Phase of Capitalist Development*, 1910, http://www.marxists.org/archive/hilferding/1910/finkap/index.htm.
10 See, for example, the most recent restatement of this position by John Milos and Dimitris P. Sotiropoulos, *Rethinking Imperialism: A Study of Capitalist Rule* (Basingstoke: Palgrave, 2009) pp. 18–20.
11 V. I. Lenin, *Seventh All-Russia Congress of Soviets*, 5–9 December 1919, http://www.marxists.org/archive/lenin/works/1919/dec/05.htm. The first several paragraphs are in fact quite instructive.
12 See for example the excellent discussion in Keith Griffin and John Gurley, "Radical Analyses of Imperialism, the Third World, and the Transition to Socialism: A Survey Article", *Journal of Economic Literature*, 23 (1985).
13 V. I. Lenin, "Draft Resolution of the Eighth Congress of Soviets on The Report on Electrification" in ibid., p. 522; cf. See the discussion in E. H. Carr, *The Bolshevik Revolution Volume 1 1917–1923*, (Middlesex: Penguin Books, 1966) pp. 366 ff.
14 V. I. Lenin, "'Left-Wing' Communism – An Infantile Disorder", in *V. I. Lenin: Selected Works*, Volume 3 (Moscow: Progress Publishers, 1971) p. 351.
15 See Tariq Ali, *The Idea of Communism* (London: Seagull Books, 2009) pp. 40–2.
16 Ibid., p. 53.
17 Charles Bettelheim, *The Transition to Socialist Economy* (New Jersey: Humanities Press, 1975); idem, *Economic Calculation and Forms of Property* (New York and London: Monthly Review Press, 1975); idem, "The Specificity of Soviet Capitalism", *Monthly Review*, 37, 4 (1985) pp. 43–61; also the exchange with Paul Sweezy in Paul M. Sweezy and Charles Bettelheim, *On the Transition to Socialism* (New York and London: Monthly Review Press, 1971).
18 Bettelheim, *Economic Calculation*, p. 149.
19 Ibid., p. 71.
20 See Stephen Resnick and Richard Wolff, "State Capitalism in the USSR? A High-Stakes Debate", *Rethinking Marxism*, 6, 2 (Summer 1993), pp. 46–48; idem, "Between State and Private Capitalism: What was Soviet 'Socialism'"? *Rethinking Marxism*, 7, 1 (Spring 1994), pp. 9–30.

21 Resnick and Wolff, "Between State and Private Capitalism", pp. 14, 18.
22 See Sweezy and Bettelheim, *On the Transition*; Paul M. Sweezy, *Post-Revolutionary Society* (New York and London: Monthly Review Press, 1980); idem, "After Capitalism – What?" *Monthly Review*, 37, 3 (1985), pp. 98–111.
23 Sweezy, *Post-Revolutionary Society*, p. 139.
24 See Ernest Mandel, "On the Nature of the Soviet State", *New Left Review* 108 (March-April 1978) pp. 23–45; idem, *Beyond Perestroika* (London: Verso, 1989); idem, *Power and Money* (London: Verso, 1992).
25 Mandel, *Power and Money*, pp. 32–3.
26 Gérard Duménil and Dominique Lévy, "Production and Management: Marx's Dual Theory of Labor", in Richard Westra and Alan Zuege (eds.), *Value and the World Economy Today: Production, Finance and Globalization* (Basingstoke: Palgrave/Macmillan 2003) pp. 153ff.
27 Gérard Duménil and Dominique Lévy, "The Dynamics of Modes of Production and Social Orders", http://www.jourdan.ens.fr/levy/dle2012n.pdf.
28 Valerie Bunce, *Subversive Institutions: The Design and Destruction of Socialism and the State* (Cambridge: Cambridge University Press, 1999) p. 28.
29 See for example Peter Clecak, "Moral and Material Incentives", *Socialist Register*, 6 (1969), http://socialistregister.com/index.php/srv/article/view/5282/2183#.Up1B77QXXbo.
30 Makoto Itoh, *Political Economy for Socialism* (London: Macmillan Press, 1995) pp. 44–6.
31 Ibid., pp. 47ff.
32 Hudis, *Marx's Concept of the Alternative to Capitalism*, p. 208.
33 János Kornai, *Economics of Shortage*, Volume A and B (Amsterdam: North Holland Press, 1980).
34 See for example Žižek, "How to Begin from the Beginning", pp. 201–10.
35 See the discussion in Cliff Durand, "The Exhaustion of Developmental Socialism: Lessons from China", *Monthly Review*, 42, 7 (1990).
36 Itoh, *Political Economy for Socialism*, pp. 151–2.
37 Westra, *Evil Axis of Finance*, p. 34.
38 This insight draws upon Kozo Uno's unpublished writing on stage theory.
39 Marx, *Contribution to the Critique of Political Economy*. The quoted line is preceded by: "Bourgeois society is the most advanced and complex historical organisation of production. The categories which express its relations, and an understanding of its structure, therefore, provide an insight into the structure and the relations of production of all formerly existing social formations".
40 Richard Westra, "Marxian Economic Theory and an Ontology of Socialism: A Japanese Intervention", *Capital & Class*, 78 (2002). Though I should point out that in this early writing I set out three ontological principles of socialism. In the more recent development of my thinking about socialism in the present book I advance four ontological principles.
41 Karl Marx, *Critique of the Gotha Program*, 1875, http://www.marxists.org/archive/marx/works/1875/gotha/.

4 Green dawn

Persuasive cases have been made for an eco-Marx by those who have ploughed through his work to unearth its wealth of detail on stewardship of the earth.[1] And, as I argue in this book, at a most fundamental level, Marxian economics offers up a very clear way of thinking about the (re)embedding of human material reproduction in the lifeworld, biosphere, and global ecosystems to ensure a livable human future. Yet, this provides little solace to critics of the disgraceful environmental records of "really existing" socialist states that lay claim to Marx's legacy. The erstwhile Soviet Union is certainly a case in point. We find even a staunch, early disparager of capitalist industrial environmental degradation resisting ideological temptation to cover his eyes and give the Soviet Union a "by" in his path breaking book.[2] And China today has raised the bar on biospheric despoiling to new heights. China surpasses the US as the world's number one carbon dioxide (CO_2) emitter (in aggregate not per capita terms, of course) and is ingloriously home to 20 of the globe's 30 most polluted cities, as well as 459 environmentally toxic "cancer villages" distributed throughout a full 29 of its 31 provinces.[3] Further, as touched on in Chapter 3 of the present book, there is the widely held apprehension of Marxism that also finds support in Marx's words, and certainly in those of many of his followers like Lenin, that paints pictures of the socialist future as one wedded to state centrally planned industrial giganticism with all latter's anti-ecological implications. Thus, as environmental movements gathered pace in the 1960s and 1970s, they began to carve out a political space for themselves increasingly critical of the role capitalist economic growth played in their shared experiences and growing awareness of potential biospheric catastrophe; but with a studied view of socialism as the "other" enemy.[4] Green social and political movements constitute a major constituency for change. It is therefore vital that their concerns and key works be addressed by socialists.

The purpose of this chapter is to do three things: First, to review up-to-date science on environmental destruction and climate change. The discussion then treats claims by prominent Green writers on how the existing economy, understood as a "kind" of "capitalism", can be tweaked in sustainable ways to meet the challenges of looming biospheric annihilation they decry. Those claims are decisively put to rest. Third, the chapter turns to select "deeper" Green schemes to remake economies for the future. We critically apply our knowledge of human economic life developed in Chapter 2, to these. As we shall see, Green designs for sustainable socio-economic change hinge upon questions of reduced economic scale. Yet Greens are fuzzy on the economic principles through which the material economic reproducibility of the ecologically sustainable societies will be managed. I argue that while questions of scale are certainly relevant to progressive future directed thinking, in the end, "small scale", "large scale", "local", "national", "global", and so forth constitute geospatial categories that offer no substitute for economic principles. Treatment of the latter devolves to questions of *qualitative* vs. *quantitative* and *ex ante* vs. *ex post* decision making in material economic life within the context of heterogeneous use value needs. After all, social schemes to ensure future eco-sustainability but which elide substantive issues of economic principles to ensure the reproduction of human material existence amount to naught. This chapter helps set the stage for our elaboration in Chapter 6 of an eco-sensitive design for a socialist successor society. Ecosocialist and eco-anarchist contributions are dealt with then.

Red sky in the morning

The millennium old adage for "sailors to take warning" has never been more apropos than now for humanity on this planet ecosystem called earth. To be sure, as discussed in Chapter 2 of this book, accepting the meaning of *science* as the pursuit of objective knowledge and truth about the workings of our world, the extent to which dialectical economic theory approaches such a lofty goal in regards to its subject matter, the deep causal inner logic of capital, is unachievable in the natural world. Unlike capital, which as an ontologically peculiar socially and historically constituted self-reifying object tells its story to us from the *inside*,[5] the natural word is *outside* us with humans having no insider information on its ultimate making or design. Nevertheless, working through revolutions in the transitive dimension of science, sciences have probed deeper and deeper with their cognitive and physical tool boxes, peeling back the layers of deep causally efficacious structures of the natural world's intransitive objects to produce knowledge in ways aspiring to capital-T truth. Of course, while uncertainties are destined to remain in our knowledge of the natural world, the business of theoretic and evidenced based prediction of *good* natural science continues to serve humanity relatively well. Let us then go to some of the authoritative sources to get a handle on the knowledge that we can use to help guide our future directed thinking.

A widely referred to method of explaining the environmental predicament of humanity is in terms of "planetary boundaries" initially outlined by Johan Rockström et al.[6] The notion of planetary boundaries captures the human shift over the last 100 years or so into a new geological era dubbed the Anthropocene – an age where human action itself emerges as a major force in shaping the biosphere. The 10,000 preceding years of the Holocene era brought relative biospheric stability to earth in ways conducive to development of its successive civilizations culminating in modern society. And it is the limited range of variability in biospheric conditions characteristic of the Holocene that constitute the benchmark for assessing the dangers inhering in current biospheric trends.[7]

The scientifically agreed upon Mother of all biospheric challenges in the Anthropocene era is climate change. Naturally occurring "greenhouse effects" of a delicate balance of gases in the earth's atmosphere is what maintained the temperature patterns associated with Holocene stability and the averting of either "ice age" or *Waterworld*-like, no ice, hot extremes. The atmospheric concentration of carbon dioxide (CO_2), the greenhouse gas (GHG) component human action is implicated in dramatically raising, held steady through the Holocene at around 275 parts per million by volume (ppm) up to the point of the industrial revolution. From there it commenced its ascent. And, by 1958 when precision monitoring equipment became available it was measured at 315.71 ppm.[8] In 2012 atmospheric CO_2 was measured at 394 ppm. Anthropogenic CO_2 from utilization of fossil fuels such as oil, gas, and coal for energy constitutes 75 percent of GHG emissions among major economies signatory to the 1992 United Nations Framework Convention on Climate Change (UNFCCC) and approximately 60 percent of total global CO_2 emissions. And fossil fuels accounted for 82 percent of global total primary energy supply (TPES) in 2011. By sector, electricity and heat is the source of 42 percent of CO_2 emissions, transport 22 percent (road transport accounts for 75 percent of that, increasing by 52 percent from 1990), and industry 21 percent in 2011.[9] With recent investigation charging just 90 major companies around the world with ultimate responsibility for two thirds of all anthropogenic CO_2 emissions![10]

The upshot of the foregoing is not that there is great uncertainty on the concatenation of effects that would follow a planetary boundary being crossed with intensified trapping of heat in the atmosphere due to excessive CO_2 concentrations (along with build-up of other GHG) but over what that boundary is, with crude computer simulations initially setting it at 550 ppm. However, as the first decade of the twenty-first century progressed, a body of increasingly incontrovertible science emerged from observed trends of each and every projected effect of global warming that, in fact, irreversible climate change was unfolding in the here and now. Evidence that led to the conclusion among the majority of experts that 350 ppm was the planetary boundary . . . and it had been crossed.[11] And the most recent report in 2013 of the Intergovernmental Panel on Climate Change (IPCC) suggests that things are going from bad to worse. That is, modeling scenarios of Representative Concentration Pathways (RCP), the IPCC report shows that under the current regime of inaction on fossil fuel emissions, worst case average global warming by 2081–2100 could well approach 6 degrees Celsius (C).[12] Let us put this in context: Averting the most "dangerous" effects of global warming, according to current international negotiations, demands preventing it rising 2 degrees C above its Holocene average. That is, international negotiations now recognize climate change *is* occurring after the surpassing of the 350 ppm planetary boundary. However following debate over what constitutes "dangerous", 450 ppm yielding the 2 degree rise is set as the line not to cross. But, Clive Hamilton declares, the chances of this "are virtually zero because the chances of keeping concentrations below 450 ppm are virtually zero".[13]

What can we expect? Melting polar ice, glaciers, permafrost (discovered not to be so "permanent" after all), along with rising sea levels, extreme weather patterns, hypertrophied instances of flooding and drought (depending on geolocation), scorching heat waves, and warmer weather generally over much of the earth, are some of the trends. Keep in mind that Paleoclimate research indicates Antarctic ice sheets formed when atmospheric CO_2 dropped to below 500 ppm while those of Greenland and West Antarctic formed as it fell below 400 ppm. With no polar ice caps or glaciers, sea levels were 70 meters higher than they are today.[14] Therefore virtually certain twenty-first-century outcomes (if society does not act now) include, rendering of highly populated coastal areas from Baton Rouge to Bangladesh unlivable, vanishing fresh water resources, desertification, collapsing ecosystems and agriculture. And then there are "feedback mechanisms" that exacerbate the impacts of climate change as giant rainforest carbon sinks are destroyed and the world's oceans acidify, annihilating coral reefs and the marine life these support. In fact, we should point out here that within the scientific community James Hansen of National Aeronautics and Space Administration (NASA) has been critical of what he sees as the IPCC tendency to occlude the factoring in of precisely such feedback mechanisms in their analysis and policy recommendations.[15]

Chemical dispersion of toxic compounds including heavy metals, persistent organic pollutants (POPs), plastics, endocrine disruptors, and radioactive wastes accumulate in the environment and perdure for extended periods. The deleterious effect of these individually is well known by science though there does not yet exist an estimate of their aggregate impact akin to the planetary boundary analysis of climate change. Nevertheless, the evidence of reductions in fertility and genetic damage for various organisms from the introduction into the environment of these toxic compounds continues to add up. So does evidence of direct links between environmental dispersion of a plethora of chemical toxicities and the recent multiplying of developmental disorders such as autism, dyslexia, and attention-deficit/hyperactivity disorder (ADHD) in children.[16] This all leading to the disturbing possibility that a planetary boundary may well be crossed behind our backs.

The large-scale emitting of such human-made toxic chemicals into the environment ratchets up in the post-WWII era of the capitalist stage of *consumerism* with the latter's religion-like ethos of ever-expanding mass consumption of consumer durables and associated electronic gadgetry. The processes euphemized as "globalization" that sliced, diced, and disarticulated consumer goods production systems across low-wage, weak regulatory regime economies of the world exacerbated the dispersion of toxicity not only in the manufacturing phase but in the waste/disposal phase.[17] In fact, as the shift of advanced economies to ICT "brain work" paralleling MNC disinternalizing of manufacturing to the third world was gathering momentum, advanced economy markets were already saturated with the mass produced consumer durables that had fuelled post-WWII growth. Thus the shift intensified MNC competition over niche markets like electronics driven by a frenetic pace of technological R&D and just as rapid product (as well as production equipment) obsolescence further intensifying the dispersion of toxic compounds around the world. China's environmental morass and rise in the global CO_2 emitter league is intimately linked to the foregoing.[18] And, while the world's media was transfixed on the collapse in Bangladesh of the Rana Plaza sweatshop complex in 2013, it is the slower death and poisoned existence of the population from the role Bangladesh plays treating and coloring garments in the global garment value chain that is the real though largely untold story of so-called globalization in increasingly fickle "fast" fashion industries.[19]

The common denominator among four of the planetary boundaries set out by the Stockholm Resilience Centre (biodiversity, hydrological cycle, land system change, biogeochemical cycles of nitrogen and phosphorous) is the chemicalization of agriculture that followed the displacement of "family" and smallholder "peasant" farming across the globe by giant agrochemical MNCs from the mid-twentieth century onwards. What have been dubbed "petrofoods" refers to the advent of petroleum based fertilizers, pesticides, and herbicides that engendered the "green revolution" chimera of heightened crop yields, the dispensing of crop rotation, and fallowing, but in the end, saddled humanity with a petroleum intense agriculture that today requires 10 calories of fossil fuel to produce but one calorie of food.[20] All the while with worldwide government subsidies to fossil fuels estimated at $630 billion in 2012.[21]

Yet this is only the beginning. While both nitrogen and phosphorous are natural substances essential to plant growth the petrofood revolution has seen excess nitrogen absorbed into the atmosphere only to then be rained out polluting both internal and coastal waterways. Phosphorous excess from petrofood production that ends up in fresh waterways results in their oxygen deprivation while runoff into rivers subsequently carried out to oceans create "dead zones" as in the Mississippi Delta that once was flush with shrimp. Then, lest we forget, is the impact of chemicalization on the soil itself, leeching out its organic nutrients. This, environmentalist Bill McKibben maintains, underpins the great hoax upon humanity perpetrated by agrochemical MNCs: that modern, urbanized societies would starve if we stopped injecting soils with their toxic synthetic brews.[22]

In fact, it is in this way that the transmutation of human agriculture into an agrochemical industry interfaces with planetary boundaries of the hydrological cycle, land system change, and biodiversity. On the one hand, vast monoculture food production demands extensive irrigation networks that constitute around 70 percent of all freshwater withdrawal globally. Supplying the irrigation and otherwise securing access to water is a major propellant of mega dam construction that exploded worldwide from the 1950s. This large-scale diverting of freshwater in turn detrimentally impacts ecosystems and their living species dependent upon natural water flows, driving many to extinction. And, when we add the wholesale emitting of toxic compounds into the mix of agrochemical pollution and agrochemical impelled water withdrawal, the sum is mounting chronic water shortages, or "water stressed" societies rendering over a fifth of the earth's population exposed to waterborne disease.[23] On the other hand, as urban growth and sprawl begins to consume prime agricultural lands (China is a poster economy for this with its loss of 22.2 million acres of arable land since 1997[24]), expanding agrochemical monoculture begins to whittle away at the world's remaining forests. And along with monoculture comes the suite of toxins, fertilizers, pesticides, and so on, which wreak havoc on the local ecosystem contributing ever more to collapse of species already fighting extinction from the ravages of climate change. One of the most ominous aspects of this is the onset of worldwide honey bee colony collapse; ominous because honey bees are not just *any* species, but responsible for about 80 percent of all pollination (the process by which plant life reproduces) globally.[25]

It must be emphasized here that agrochemical reorganization of agriculture worldwide becomes ever more frenetic in the neoliberal era. As the process discussed in the Introduction to this book unfolded (advanced economies led by the US abdicating their real economies in favor of surrogate economies of casino finance and services), the plummeting of real wages and rising inequalities that trailed the eviscerating of real economy jobs had to be managed. For categories of material goods, the holding of ever-expanding mass consumption as tantamount to "freedom" effectively meant the "American way of life" would necessarily have to be "Made in China". As the "China's", "Bangladesh's" and other low wage producers through which global value chains are routed ramped up their biggest export – price deflation.[26] Food prices tell a similar deflationary tale. In domestic agricultural sectors of advanced economies, the US and European Union (EU) particularly, the neoliberal policy tool was "big government" subsidies. Whether to agribusiness directly or through fossil fuel subsidies, average subsidies in the EU per cow, for example, are greater than the $2 dollars a day on which according to the World Bank almost half the world's population lives. In the US "big government" subsidies allow farmers to export rice at 25 percent less than its production cost, wheat 28 percent less, and corn 10 percent less.[27] Indeed, in the neoliberal decades from 1975 to 2003 food became cheaper than at any point in recent history going back to the sixteenth century.[28]

Neoliberal policy for agriculture across the non-developed third world entailed brutal enforcement of the so-called Washington Consensus that came into being following the 1982 global debt crisis.[29] The debt crisis brought to a screeching halt the third-world quest for a New International Economic Order (NIEO) in which each third-world state would strive to achieve full-scale industrialization according to the post-WWII advanced economy "economic nationalist" model.[30] The hallmark of so-called Washington Consensus policy is "export-oriented growth". Under the gun of crushing debt burdens third-world states were forced to eliminate every neoliberal perceived market "distortion" ranging from state regulatory regimes favoring urban industrialization, state development banks, subsidies for business technological upgrading, public funding for education, health care, infrastructure (both rural and urban), protectionist trade measures, and so on. Instead, the third world was to revert to its "comparative advantage" that effectively meant producing one or two globally traded crops for export. The Washington Consensus fable was that with wholesale external orientation of third-world economies sufficient foreign exchange would be generated to service debts as well as import necessary industrial goods (as agriculture pulled up light manufacturing in its wake).

Of course, this is nonsense. Agribusiness MNCs driven by global profit horizons pounced on vulnerable third-world economies using their worldwide sourcing, transport, processing, and marketing prowess to play third-world countries off against each other in lowering costs of agricultural goods. The reorienting of agriculture away from domestic food provision and subsistence increased overall commercialization of agriculture benefiting parasitic landed classes, large-scale plantation operators, and foreign MNCs. In turn, it fostered growing landlessness among peasant/small farmer cultivators and spawned an ever bloating casual workforce. Besides the perverse land use outcome that sees "poor people go hungry while surrounded by fertile land that produces luxury crops for the rich on the other side of the world".[31] The so-called Washington Consensus accelerated the tendency toward crossing planetary boundaries in land use change touched on above. While critical of state subsidies for third-world industrial modernization, the neoliberal Washington Consensus impelled hordes of rural disenfranchised into bloating urban slums, expected to encompass 1.4 billion people by 2020.[32] And it is the explosion of slums ringing third-world cities that in part encroaches on arable lands; which in turn factors into the aggressive agrochemical monoculture devastation of the terrestrial biosphere.

The final insult to third-world humanity here is that with available global food provisioning under multipronged attack from climate change, toxic chemicalization, and skewed land use patterns, coveting food access through a practice known as "land grabbing" is emerging as one of the "fiercest struggles" of the "race for what's left" of the world's resources. Where a motley cabal of state sponsored agribusinesses from the likes of China, South Korea, Saudi Arabia to international private investors and even hedge funds are scrambling to grab land, the "new gold", across impoverished Africa and around the world.[33] As Frank Pearce puts it in the opening pages of his exhaustive study:

> ... Over the next few decades I believe land grabbing will matter more, to more of the planet's people, even than climate change. The new land rush looks increasingly like a final enclosure of the planet's wild places, a last roundup of the global commons.[34]

Greening the augmentation of abstract mercantile wealth?

We need not immediately reprise the argument made in the Introduction to this book, that there is less and less in current economic trends that are substantively *capitalist*. The fact that there is scant recognition of the operation of "the market" today as largely a façade behind which "big government", "big bank", and "big MNCs" functioning much like Soviet-style command economies, toy with economic life for the aggrandizement of a relatively small global cohort is a neoliberal ideological coup of biblical proportions. For the purpose of the following discussion, that the neoliberal policy "toying" with economic life continues to be in the service of the abstract, quantitative, capitalist-like social goal of augmenting mercantile wealth, we can still can still mount our critique of Green argument on tweaking capitalism for environmentally sustainable ends particularly given Greens' own reference to the economy as a "kind" of "capitalism".

So-called "green capitalist" argument essentially appears in three broad genres: One is the "internalizing of externalities". Two is the technological fix/adaptation claim. Three is the "steady state" or degrowth answer.

The notion of "externalities" enters mainstream economics parlance with the rise to ideological dominance of the neoclassical tradition. It is part and parcel of neoclassical inheritance from classical political economy – the naturalizing of capitalism and belief in the ultimate perfectibility of "the market". Hence the position advanced in the landmark Stern Review, of climate change as an "externality" and reflection of the "greatest market failure the world has ever seen", was universally accepted by neoclassical economics.[35] Such acceptance of climate change as the "greatest market failure", of course, bolsters neoclassical claims about market perfectibility and capitalism as a natural order. This is the case because it circumscribes debate over climate change or biospheric despoiling generally to that of "internalizing" into market operations their wider social costs by "getting prices right" for market participants who generate those costs to pay for them.

As prominent environmentalist James Gustave Speth observes, from the 1970s the environmentalist case for a modicum of government intervention as, for example, in the regulation of stock market activities in the US by the Securities and Exchange Commission had been accepted by even the most market enraptured public and private actors. However, beginning in the 1980s, our neoliberal decades, environmental economics emerged as modern economics' "answer to the failure of the market to care for the environment". Utilizing economic incentives to achieve environmental ends was a first step. And, by the early twenty-first century, the price "mechanism" became "the default position in environmental policy", embraced by both business and the environmental community.[36] Even Speth himself believes "[t]he market can be transformed into an instrument for environmental restoration".[37] All which brings us back to the issue of market perfectibility lent credence to by the Stern Review. For "getting prices right" is simply a quibble over setting a supposed "discount rate", or rate for assessing current costs and benefits in relation to costs and benefits among courses of climate action into the future. So the more seriously we take the crossing of planetary boundaries and concern ourselves with dire climate change impacts on the planet's future, in this view, the lower the discount rate will be. And the higher the social costs market participants generating the biospheric despoiling externalities are to be saddled with compensating for today.[38]

Of course no consensus has ever been arrived at on where the discount rate should be set. But let us bracket this question for the moment. Much of the critique of the whole charade has turned on the fact that even if one was agreed upon, it is not clear how in the current political and economic circumstances its policy implications could be effectively acted upon. Even Speth tries to come to terms with the reality that outside of neoclassical models the world of benignly referred to "market participants" is dominated by giant MNCs. This forces Speth to lapse into fantasies about government action over things like "eliminating corporate personhood" or "expelling unwanted" MNCs.[39] All the while as secret negotiations between major governments and cabals of elite lawyers representing MNC behemoths are hatching a new generation of environment throttling international investment rules governed by "investor-state arbitration tribunals". These will dominate the upcoming global trade agreements between US and Asia (Trans-Pacific Partnership or TPP), US and the EU (Transatlantic Trade and Investment Partnership or T-TIP), and empower MNCs to bring ruinous legal action against governments for even thinking about environmental strictures that Speth wishfully hopes might come to pass.[40]

In his sweeping critique of so-called green capitalism as "the god that failed", democratic socialist Richard Smith pillories every single policy initiative in terms of the impossibility of breaching the capitalist bulwarks marshaled against them. Kyoto Protocol emission targets became anathema when the realization dawned that complying would reduce GDP in many major economies from upwards of 1 percent, such impelling prominent national polluters to race for the exists; "cap and trade" solutions where environmental despoilers are awarded "permits" to pollute based on their reductions that could then be "traded" with overpolluters, the latter then facing the rising costs of "permits" finally being forced to tow eco-sustainable lines, proved "designed to fail" as countries and MNCs garnered litanies of "exemptions" from this new so-called market force; and carbon taxes. As Smith points out, though vehemently opposed in many quarters, carbon taxes managed to find big business support because they ended up being "revenue neutral" through "offsets" (such as lower corporate taxes), or "impact neutral" where, for example, rebates given to those that swap clunkers for eco-cars are then spent jetting the family to Barbados! Smith concludes: "Sustainable production is certainly possible – but not under capitalism . . . The problem is capitalist private property in the major means of production, especially in the corporate form . . . concerned only to maximize profits . . . [from which] all evils of capitalism inevitably follow".[41]

But even market remedy pushing environmentalists like Speth recognize similar deep-seated elements of the capitalist bulwark marshaled against eco-sustainability: along with its drive toward expanding profits, Speth remarks on its related "biases" that favor the present over the future and the private over the public ("economists have had to invent theories of . . . public goods to justify the public sector's existence" he laments).[42]

However, while Marx does not advert directly to "externalities", dialectical economic theory foregrounds the elaboration of a more fundamental conceptualization of the term that helps us cut to the crux of the anti-environmental thrust of capitalism beyond critiques shared by much of the Left and Greens. Remember, commencing with classical political economy, bourgeois economics has always viewed capitalism as a transhistorical order. Hence, it never problematizes capitalist abstracting from the sensuous qualitative heterogeneity of things to interrelate them according to its homogenizing quantitative chrematistic. Put differently, bourgeois economics conflates "value" in *use* based on the discrete qualities of the thing in question with *value* in "exchange" where things are differentiated only numerically in abstraction from their qualitative heterogeneity. For Marx, the possibility of capitalism as an historical society is inexorably tied to the emergence of social demand for a particular constellation of material use values and productive technologies that lend themselves to the suppression of qualitative determinants in economic life in favor of quantitative ones. And, as with past historical societies, Marx understood that capitalism will pass from human history with the exhaustion of its historical role and as new human use value possibilities emerge on the horizon. Marx addresses the historical transience of capitalism in his economic formulations in terms of a fundamental tension that exists between value and use value. That is, inhering in the commodity, the basic economic category of capital with which dialectical economic theory commences, is precisely this contradiction between value representing abstract-general, quantitative mercantile wealth and use value representing concrete-specific, qualitative material wealth. It is in this sense, therefore, that for capital, *qualitative human use value life itself* constitutes an *externality* that must be *internalized* or neutralized in a way conducive to its social goal of augmenting abstract-general mercantile wealth or profit-making.

As discussed in Chapter 2 of this book, to consummate the reificatory tendencies of capital in the thought experiment of a purely capitalist society, dialectical economic theory assumes an ideal use value space where externalities or recalcitrance use value dimensions of material life pose for value are internalized to permit *in theory* capital getting its way with the world (see Box 4.1). Again, theorizing a bourgeois utopia as such, where all inputs and outputs of the production process are commodified, subject positions are personifications of economic categories, prices set objectively by integrated systems of self-regulating markets, and human material existence reproduced as a byproduct of value augmentation, is intended as a timeless definition of what capital in its most fundamental incarnation *is*. And, as a definitive critique of classical bourgeois political economy (and "vulgar" bourgeois "economics" that follows) given the way dialectical economic theory exposes each and every dark secret of capital its ideologues seek to conceal. To be crisply clear on this, in a bourgeois utopia that assumes an ideal use value space, where all externalities are internalized, and prices are set objectively in self-regulating markets, it is impossible for capital to yield a "discount rate" for the future. As emphasized by political economist Robert Albritton, this is the case because inhering in capitalist "rationality" is a fundamental irrationality that renders capitalist prices "backward-facing". That is, prices set in the capitalist market reflect the prices of commodified material inputs and labor power incurred by capital in the past or recent present as such factor into capital's immediate turnover profit horizons. To be sure, social investment in the future for things like education or health care weaken capitalist "rationality". But to account for biospheric annihilation would "overwhelm" capitalist pricing with its market irrationality.[43]

> **Box 4.1**
>
> It is worth quoting Thomas T. Sekine at length here (see Sekine, "Towards a Critique of Bourgeois Economics", pp. 247–8):
>
>> [E]conomic theory must always presuppose an "ideal" working of the capitalist market, which means use-values must be neutralized, or "nominalized", therein. In theory, in other words, they are viewed only as names of different objects for use or consumption (direct and productive), and conform always to capital's wish to treat them as value (i.e., as abstract-general, mercantile wealth). The difference between Marxian and classical approach lies in how such an image is obtained. In the Marxian case . . . it is obtained by copying the real movement toward pure capitalism, which could be observed in the development of capitalism in history. When capitalism passes near the saddle-point of its growth curve, an ideal working of the capitalist market can be perceived (foreseen), as a state in which the use-value resistance against the dictates of the value principle "asymptotically approaches zero" (i.e., almost evaporates). There is, in this case, nothing normative about letting capital pose its own ideal state. In the classical [bourgeois] case, in contrast, the ideal state of the capitalist market (the pre-established harmony) is a norm or "ought" (perhaps ordained by Providence or the Infinite), which can be disturbed only by the aberrant behavior of finite human beings . . . [H]owever, when the real and the ideal of capitalism diverge from each other, the two approaches manifest completely distinct responses. If the real diverges from the ideal, the Marxian response will be that use-values turn out, in reality, to be more recalcitrant (less amenable) to the aim of capital than is supposed in theory, while the classical response will be that there are aberrant interferences with God's plan, where the latter must be obeyed by removing the former.

The raison d'être for levels of analysis in Marxian political economy where dialectical economic theory is supplemented by *stage theory* and *historical analysis* of capitalism is precisely the fact that capital in history *never* internalizes all externalities to "perfect" itself. And, as we point out in Chapter 2, while the mid-nineteenth-century light use value complex of cotton textile production existing in Marx's day offered little use value resistance to subsumption by capital, the heavy use value complex characteristic of the stage of imperialism commences a process where capital accumulation moves asymptotically *away* from its ideal image. The import of this for the present discussion is that the manifestation of the asymptotic movement of capital away from "perfection" in gathering extra-economic, extra-capitalist superstructure support for accumulation leads to the inescapable reality of capitalist prices being set *less* by any kind of market "mechanism" and *more* by political and ideological policy driven mechanisms.

In the Introduction to the present volume we discuss the extent to which the golden age economy of the capitalist stage of *consumerism* maintained capitalist relations of production by paradoxically decommodifying considerable parts of economic life. Whether through countercyclical macroeconomic aggregate demand management or welfare state social wage provision, prices were manipulated by governments for socially beneficial ends. Nevertheless, because expanded reproduction of the golden age economy was still heavily weighted toward mass producing of consumer durables, and state economic programming operated ex post, a significant element of objective capitalist market pricing remained. Into the neoliberal decades, I further argued, the capitalist substance of advanced economies was rapidly leeched out. Capitalist market pricing, I noted, is attuned to direct costs of material inputs and labor power. However, the shifting of advanced economies and commanding heights business toward expanding ICT knowledge intensity and services saddled the economy at large with increased haphazard pricing of goods due to growing proportions of indirect costs in production and marketing. The decommodifying of money with its "paper standard" policy issuance under generalizing conditions of OTD banking tilted world economies toward debt fuelled casino games played with idle M. Government complicity in this gaming amounts to monstrous political and ideological manipulation of prices on everything running the gamut from inflation of asset prices to food price spikes wrecking further havoc on real economic life. Thus in the neoliberal decades policy orchestration of economic outcomes whether emanating from "big government", "big bank", or big MNC (or all in concert) exceeds that of the golden age, but now for pernicious ends of the "1 percent" (as expressed by recent protest movements) with little broader socially redeeming value.

Like Don Quixote seeking to revive knight errantry in the seventeenth century, neoliberal ideological chants applauded by environmental economics that advocate "the market" as "the default position in environmental policy" in the twenty-first century are daft. So narcotized by neoclassical ideological opium are Speth and others calling for "getting environmental prices right" or for markets to "tell the ecological truth",[44] that they are blind to how as the neoliberal era unfolded "the market" has not even been able to "tell the capitalist truth" about prices. Putting this in terms with which the section began, if such a thing as "market failure" has any coherent meaning it is that the capitalist market *fails* to account for the heterogeneous use value dimension of human material life. Capitalism thus constitutes an "alien", "upside-down" society, as Marx described it, or the limit form of what a human society should *not* be.

Notwithstanding the forgoing, the transient march of capital in human history coincided with an historical period where the satisfying of social demand for a relatively narrow range of standardized material and mass produced goods was "efficiently" accommodated under the value principle of indifference to use value: this roughly century and a half epoch then generating a manageable, though ever mounting quantum of externalities or use value oppositions. But where capital nevertheless managed to reproduce human economic life as a byproduct of value augmentation. If the exhaustion of capitalism as a mode of reproducing human economic life is signaled by the waning of standardized material goods producing societies and their replacement by rent seeking, casino money game, expropriation, surrogate economies, it is the specter of exploding biospheric planetary boundaries that constitutes the ultimate revenge of use value against continued political and ideological wielding of human material life for purposes of quantitative value augmentation.

In this light, we are able to more summarily treat remaining "green capitalist" arguments over technological fix/adaptation and so-called degrowth. It goes without saying that the first question does not disappear for creative socialist future directed thinking. Thus, it is revisited in Chapter 6. Here our consideration is limited to views of extending what is metaphorically referred to as "the American way of life" through the above.

On the adaptation side of the issue, Clive Hamilton reminds us that our climate "is not like a central heating system that can be smoothly adjusted to the desired temperature".[45] Hence, even if the entire globe springs into Superman-like radical climate action *today*, humanity still has to deal with a trajectory of 2 degree C warming as CO_2 we have heretofore injected into the atmosphere does not suddenly dissipate. But with the sorts of phasing being discussed where wealthy states cut emissions 25–40 percent by 2020 with the non-developed world following by 2030, the evidence points to at least a 4 degree C warmer world. Hamilton alludes to the Netherlands where futuristic planning over rising sea levels includes floating cities and greenhouses along with towns built on raised dikes. But for the much of the world's coastal populace located in South and East Asia the prospects of constructing such accouterment is slim. Island nations are certain to disappear, forcing waves of climate refugees across the globe.[46] Projections of 200 million people displaced by climate change in the 4 degree C warming trajectory world of 2050 are seen as conservative.[47] Then there are the other planetary boundaries the crossing of which is certain to be accelerated by a much hotter planet. These dramatically impact water availability and agriculture especially in current tropical/subtropical zones. Hamilton opines depressingly:

> One thing is certain: the transition to some new stage of stability will be long and brutal, especially for the poorest and most vulnerable whose survival will be threatened by food shortages, extreme weather and disease. Yet in a world that is now densely interlinked, everyone will be affected profoundly.
> ... It almost goes without saying that the capacity of individuals to adapt is limited, the more so if social order breaks down. Societies must collectively transform themselves if we are to manage and alleviate the impacts of a world at four degrees and beyond.[48]

Despite the fact that a high road out of this morass exists, which entails the sort of collective transformation those like Hamilton call for (we will get to that in a moment), there is also a low road that mainstream policy makers in advanced states seem increasingly inclined to maneuver thinking towards. What scientists grandly dub geoengineering and critics, "geo-tinkering", on the one hand, entails a suite of climate actions known as solar radiation management (SRM).[49] Quite simply, the idea here is to increase the earth's *albedo* or rate at which it reflects incoming sunlight. Literally, the bottom level plan here is to do things like genetically modifying crops with shiny, reflective leaves and putting reflective or white roofs on all buildings. Creating reflective foams or bubbles for the world's seas and oceans is another idea being floated in this regard. Moving upwards, there is cloud whitening. But the SRM technique gathering the most interest in power circles is injecting sulfate particles into the stratosphere simulating proven effects of volcanic eruptions for cooling the earth. The current economic attractiveness of this approach is first, that sulfur may be drawn from coal-fired power plants and dispersed by way of jet travel; thus rendering two of the prime culprits in climate change part of the solution. And second, the "bang for the buck" is estimated to be a mere $25 to $50 billion annually, a fraction of the diminution of global GDP advocated in the Stern Review.[50]

It is hardly surprising, though certainly oozing with irony, to see geoengineering being touted so zealously by the right-wing think tanks involved in the climate change denial business. They are accompanied by "weaponeering" physicists including veterans of Ronald Reagan's Star Wars missile shield fantasy whose ideology of "domination over nature" perpetually compels their search for the next "killer app", as Clive Hamilton puts it.[51] Joining the chorus is billionaire Virgin Group CEO Richard Branson who sees geoengineering as ultimately rendering climate change conferences unnecessary.[52] Branson, however, is enamored with the other low road geoengineering panacea for not only lowering earth's temperature but actual carbon dioxide removal (CDR) to forestall "feedback mechanisms" of CO_2 concentrations. CDR plans range from "capturing" carbon directly from fossil fuel plant emissions to creating "scrubbers" to "pull" CO_2 out of the atmosphere. Of course, where to store what would amount in the US alone to the equivalent in daily volume of US oil consumption (if and when the technology for this is developed), is a dirty sticking point. But what unites both SRM and CDR is that their effective operationalizing requires technocratic centralized political authority and the fact that there is really no possibility of really testing them or truly assessing their varied, potentially deleterious bioregional weather system impacts, prior to full-scale implementation. And they reek of self-fulfilling prophesy where substantive climate action social change is delayed to the point where planetary geoengineering emerges as a forced authoritarian final solution.[53]

The high road, of course, and we will revisit it once more in Chapter 6, revolves around the raft of renewable alter-energies including solar – both photovoltaic (PV) and concentrating solar power (CSP) – wind, small hydro, geothermal, wave and tidal, biomass. Fossil fuels, as detailed above, maintained 82 percent of global TPES in 2011: how to replace it as the current energy matrix for those endeavors cumulatively responsible for 85 percent of CO_2 emissions – electricity and heating, transportation, and industry – is a Himalayan question. One made more pressing to answer given the finite supply of fossil fuels.

Without getting into debate over but another recent bourgeois calculus (combining thermodynamics with neoclassical economics) that yields a so-called energy return on investment (EROI) ratio (which is plagued by conflations of value and use value along with neoclassical economics hackneyed grasp of what "factors of production" produce *use values* and the factor capable of producing *value*) it is nevertheless the case that readying renewable alter-energies for tomorrow must draw upon energy resources today.[54] And, what is explained in terms of the "energy trap", that to maintain what we think of as "the American way of life" while shifting to alter-energies, societies need to ratchet up their exploitation of fossil fuels to backstop the shift. But, this becomes exceedingly difficult under conditions where fossil fuel production passes its "peak" point.[55] In fact, Michael T. Klare in his chilling study *The Race for What's Left* captures the way this realization seems to have dawned on powerful state actors driving policies to invade the most inhospitable ecologically fraught environs in search of fossil fuel El Dorado (deep offshore drilling, the Arctic), as well as turn toward "unconventionals" (tar sands, shale gas), with such extractive efforts gobbling up their own share of resources. The use of natural gas to produce oil from Canadian tar sands, for example, has been equated with "using caviar to make fake crab meat".[56] Unconventionals also increasingly lay waste to the terrestrial biosphere.

While renewable, our high road alter-energies are not without their resource dependencies or environmental impacts. However, with planning and care, studies show solar PV and CSP could meet 40 percent of global energy demand by 2030 with the use of only 0.29 percent of the world's land area. Existing roof area with sun exposure in the US alone can immediately supply 20 percent of current US electricity demand through solar PV. Wind energy is estimated to be able to supply 50 percent of the world's energy by 2030 utilizing only 1.17 percent of global land area. Wind energy is also far less water intensive than solar CSP. And it may be utilized flexibly for both centralized and decentralized energy applications. Other alter-energies, for example geothermal, which already supplies 12 percent of Nicaraguan power, are also relatively ecologically clean, and we will return to them.[57]

The problem with this, again, is entrenched interests in political orchestrating of abstract mercantile wealth augmentation as the social goal. And it is not just the sunk costs in petroleum infrastructure that amounted to around $10 trillion at the dawn of the twenty-first century with up to a 50-year amortization requirement.[58] Environmental consultant Trucost used the MSCI All Country World Index (ACWI) listing of 2,439 companies from major economies around the world to hypothetically assess what saddling investor portfolio earnings with environmental costs would amount to in 2008 (just as the meltdown was striking); and came up with a figure of 50 percent (*before* other deductions).[59] That the fossil fuel energy that undergirds such investor earnings requires no major new up-front costs offers false comfort that the so-called energy trap is surmounted. As Tom Murphy puts it:

The fact that fossil fuels don't trap us encourages us to stick with them. But being a finite resource, their attractiveness is the sound of the Siren, luring us to stay on the sinking ship. Or did the Sirens lure sailors *from* ships? Either way, fossil fuels are already compatible with our transportation fleet, strengthening the death-grip.[60]

Then there is the question of the role fossil fuels play in supporting the military power required to defend "our way of life". The US Department of Defense (DoD) in 2012 was the largest single consumer of oil in the world. It may be noted that there are only 35 nation-states in the world that consume more oil than the US DoD: with oil accounting for 77.4 percent of DoD energy consumption in 2012 despite a concerted effort by the military to go "green" over the past half decade. In 2012 the US DoD thus emitted 70 million metric tons of CO_2, about the same amount as emitted in a year by countries like Colombia or the Philippines (and, importantly, this footprint does not factor in energy usage by military contractors supporting the US military domestically or abroad)[61] We may note as well here that in 2012 the US was responsible for a full 39 percent of total global military expenditure.[62]

And, putting alter-energies into play under the current economic dynamic according to Smith will "just give a huge solar-powered green light to the manufacturers of endless . . . new toys we can't even imagine yet . . . [that] would end up in some landfill somewhere".[63] This does not bode well for sustainability as the reality of "peak oil" also impacts the assortment of rare earths and critical minerals the alter-energies such as solar PV and CSP as well as wind need to operate effectively. Klare sums it all up well:

> In recent years, many analysts and politicians have spoken optimistically about a "green" high-tech future in which our current reliance on heavily polluting fuels will give way to new, environmentally friendly alternatives. That scenario may indeed come to pass, but getting there will not be a simple task – and critical minerals are one potential major problem . . . [M]any advanced green technologies depend on relatively scarce, hard-to-acquire specialty elements whose future availability cannot be ensured. As time goes on, struggles over control of these minerals could prove no less intense and significant than past battles over . . . commodities of the Industrial Age.[64]

Finally, we come to degrowth. The merit of this approach as reflected in the work of Richard Heinberg is that it takes account of the confluence of peak fossil fuel energy along with other "peaks" in resources, agrochemical output, pollution, and so on, *and* the limits inhering in the neoliberal economy of debt leveraged casino games.[65] Heinberg queries: "Perhaps the meteoric rise of the finance economy in the past couple of decades resulted from a semi-conscious strategy on the part of society's managerial elites to leverage the last possible increments of growth from a physical, resource based economy that was nearing its capacity".[66] But, where degrowth reveals its fundamental inadequacy, is in its solution. According to Heinberg:

> A steady-state economy would aim for stable or mildly fluctuating levels in population and consumption of energy and materials; birth rates would equal death rates, saving/investment would equal depreciation.
> ... Markets would still allocate resources efficiently, but some vital decisions (such as permissible rates of resource extraction and the just distribution of resources, especially those created by nature or society as a whole) would be kept outside the market.[67]

Heinberg then retreats into the same dreamscape as Speth over governments and commanding heights economic institutions shifting their behaviors away from fixation on growth and rising GDP; in fact, suggesting "solutions to our growth-based problems [all] involve some form of self-restraint".[68]

It goes without saying here that adding the population factor into the mix is spurious. In their sweeping critique of the populationism literature as it interfaces with Green argument, Ian Angus and Simon Butler reword the iconic Bob Dylan song as *"it ain't we babe"* to make the point that there is no question of moving forward on climate change and eco-sustainability without directly confronting the way extreme wealth disparities not only between countries but within them yield vastly divergent environmental footprints.[69] And the neoliberal era has only hypertrophied inequalities. In the world as a whole 1 percent of families own 46 percent all wealth while the wealthiest 85 people across the globe own more than the bottom half of the world's population; even as 2012 ushered 210 new billionaires into the fold. In the US, the richest 1 percent increased their income share by almost 150 percent between 1980 and 2012.[70] Indeed, by the opening decade of the twenty-first century, the estimate is that only 7 percent of the global populace is responsible for 50 percent of all global CO_2 emissions with the bottom 50 percent responsible for 7 percent of CO_2 emissions.[71] It is thus the ecological footprint of the swelling pack of über-rich that will necessitate a wholly different universe of "self [or otherwise] restraint". And "steady-state" ... "Are Toyota or General Motors looking to produce the same number of steel cars next year as this year" asks Richard Smith? "To ask the question is to answer it".[72]

But besides the foregoing, along with the sort of political body that might make the "vital decisions" over what is to be "kept outside the market" as adverted to by Heinberg, we once more find ourselves assaulted by neoclassical economics phantasmagoria of markets: the "efficient allocation of resources" in the *capitalist* market (discussion of potentially other "kinds" of "markets" will take place below and in Chapters 5 and 6) is inextricably bound to *the efficiency of value augmentation*. That is, to say that resources are allocated efficiently is to show, as per our Chapter 2 treatment above of the *doctrine of production* in dialectical economic theory, how through its circulation process, entailing the coordination and non-interruption of its operations across all separate units in producer and consumer industries, capital is able to meet the general norms of economic life. But the possibility of such coordination is predicated upon the assumption that whether we are talking about components of producer goods, the goods themselves, or goods destined for consumption, all are produced as value objects with indifference to their use value (except to the extent the latter impacts profit). And goods are produced by commodified labor power available for purchase in the market to then be applied by capital (again indifferently to use value) to the production of *any* good according to shifting patterns of social demand and opportunities for profit-making. In other words, capital meets the general norms of economic life to materially reproduce a human society *only* as a byproduct of value augmentation.

Yet, this is not the end of the matter. The "perfection" of the capitalist market as the medium for human material reproduction is arrived at in dialectical economic theory only by holding use value implicit. However, even here, with the ideal use value accouterment of industrial capital and tractable commodities, what the *doctrine of distribution* demonstrates is that the so-called efficient allocation of resources is never a fait accompli. With no ex ante coordination, decisions made by the separate units of capital are validated only ex post in the maelstrom of capitalist competition as such plays out in the course of capitalist business cycle oscillations between prosperity and depression phases. From the perspective of use value needs of society as a whole, such an anarchical process can hardly be considered "efficient" because the labor power expended (remember, we are talking about the life energy of human beings) and resources utilized (material resources ultimately entail the refashioning and exhausting of nature) will have been wasted if competitive conditions of value augmentation are not met by this or that individual business.

But the kicker here is this: As has been emphasized, when we leave the rarified environment of abstract theory and "reactivate" use value in the context of stage theory, it becomes quite evident that the value principle or market grip on human material life is not only never absolute, even in the stage of *liberalism*, but becomes subject to burgeoning tensions with the stage of *imperialism*. The issue here is not just that of the efficiency of value augmentation and allocation of social resources for that purpose requiring a growing array of extra-market, extra-capitalist supports, or that with the advent of the stage of *consumerism* and its petroleum energy infrastructure the externalities begin to overwhelm the economy, as Albritton avers. The fact is that the use value complex beckoning humanity in the twenty-first century, along with the alter-energies that will operate it into the future, simply cannot be managed capitalistically. That is, by a "mechanism" that works "optimally" to process a relatively narrow range of standardized material goods that society could produce with indifference to their qualitative heterogeneity and for the abstract, extra-human purpose of value augmentation. This point is the foundation for Marx's view of capitalism as a transient social order. We will return to it in the following chapter.

Can "small is beautiful" satisfy the general norms of economic life?

In his landmark contribution to Green theory, E. F. Schumacher scathingly critiqued the eco-pedigree of industrial giganticism in both its Soviet style and capitalist forms. He then offered a model for future eco-sustainable societies based on reduced-scale, "small" communities operating "appropriate" technologies and reembedded in a dechemicalized agriculture.[73] While Schumacher's emphasis upon the eco-sanctity of small scale continues to be an animating factor in Green and even ecosocialist/eco-anarchist thinking (we will get to the latter in Chapter 6), his advancing of a "Buddhist economics" as the economic alternative to socialism or capitalism (as he understood them) has not travelled well through time (for example, Paul Hawken who wrote the introduction to the 1999 reprint of Schumacher's 1973 book is a proponent of so-called green capitalism). However there are Green writers in the Schumacher tradition, who build on powerful Green critique of the current environmental morass by Speth and others, yet push well beyond so-called green capitalism and degrowth toward small-scale, local economy alternatives as the necessary Green outcome. And they combine their vision of localism with a more clearly articulated economic principle than "Buddhist economics". I will bring this chapter to a close by taking up issues of material economic reproducibility their work raises.

Environmentalist Bill McKibben opens the discussion in this way:

> In the new world we've created, the one with hotter temperatures and more drought and less oil, big is vulnerable. We are going to need to split up, at least a little, if we're going to avoid being subdued by the forces we've unleashed. Scale matters, and at the moment ours is out of whack with our needs . . . As we lose climactic stability that's marked all of human civilization . . . [t]he changes to our lives will be ongoing . . . and will require uncommon nimbleness . . .[74]

But, he adds: "Shifting our focus to local economies will not mean abandoning Adam Smith or doing away with markets".[75] Rather, he suggests "we may be able to re-create some of the institutions that marked, say, Adam Smith's Britain".[76]

Vehement critic of "Wall Street capitalism" David Korten concurs: "Ironically, it turns out that the solution to a failed capitalist economy is a real-market economy much in line with the true vision of Adam Smith".[77] Korten continues, "Smith envisioned a world of local-market economies populated by small entrepreneurs, artisans, family farmers with strong community roots, engaged in producing and exchanging goods to meet the needs of themselves and their neighbors".[78] McKibben similarly emphasizes that the corollary of markets for Smith was always the ethically grounded local community "where the baker and butcher actually knew each other, and . . . had to show themselves good citizens because they wanted credit from the banker".[79] Korten further notes how in his "real" or "Main Street" market economy "democratically accountable" governments will set rules for economic actors in local markets to meet their "needs in socially and environmentally responsible ways".[80] In the end, as summed up by McKibben, "Adam Smith, watching the butchers and bakers of his English village making each other richer through the invisible hand of economic exchange, never imagined that the skids would be so thoroughly greased".[81]

To give away some of what will figure into the Chapter 6 design I offer for a material economically reproducible or "viable" eco-sensitive, socio-economically progressive future order, I wholeheartedly agree with McKibben that this will require extraordinary "nimbleness" and that geospatial scale *does* matter. Though, I will add (with elaboration reserved to Chapter 6), that in themselves, "local economies" do not have any inbuilt propensity toward environmental benignity. But, to restate our point from the introduction to this chapter, questions of eco-sustainability amount to naught if the material economic reproducibility of human society cannot be ensured. And this brings us back to the fundamental conflation in work of classical economists like Adam Smith that has remained unproblematized across the mainstream economic tradition – that of value in use, and value in exchange: Which in turn entails a conflating of two very different meanings of "exchange".

To take this up schematically, C-C (where C represents a good) involving "exchange" of C for C, is a relatively rare occurrence *within* precapitalist communities or societies as economic historian Karl Polanyi shows.[82] The reason for this, quite simply, is that across the sweep of human history material life of social communities is reproduced largely through varying forms of interpersonal extra-economic relationships (Chapter 6 will elaborate further on this by developing typologies of economic principles at the core of human material reproduction across history). Anthropologist David Graeber is at similar pains to dismiss "the myth of barter".[83] And to the extent C-C does occur in the context of interpersonal relations of domination and subordination or "hierarchy" Graeber explains, it "seems to be that the sorts of things given on each side should be considered fundamentally different in quality, their relative value impossible to quantify . . . Nor did anyone ever consider making such a calculation".[84] On the other hand, when "exchange" of any *impersonal* kind took place involving C-C, it did so *between* bounded communities. And historic communities took care to ensure their discrete material reproductive modalities were never infiltrated by such "trading" activity. A clear example of this practice is the creation by the Tokugawa Shogunate in 1634 of Dejima, or "protruding island", in the bay of Nagasaki to accommodate first Portuguese then Dutch merchants. Neither was permitted to cross into Nagasaki. In effect, Dejima maintained a firewall separating the economic practices of Japan and that of foreign merchants.[85]

Marx, for his part, dealing with the notion codified in classical political economy, and then refined by neoclassical economics, that money is simply an extension of C-C, schematizes this as C-M-C (where M is money). C in this sense may be a crafted leather coat that the producer seeks to "exchange" for horseshoes from a blacksmith, for example. But, because wants of the blacksmith do not coincide with our leather crafter, the coat is sold for money that is then tendered to the blacksmith for horseshoes. Marx, however, emphasizes that such "exchange" is always of use values a limited surplus of which in the hands of their owner being possibly offered up for "trade". And the purpose of the "exchange" is use value need where the heterogeneous qualities of the goods to be consumed are still foremost in mind of each party. Hence not only is C-M-C a one-off occurrence in each case. It ends exactly where it started – with C. In other words, pace McKibben, there is no mechanism inhering in such "exchanges" to make anyone "richer", at least in any objectively measurable fashion. As was remarked in Chapter 2 on the phantasmagoria of Marxist Karl Kautsky's petty commodity society, to the extent C-M-C depicts an actual precapitalist historical situation, it contains no dynamic whatsoever beyond a single "exchange".

Most importantly, C-M-C offers no foundation for the material reproduction of a human society (even a so-called steady-state one) today. The reason is that in a local economy composed of presumably *self-employed* "small entrepreneurs, artisans, family farmers" (as Korten sees it), there exists virtually no elasticity of labor supply given how each self-employed operator is tied to a concrete-specific use value skill. Given the antipathy of McKibben and Korten to any form of socialism, we can assume that that they envision no recourse to ex ante economic decision making. Rather, with each self-employed economic actor pursuing their own self-seeking proclivities à la Adam Smith, whether in the end each individual decision on the what, how, and how much of production is valid in any "community" sense, is only established ex post. But because each C-M-C is simply a one-off "trade" filling in for a dearth in coincidence of use value wants (otherwise C-C is all that would be required in this schema), by the time all the wants worked their way through the division of labor based on self-employed artisans and the realization dawned that so many were unsatisfied, there would be no social basis for "efficiently" adjusting supply to demand therefore ensuring that society was mired in shortages. To take an example on the supply side of C-M-C, the historical record of early modern European transition to capitalism with its loosening of feudal interpersonal bonds is replete with accounts bemoaning the ethic of artisans or preindustrial craft workers who having worked enough to satisfy their own needs simply went on vacation.[86] And, in the end, any society unable to allocate basic goods to meet shifting patterns of social demand will die out.

Given Adam Smith's temporal emplacement, he would have witnessed only the process of "formal" subsumption of use value life by capital remarked upon in Chapter 2. The eighteenth-century *mercantilist* period as per stage theory was still marked by vestiges of precapitalism including the fact that nascent capitalist "cottage" and "putting-out" industry would not have as yet shifted to urban areas. Nevertheless, as reproduction of economic life increasingly came to rely on a class of laborers divorced from means of production and land and making their labor power available in the market for hire, the cost of food loomed as an increasingly important question. Thus the one genuine example from the "English village" of Smith's time where "greedy" self-seeking market behavior made a cross-section of people better off in the absence of any visible hand of government policy, was with capitalist farmers that rented the land from landlords fostering a range of improved farming practices to increase their profits while lowering the price of food.[87]

But this dynamic cannot be captured by C-M-C. Rather, it is part and parcel of capitalist subsumption of use value life and the circulation form specific to capital that is M-C-M`. As Marx makes so abundantly clear in Volume 1 of *Capital*, and dialectical economic theory displays in the *doctrine of circulation*, the C in Smith's bourgeois ideological fantasy of frictionless barter or trade is, in the reality of the *capitalist* market, always an in-the-closet M! That is, as a commodity, C's owner, the seller (and initiator of all "exchanges"), is interested *not* in its use value but in its value or "moneyness". Money, as we point out in Chapter 2, emerges as the social connector in capitalist society because it can purchase any commodity without qualitative use value restrictions. As the commodification of material life proceeds apace, whether "the baker and butcher" are neighborhood friends is neither here nor there. In the substantive socio-economic sense the nexus that brings qualitatively divergent heterogeneous use value life into "order" in the capitalist market is its abstract, quantitative chrematistic of value augmentation and "price signals". This is perfected *only* to the extent the sensuous qualitative use value characteristics of goods are suppressed. And, in turn, it is based upon a division of labor where a social class of workers makes their labor power available in the market for capital to purchase and set into motion producing *any* good as opportunities for profit-making arise. This is what imparts the flexibility to capitalism, absent in the mythical C-M-C economy, to meet social demand and satisfy general norms of economic life to reproduce a human society.

But such flexibility or "efficiency", along with ex post coordination that McKibben and Korten want to harness for the Green future, is a deal with the devil. There *is* a way out of this as we shall see in Chapter 6 of this book. And it potentially can bring to bear small-m market operations as part of a more nuanced design. But for those whose hearts are certainly in the right place I have to say unequivocally that we cannot have our bourgeois cake and eat it too.

Notes

1 John R. Bell, "Marx's Anti-authoritarian Ecocommunism", in Robert Albritton, Shannon Bell, John R. Bell, and Richard Westra (eds.), *New Socialisms: Futures beyond Globalization*. Routledge Studies in Governance and Change in the Global Era (London: Routledge, 2012).
2 See Harry Rothman, *Murderous Providence: A Study of Pollution in Industrial Societies* (London: Rupert Hart-Davis, 1972).
3 Judith Shapiro, *China's Environmental Challenges* (Cambridge, UK: Polity, 2012) pp. 6–7.
4 On some of the questions of environmentalism as a social or political movement see Luke Martell, *Ecology and Society: An Introduction* (Amherst, MA: University of Massachusetts Press, 1994).
5 As put by Robert Albritton, "it is as though [capital] tells its own story without our interference. But this story is not told to us directly and immediately, but must be deciphered by theoretical practice. We can carry out this theoretical practice because we are objectified by capital but still have the potential cognitively to become knowing

subjects capable of theoretically grasping what is happening to us. We can know capital as a subjectified object because we are objectified subjects". See Albritton, *Dialectics and Deconstruction in Political Economy*, p. 35.

6 Johan Rockström et al. "A Safe Operating Space for Humanity", *Nature*, 461 (24 September 2009); idem, in more detail as, "Planetary Boundaries: Exploring the Safe Operating Space for Humanity", *Ecology and Society*, 14, 2 (2009), http://www.ecologyandsociety.org/vol14/iss2/art32/; and summarized on the website of the Stockholm Resilience Center, http://www.stockholmresilience.org/research/researchnews/tippingtowardstheunknown/thenineplanetaryboundaries.4.1fe8f33123572b59ab80007039.html; and treated more recently by Carl Folke, "Respecting Planetary Boundaries and Reconnecting to the Biosphere", in Worldwatch Institute, *State of the World 2013: Is Sustainability Still Possible?* (Washington, DC: The Worldwatch Institute, 2013).

7 Folke, "Respecting Planetary Boundaries and Reconnecting to the Biosphere", pp. 21–2.

8 Westra, *Evil Axis of Finance*, p. 205.

9 International Energy Agency Statistics, CO_2 *Emissions from Fuel Combustion*, International Energy Agency 2013, http://www.iea.org/publications/freepublications/publication/CO2EmissionsFromFuelCombustionHighlights2013.pdf.

10 Suzanne Goldenberg, "Just 90 Companies Caused Two-Thirds of Man-Made Global Warming Emissions", *The Guardian*, 20 November 2013, http://www.theguardian.com/environment/2013/nov/20/90-companies-man-made-global-warming-emissions-climate-change?

11 Bill McKibben, *Eaarth: Making Life on a Tough New Planet* (New York: St. Martin's Griffin, 2011) pp. 13–20.

12 IPCC, *Climate Change 2013: The Physical Science Basis. Contribution of Working Group I to the Fifth Assessment Report of the Intergovernmental Panel on Climate Change* (Cambridge, UK: Cambridge University Press, 2013), http://www.climatechange2013.org/images/report/WG1AR5_ALL_FINAL.pdf.

13 Clive Hamilton, *Requiem for a Species: Why We Resist the Truth about Climate Change* (London: Earthscan, 2010) p. 12.

14 Ibid., p. 13.

15 Mike Davis, "Who Will Build The Ark?" *Countercurrents*, 29 January 2010, http://www.countercurrents.org/davis290110.htm.

16 Johan Rockström et al., "Planetary Boundaries: Exploring the Safe Operating Space for Humanity", pp. 18–19.

17 In 2004, for example, scrap worth $3.1 billion was the single biggest export from the US to China. See Westra, *Evil Axis of Finance*, p. 204. And so-called e-waste continues to accumulate in a booming business across the non-developed world. See RT, "Illegal Trash Trade: E-waste Smuggling Contaminate Developing Countries", 5 August 2013, http://rt.com/news/e-waste-illegal-environment-uk-043/.

18 See Shapiro, *China's Environmental Challenges*.

19 Jim Yardley, "Bangladesh Pollution, Told in Colors and Smells", *New York Times*, 14 July 2013, http://www.nytimes.com/2013/07/15/world/asia/bangladesh-pollution-told-in-colors-and-smells.html.

20 Robert Albritton, *Let Them Eat Junk: How Capitalism Creates Hunger and Obesity* (Winnipeg: Arbeiter Ring, 2009) pp. 58, 149.

21 Shelagh Whitely, *Time to Change the Game: Fossil Fuel Subsidies and Climate* (London: Overseas Development Institute, 2013), http://www.odi.org.uk/subsidies-change-the-game.

22 McKibben, *Eaarth*, pp. 164–6.
23 James Gustave Speth, *The Bridge at the Edge of the World: Capitalism, the Environment, and Crossing from Crisis to Sustainability* (New Haven: Yale University Press, 2008) pp. 32–3.
24 Shapiro, *China's Environmental Challenges*, p. 45.
25 Rex Weyler, "Honey Bee Collapse: A Lesson In Ecology", *Countercurrents*, 14 June 2013, http://www.countercurrents.org/weyler140613.htm.
26 Westra, *Political Economy and Globalization*, p. 185.
27 Peter Dicken, *Global Shift: Mapping the Changing Contours of the World Economy*. Sixth Edition (London: Guilford Press, 2011) p. 288.
28 Jason W. Moore, "The Socio-Ecological Crises of Capitalism", in Sasha Lilley, *Capital and Its Discontents: Conversations with Radical Thinkers in a Time of Tumult* (Oakland, CA: PM Press, 2011) p. 146.
29 See the discussion in Westra, *Evil Axis of Finance*, pp. 88ff.
30 Explained in Westra, *Political Economy and Globalization*, pp. 89–90.
31 Helena Norberg-Hodge, Todd Merrifield, and Steven Gorelick, *Bringing the Food Economy Home: Local Alternatives to Global Agribusiness* (London: Zed, 2002) p. 75.
32 International Federation of Red Cross and Red Crescent Societies, *World Disasters Report 2010: Focus on Urban Risk*, http://www.ifrc.org/Global/Publications/disasters/WDR/WDR2010-full.pdf, p. 15.
33 Michael T. Klare, *The Race for What's Left: The Global Scramble for the World's Last Resources* (New York: Picador, 2012) pp. 11–12, Chapter 7.
34 Frank Pearce, *The Land Grabbers: The New Fight over Who Owns the Earth* (Boston: Beacon Press, 2012) p. x.
35 See Hamilton, *Requiem for a Species*, pp. 51–6. The report itself, *Economics of Climate Change*, is available at http://webarchive.nationalarchives.gov.uk/20130129110402/http://www.hm-treasury.gov.uk/stern_review_report.htm.
36 Speth, *The Bridge at the Edge of the World*, pp. 89–94.
37 Ibid., p. 12.
38 See the discussion of the response to the Stern Review by Yale economist William Nordhaus in Hamilton, *Requiem for a Species*, pp. 56–62; also Speth, *The Bridge at the Edge of the World*, 100–6.
39 Speth, *The Bridge at the Edge of the World*, pp. 165–82.
40 See Thomas Mc Donagh, *Unfair, Unsustainable, and Under the Radar: How Corporations use Global Investment Rules to Undermine A Sustainable Future* (The Democracy Center, 2013), http://democracyctr.org/new-report-unfair-unsustainable-and-under-the-radar/.
41 Richard Smith, "Green Capitalism: The God That Failed", *Truthout*, 9 January 2014, http://www.truth-out.org/news/item/21060-green-capitalism-the-god-that-failed.
42 Speth, *The Bridge at the Edge of the World*, pp. 61ff.
43 Robert Albritton, "Buy Now, Pay Later: Resisting the Powers of the Commodity Form", unpublished typescript.
44 The latter point quoted in Smith, "Green Capitalism".
45 Hamilton, *Requiem for a Species*, p. 62.
46 Ibid., pp. 194–203.
47 Michael Renner, "Climate Change and Displacements", *State of the World 2013*, p. 349.
48 Hamilton, *Requiem for a Species*, pp. 204–6.
49 Simon Nicholson, "The Promises and Perils of Geoengineering", *State of the World 2013*, p. 326.

50 Ibid., pp. 319–21.
51 Hamilton, *Requiem for a Species*, 182–8.
52 Nicholson, "The Promises and Perils of Geoengineering", p. 324.
53 Ibid., pp. 322ff.
54 Eric Zencey, "Energy as a Master Resource", *State of the World 2013*, p. 77.
55 Ibid., pp. 80–2.
56 Quoted in Klare, *The Race for What's Left*, p. 104. See Chapters 3 and 4.
57 See the excellent discussion in Shakuntala Makhijani and Alexander Ochs, "Renewable Energy's Natural Resource Impacts", *State of the World 2013*, pp. 85–91.
58 McKibben, *Eaarth*, p. 55.
59 Trucost, "Universal Ownership: Why Environmental Externalities Matter to Institutional Investors", United Nations Environmental Program Finance Initiative (UNEP FI) and Principles for Responsible Investment (PRI), 6 April 2011, http://www.trucost.com/published-research/43/universal-ownership-why-environmental-externalities-matter-to-institutional-investors-full-report, p. 28.
60 Tom Murphy, "The Energy Trap", *Do The Math* (blog), 18 October 2011, https://physics.ucsd.edu/do-the-math/2011/10/the-energy-trap/.
61 Sohbet Karbuz, "US Military Addicted to Energy", OilPrice.com, 2 September 2013, http://oilprice.com/Energy/Energy-General/US-Military-Addicted-to-Energy.html. For country figures, see the graphic from the *Guardian*, "World Carbon Dioxide Emissions Data by Country: China Speeds Ahead of the Rest", 31 January 2011, http://www.theguardian.com/news/datablog/2011/jan/31/world-carbon-dioxide-emissions-country-data-co2#zoomed-picture.
62 Stockholm International Peace Research Institute (SIPRI), "Recent Trends in Military Expenditure", http://www.sipri.org/research/armaments/milex/recent-trends, accessed 20 March 2014.
63 Smith, "Green Capitalism".
64 Klare, *The Race for What's Left*, pp. 181–2.
65 Richard Heinberg, *The End of Growth: Adapting to Our New Economic Reality* (Gabriola Island, BC: New Society Publishers, 2011).
66 Ibid., p. 152.
67 Ibid., p. 250.
68 Ibid., p. 265.
69 Ian Angus and Simon Butler, *Too Many People? Population, Immigration, and the Environmental Crisis* (Chicago, IL: Haymarket Books, 2011) p. 145.
70 Oxfam, "Working for the Few: Political Capture and Economic Inequality", Oxfam Briefing Paper 178, 20 January 2014, http://www.oxfam.org/sites/www.oxfam.org/files/bp-working-for-few-political-capture-economic-inequality-200114-en.pdf.
71 Chris Williams, *Ecology and Socialism: Solutions to Capitalist Ecological Crisis* (Chicago: Haymarket Books, 2010).
72 Smith, "Green Capitalism".
73 E. F. Schumacher, *Small Is Beautiful: Economics as if People Mattered* (Point Roberts, WA: Hartley and Marks, 1999).
74 McKibben, *Eaarth*, pp. 146–7.
75 Bill McKibben, *Deep Economy: The Wealth of Communities and the Durable Future* (New York: Henry Holt and Company) p. 2.
76 Ibid., p. 125.
77 David C. Korten, *Agenda for a New Economy: From Phantom Wealth to Real Wealth* (San Francisco: Berrett-Koehler, 2009) p. 2.

78 Ibid., p. 119.
79 McKibben, *Deep Economy*, p. 127.
80 Korten, *Agenda for a New Economy*, p. 32. Korten follows with a point-by-point elaboration of how "Main Street" markets differ from those of "Wall Street".
81 McKibben, *Deep Economy*, p. 123.
82 Polanyi, *The Livelihood of Man*.
83 David Graeber, *Debt: The First 5,000 Years* (New York: Melville House, 2012) Chapter 2. The actual historical record is exhaustively surveyed by Graeber to prove the phantasmagoria of "barter" societies. Adam Smith's work is also explored to demonstrate the spurious way Smith jumps from his ahistorical construct of "state of nature" to an eighteenth-century English village.
84 Ibid., p. 112.
85 This example was brought to my attention by Makoto Nishibe, "What Is Globalization and What Does It Do? Evolution of Capitalism", unpublished, n.d.
86 Robert S. Duplessis, *Transitions to Capitalism in Early Modern Europe* (Cambridge: Cambridge University Press, 2004) pp. 262–6.
87 Colin A. M. Duncan, "Adam Smith's Green Vision and the Future of Global Socialism", in Albritton, Bell, Bell, and Westra (eds.), *New Socialisms*, pp. 98–9.

5 Neoclassical rapture in *Jurassic Park*

In case you missed it, the film *Jurassic Park* cast a world, long-lost, of roaming dinosaurs, recreated on isolated islands through cloning of fossilized DNA. It is a fitting metaphor for treatment in this chapter of a debate over *market* or *state* as principles of economy for a future of human flourishing. To backtrack a bit, so as to set the debate in context, we had emphasized in Chapter 2 that Marx never completed *Capital*. Only the first of its three volumes was actually prepared for publication during his lifetime (the original German edition of Volume 1 appeared in 1867). The following two volumes were then edited by Friedrich Engels and published in 1885 and 1894 respectively. The process of editing Volume 3 would ultimately prove extremely problematic for Engels and fomented intense controversy. This swirled around the infamous *transformation problem* where Marx shifts the terms of dialectical exposition in *Capital* from *value* to *price* (see Box 5.1). Marx's Volume 3, however, was left in the most rough and unfinished state. To deal with questions that resolution of the *transformation problem* demanded, Engels orchestrated a "Prize Essay Competition", ostensibly to gauge the wider state of knowledge on it. Engels, interestingly, refused to expose debate contributors to Marx's most advanced work on this topic. Also, in responding to entries to the competition, Engels was recorded as being evasive and even obstructive. And, Engels ended up merely confirming what *he* understood as Marx's position on the problem despite the immense gaps Marx left in Volume 3. Engels eschewed the assistance of numerous gifted Marxian economists in readying Volume 3 for the printer under circumstances where given the division of labor he and Marx shared, it was quite probable that Engels was somewhat out of touch with developments in political economy by that time.[1]

During the period in which publication of *Capital* was delayed, the new species of bourgeois economics – neoclassical economics – ascended to a position of unrivaled hegemony particularly in the Anglo-American world. It would be the theoretical core of neoclassical theory that came to plague *Capital*. Stated succinctly, neoclassical economics switched the course of economic theory away from the classical political economy concern with the production of wealth towards the narrow question of distributing "scarce" resources among competing ends. The centerpiece of neoclassical analysis here was its theory of relative prices that backstopped claims about an "optimal" allocation of resources in a static equilibrium.[2]

It was on the basis of neoclassical price theory then that the assault upon Marx's *Capital* was mounted. Nevertheless, the early twentieth-century attacks on Marxian economics, for its undeveloped price theory, never spilled out beyond a narrow group of specialists.[3] This changed following WWII. By the 1950s, the "formalist revolution" in neoclassical economics transformed even the stultified neoclassical concern with distribution in a *real* economy into "a mathematical problem about a virtual economy" as the late Mark Blaug so aptly describes it.[4] Of course, from the perspective of this book, the neoclassical move to high quantitative artifice on "the market" at precisely the time when the capitalist market managed economic life only with Herculean superstructure support is instructive in itself: and we will return to this. In any case, the new quantitative calculus mesmerized economists of all stripes including Marxist economists. Steeped in neoclassical price theory, and armed with its techniques, all pounced on Marx's Volume 3, setting off a second round of "value theory" debate that continues today.[5] As alluded to in Chapter 1 of this book, much of the Marxist profession had by this time abandoned "economics" in any case, largely for HM and its philosophical debates over historical directionality. Or, for the sort of fuzzy "multidimensional political economy" à la Fine and Milonakis adverted to in Chapter 2 and that, as I also argue at length elsewhere, tends en masse to be self-styled with little direct connection made to Marx's *Capital* beyond the requisite radical quotations.[6]

Box 5.1

The fact of the matter is that there actually is *no* transformation problem per se (though the important technical task of transforming values into prices *and* vice versa is very real) when the dialectical architecture of Marx's *Capital* is taken into account. Nevertheless, its resolution only occurred in the hands of Japanese Marxian economist Kozo Uno who completed and refined Marx's unfinished work. And it is Uno's student Thomas Sekine who ultimately elaborated it in relation to the raft of purported difficulties faced by Marxian economics re: choice of technique; heterogeneous labor; joint production (see Thomas Sekine, "The Law of Market Value", in Bell (ed.) *Towards a Critique of Bourgeois Economics*, pp. 139ff).

"Transformation" is utilized in a twofold sense by Marx. In the first instance it refers to a *qualitative* operation where, with its unraveling of all the categories of capital, dialectical economic theory treats their further concrete (in thought) specification as in: "the transformation of the commodity form into the money form", "the transformation of money into capital", "the transformation of surplus profit into rent", "the transformation of capital into a commodity", "the transformation of value into price", and so forth. But these conceptual operations must *not* be confused with the particular instance of the *quantitative* operation transformation refers to which involves the mathematical transformation of value into price and the *rate* of surplus value into the *rate* of profit and the *inverse* calculation or movement between these categories. That is, given the dialectical architecture of *Capital*, it is not a question of there being two "systems" of value and surplus value *and* price and profit, the separate workings of which are *empirically* verifiable. Rather, in the *doctrine of production*, tasked with dialectically elucidating capital accumulation from *inside* the production process (and the circulation process of capital "outside" of that), the specific conditions are not as yet posited for the *quantitative* determination of either value or price. In the *doctrine of distribution*, which explores accumulation from the *outside* in the surface manifestations of capital in the market, the necessary specification of the *technology complex* and the *organic composition of capital* permit the simultaneous quantitative determination of both values and prices. And on the basis of specific information about these factors it is possible to produce the bedeviling inverse calculations or movements between rates of profit and prices *and* surplus value and values (*and* vice versa) as in the plotting of coordinates across two differing spaces.

Prices, then, though diverging from values, necessarily remain *tethered* to them as a requisite of the fundamental economic reproducibility of capitalism as an historical society. What dialectical economic theory proceeds to capture is the fashion in which such tethering is manifested through the *law of market value* under which supply and demand production price fluctuations induce the flow or reallocation of resources *at the margins* of all capitalist industries (with their differing organic compositions of capital and so forth). Dialectical economic theory, therefore, through the transformation of value into price, resolves the contradiction between value and use value as it is expressed in both the inter- and intrasector variability of technique utilized by diverse capitalist enterprises in the production of discrete use values (see, here, Sekine, *An Outline of the Dialectic of Capital*, Volume 2, pp. 33–42. This is based on the fragmentary discussion in Karl Marx, *Capital* V III, Chapters 10, 11, and the "Supplementary Remarks" that constitute Chapter 12, http://www.marxists.org/archive/marx/works/1894-c3/index.htm, 2014).

Economic calculation

It is certainly instructive, though not surprising, that early twentieth-century debate over the feasibility of socialist state planning would unfold on the basis of neoclassical price theory and the prime concern of the latter over balancing supply and demand in an "optimal" equilibrium. Or that probing economic questions of socialism's feasibility would initially be undertaken *not* by Marxists but those critical of the socialist project.[7] What was perceived to be at stake is the question of whether a *state* centrally planned economy predicated upon public ownership of the means of production, as readings of Marx suggest is the formula for a socialist alternative to capitalism, could reproduce the purported "rational" economic calculations of the capitalist *market* to allocate resources efficiently. The work of Japanese economist Makoto Itoh contains a succinct play-by-play here.[8] Let us deal with the main questions. The first salvos launched against central planning hit on three points: a) the problem for planning constituted by heterogeneous labor in tailoring supply of consumer goods to demand; b) the problem for state ownership of the means of production in choosing the most cost-efficient methods in the absence of market prices; and c) the sheer impracticability for state planners to perform calculations for all inputs and outputs in a complex economy so as to optimally allocate resources. As Itoh notes, main calculation debate player Austrian economist Ludwig von Mises, operating with a hackneyed understanding of Marx's *Capital* derived from intervention in the early value theory debate of his professor Eugen Böhm-Bawerk, rejected the possibility of labor as a standard of measure. Of course, we know such rejection to be to be foolish as the reducing of concrete-specific labor to homogenous abstract human labor is easily handled by Marxian economics. And Marx's theory of prices of production predicated upon the labor theory of value adequately treats questions of the competitiveness of techniques.[9]

In any case, as socialist defenders of state planning fired back, they did so remaining on the terrain of bourgeois economics with models showing how based on demand curves for both consumer goods and major means of production, trial and error procedures similar to that occurring in competitive markets can arrive at sets of equilibrium accounting or "shadow" prices. And, the fact that state planners had a more complete grasp of what was going on in the economy as a whole, the trial and error process of observing decisions of both consumers and managers of socialist enterprises would lead to a quicker ascertaining of equilibrium prices in a socialist economy than a capitalist one. Oskar Lange, who played a major part in the rebuttal of von Mises, followed up decades later on his earlier work with a then extremely optimistic argument over the use of computers to solve the simultaneous equations necessary to process the required "feedback" to planners of economic activities. Lange, in fact, viewed "the market" and computers as devices that could be substituted for each other.[10]

We should bear in mind, the Soviet Union, the first socialist country, did not organize its economy according to the neoclassical inspired model of Lange. Initial formation of prices in the Soviet Union was guided by the pre-WWI price configuration and thereafter (except during the brief period of Lenin's New Economic Policy or NEP[11]) prices were for the most part officially fixed. Indeed, as Lange himself acceded to government in his native Poland following Poland's integration into the Soviet bloc in the post-WWII era, he also never pushed the socialist government to implement his model. While it is generally recognized that defenders of state planning and public ownership of the means of production represented by Lange won the early calculation debate, Lange's model has never actually been adopted anywhere. It is rather viewed as a piece of intellectual history "proving" that neoclassical price theory and claim of "optimal" market equilibrium outcome does not ceteris paribus exclude a planned socialist economy with public ownership of the means of production.[12]

The fact that the Soviet Union avoided the effects of the Great Depression that ravaged the capitalist world economy in the 1930s, and then proceeded in the aftermath of WWII to grow impressively, no doubt contributed to the paucity of interest among economists in continuing to debate the feasibility of socialist planning. However, by the 1980s, with the Soviet Union clearly facing economic duress, amplified by political stresses that would prompt its rapid and unceremonious collapse by 1989, the calculation debate revived.

We may recall our discussion in Chapter 3 of debate over how the "really existing" socialism of Soviet-style societies should be characterized – as a kind of capitalism, deformed socialism, or something divergent from both capitalism and socialism. The parameters of this debate were set, I argued, by the understanding of socialism deriving from HM that socialism realizes the historical telos of capitalism and will spring from the so-called socializing tendencies of the latter. This helped galvanize the view of socialist revolution as wresting political power embodied in the state along with commanding heights economic power from the bourgeoisie to be then wielded by the organized working class and its representatives in state planning based on public ownership of the already partially "socialized" means of production inherited from capitalism. It is true, as chronicled by Peter Hudis, that Marx's views on the state morphed considerably from the time of writing the *Communist Manifesto* to that of *The Civil War in France* and Marx's analysis of the Paris Commune toward dismantling centralized state power and remaking it to support decentralized popular empowerment.[13] Nevertheless, it is arguably the case that socialist political parties that either acceded to power or aspired to, along with social democratic political parties through the golden age, both identified with state economic planning (or significant state programming in social democracies) as the socialist goal.

But as incontrovertible evidence of both economic stagnation of Soviet-style central planning and the authoritarian bent of Soviet-style societies (with the latter seen as going hand-in-hand with the former) spread, socialists were pressed to seek a new orientation. It is in this vein, then, that the calculation debate revived with the proffering by committed socialists of that which decades earlier would have been seen as anathema by comrades, models of so-called market socialism. One of the earliest defenses of this was made by British economist and specialist on the Soviet economy, Alec Nove.[14] Nove dwells in particular on our point "c" from the early calculation debate, the sheer impracticability for state planners to perform calculations for all inputs and outputs in a complex economy. Soviet planning, Nove argues, proved successful with targeted sectors of the economy such as military production. But, he maintains,

> [W]hether the decision is that of a consumer, a producer, a would-be innovator, a commune . . . [t]hey all have one thing, one requirement, in common: the need for a number of material inputs. . . . How . . . are they to be obtained? By application to the "associated producers" or some planning office? Bearing

in mind that each decision involves several different inputs, provided by a number of different enterprises each of which in turn requires different inputs. . . . The use of computers can speed up calculations and help achieve material balance. But it will be human beings, not computers, who administer priorities . . .[15]

In developing his market model Nove envisioned targeted non-market public sectors such as water or electricity where predictability of supply and demand conditions are uncomplicated along with education, health, postal service, public transportation, and like sectors that are sheltered from market profitability criteria.[16] Nove further specified the workability of his model populated by a diverse array of production unit types including state enterprises, cooperatives, worker self-management, the latter Nove seeing as a core socialist principle. After all, rendering workers cogs in the bureaucratic plan, for Nove, could only but foster worker alienation. Nove supported multiparty democracy. And Nove foresaw a modicum of centralized planning for large-scale investments.[17]

Most recently, a model of so-called market socialism has been advanced by David Schweickart.[18] As per the participants in the early calculation debate, Schweickart finds himself enamored with the technical "elegance" of neoclassical economics theory of distribution. While unassailable in economic terms for Schweickart, the problem is its "ethical" elision. That is, capitalists and landlords are "absent" from the production process yet receive a "healthy cut".[19] For the successor society to ameliorate this key distributional ill of capitalism, Schweickart advances "Economic Democracy", which simply plucks capitalist and landlord out of the market equation. To this effect, he throws down the gauntlet:

> Economic Democracy is a market economy . . . centralized planning, the most commonly advocated socialist alternative to market allocation, is inherently flawed, and schemes for decentralized, nonmarket planning are unworkable. . . . Without a price mechanism sensitive to supply and demand, it is difficult for a producer or planner to know what and how much to produce, and which production and marketing methods are the most efficient.[20]

Schweickart then outlines his market model in terms of worker self-managed firms and social control of investment. The latter is the socialist crux of the model. It operates through a flat tax on capital assets that amounts to "a leasing fee paid by workers of the enterprise for use of social property that belongs to all". Investments are to be allocated in two possible ways: one, by a "market conforming" planning board, as practiced by Japan and South Korea during their development spurts; two, by a system of publicly owned yet competing, privately managed banks.[21] As in the case of Nove's model, Schweickart also maintains that as with existing capitalism, there will be a less competitive "public" sector providing goods and services such as transportation infrastructure, health care, and so forth; where investment in each sector is to be made democratically by national, regional, and local legislative bodies.[22]

Again, as per the early calculation debate, socialist planners fired back. The central players here – Michael Albert and Robin Hahnel,[23] W. Paul Cockshott and Allin Cottrell,[24] Fikret Adaman and Pat Devine[25] – all advance models of *democratic participatory* planning, which range in degree of centralization yet adopt measures that arguably translate popular participation into efficient allocations of resources. Albert and Hahnel maintain a market simulating efficient equilibration of supply and demand can be effectuated through a decentralized iterative planning process where microlevel consumers' and workers' councils adjust demands that are subject to revision according to information transmitted from relevant meso- and crucial macrolevel "facilitation" bodies. Cockshott and Cottrell envision democratic central planning that recruits advanced ICT networks to balance inputs and outputs (equilibrium-like with what they refer to as a "marketing algorithm"[26]) through information derived from direct calculation of labour time. In recent writing they have also adopted the buzzword "iteration" as in their "iterative coordination" to explain how popular participation through "plebiscites" at various "levels" manifests itself on the democratic side of central planning.[27] Pace Nove, Cockshott and Cottrell conclude:

> Given the advances in computation and information technology . . . we can envisage a flexible and responsible planning system covering the whole economy, with iteration built in and negotiation as a necessary adjunct.[28]

Finally, Adaman and Devine are outliers in the democratic participatory planning response in that they do not propose simulation of a neoclassical equilibrium. Rather, they advocate "social ownership" where property is owned neither by state nor privately but by those affected by the use of the property in question. Participatory planning is effectuated by "negotiated coordination" among "stakeholder" representatives at enterprise, community, regional, national, and so on, levels. The economic modus operandi of this decentralized participatory scheme derives from a distinction Adaman and Devine draw between "market exchange" and "market forces". They understand the former in terms of "use of existing capacity" and maintain transactions predicated upon it between producers and users (with prices calculated by units on the basis of labor costs, "capital charge", and input costs) would not be coordinated ex ante. The latter, on the other hand, which Adaman and Devine identify with how "changes in capacity" occur in capitalism, is what will be subject to ex ante "negotiated coordination".[29] However, there is another controversy Adaman and Devine address in their model. Let us turn to it.

Motivation, innovation, and discovery

What started as a *calculation* debate over the possibility of a centrally planned economy with publicly owned means of production efficiently allocating social resources had actually opened two further channels for critique of socialism. Von Mises, for example, had also emphasized that without price competition as engendered in actual functioning markets and freedom for economic agents to take advantage of it there would be little to motivate investment in innovative technique. Friedrich Hayek, in his review of the early debate, added to von Mises's point, that not only does socialist planning and public ownership strangle motivation to innovate, the very character of knowledge that grounds innovation is not readily accessible by a planning authority as its existence in society is always dispersed and held tacitly. Hayek would then move from his concern with knowledge as such and the relation of the individual to it to arguments for the innate incompatibility of socialism with human liberty that has become the neoliberal refrain.[30]

It is the work of von Mises and Hayek then that foregrounds the "Austrian approach" to bourgeois economics, which questions the ability of the "static" equilibrium theory of Léon Walras to adequately treat the purported real-world dynamism of "the market". For the Austrians, the fount of market vitality is not the routine of price informed action of social agents that the notion of a general equilibrium captures, but a process of *entrepreneurial discovery* unfolding in an environment of "rivalrous" competition. The entrepreneur is presented as the indomitable hero of capitalism, forever "scanning" the economic "horizons" to mobilize the dispersed, tacit, or "un-thought-of" knowledge of economic life to produce the profit-making, market-driving discoveries that constitute the fountain of capitalist innovation and growth.[31] According to Geoffrey Hodgson, as the calculation debate revived at the dawn of the neoliberal era with the Soviet economy convulsing in death throes as we note, it did so with the view that argument based on the Lange model occluded what von Mises and Hayek grasped as "the real mechanisms of a market economy" and that the socialist planning side of the debate never fully came to grips with the fundamental challenge to non-market economy posed by the character of knowledge for economies.[32]

Hodgson proceeds on the basis of the above to attack recent proposals for democratic participatory planning. His targets are Adaman and Devine along with Cockshott and Cottrell though his arguments certainly apply to Albert and Hahnel as well. Let us briefly look at what Hodgson has to say about calculation to set the stage for his major intervention. Hodgson is adamant that *any* kind of planning is destined to allocate resources in laborious, suboptimal ways. I intend to deal with the substantive question of Adaman and Devine's notion of "market exchange" vs. "market forces" in the following section. But, on the face of their explanation here, Hodgson believes he has caught them out trying to have things both ways. That is, "impelled to advocate some version of the market mechanism. Yet this pill was sweetened with layers of sweet-sounding proposals . . . In all, the layers are so thick it is difficult to find the bitter pill itself".[33] Hodgson admits he is all for Adaman and Devine's "negotiated coordination" among "stakeholders". But to the extent that this entails more than "transforming" the market, even in the case of demarcating "market exchange" as supposedly outside the ex ante plan, Hodgson argues when questions of new products arise that bring to bear decisions on investment (an inevitable regularity given people's changing tastes and profiles, he notes), the result is sure to be a meeting "overload" that will leave no time "for work, leisure or consumption".[34] Hodgson further takes issue with Adaman and Devine's pegging of "the market" as an ex post mechanism of economic coordination. Hodgson unabashedly declares: "All costs in markets involve calculations by social agents concerning the future".[35] Finally, Hodgson raises the tone to conclude. "The existence of conflicting plans is an endemic problem, and it would be a dangerous mistake to assume that any system of participatory or democratic planning will at some point remove these conflicts."[36]

To Cockshott and Cottrell, Hodgson has little to say on the calculation matter per se. And what he does say is confused and redundant but worth us spelling it out now before we move on. First, he talks about Cockshott and Cottrell's computer models calculating "socially necessary labor time". Actually, in their book *Towards a New Socialism* they *never* use that term. They refer to *labor time*, something we will return to in the following section. In dialectical economic theory, *socially necessary labor* is the only *real* (new) cost incurred by society in the production of commodities. It refers to the ex post way in which capital validates whether labor power expended in the production of commodities is productive of value. Marx emphasizes the "social necessary" aspect of labor in this context, of course, because in bourgeois society where means of production are in private hands Marx wants to explain how private labor that is never directly social can be made so. Thus, when commodities are produced in equilibrium quantities, that is, neither overproduced nor underproduced in relation to the existing pattern of social demand, it can be said that socially necessary labor has been expended in their production. The question of socially necessary labor cuts to the very heart of the *law of value* (see Box 5.2).

Box 5.2

As summarized by Sekine:

> In capitalist society the production of commodities is universal and not partial. In other words, all use-values that society needs are produced as value objects because even labour-power is converted into a commodity. Value-objects tend to embody only socially necessary labour. When all commodities embody socially necessary labour, they are all produced in quantities that meet the social demand (none being overproduced or underproduced). This further implies that the allocation of productive labour in society is optimal and a uniform rate of profit obtains in all spheres of production. The law of value, on this ground, claims that all commodities tend to be exchanged at equilibrium prices, which presuppose an optimal social allocation of productive labour, and, consequently, also presuppose the expenditure of only socially necessary labour for the production of all commodities.

See Thomas T. Sekine, "The Necessity of the Law of Value, Its Demonstration and Significance", in Bell (ed.), *Towards a Critique of Bourgeois Economics*, pp. 107–8 (though the chapter as a whole is compelling for those craving to "do the math".

Second, Hodgson goes back to the early von Mises's misapprehension of Marxian economic theory that von Mises obtained from his professor, Böhm-Bawerk, that reducing skilled or concrete-specific labor to homogeneous abstract human labor is problematic for theory and would undo economic calculations of labor time. That is simply wrongheaded.

However, the issues Hodgson is gnawing at the bit to belabor are these. Along with Hayek's concern with the dispersed nature of knowledge for economies, Hodgson draws scientist and philosopher Michael Polanyi into the fray hoping thereby to slam dunk his case for "the market" is forever. Without straying too far afield in philosophy of science debate here, we may recall our Chapter 2 discussion of CR critique of positivist methodological reductionism where science is equated with the making of "value free" claims about empirical regularities for purposes of prediction. Michael Polanyi is part of a trend challenging positivism known broadly as *constructivism*. Quite simply, constructivist theories are part of the "social turn" in science that sees the results of experiments, for example, as not confirming a correspondence between our ("value free") theories of the world and a mind-independent reality but "constructed" by us with the instruments, concepts, thought schemes we deploy. Polanyi's intervention entails argument over the deeply "personal" constructed quality of knowledge, defying articulacy in the fashion construed by positivism, and Hodgson reproduces the ubiquitous Polanyi quote here that *"we know more than we can tell"*. Following Polanyi, Hodgson further maintains that given how *all* knowledge of nature and society is incised with this tacit dimension, ultimately "the foundation of all knowledge must remain inexplicit". As such, any "attempt to dispense with tacitness, and to attempt to subject *all* human affairs to open reason and discussion, would be . . . dangerous".[37]

What then does this all mean according to Hodgson for new socialist models of democratic participatory planning? First, given that scientific advance and technological innovation relies on tacit knowledge, though this is potentially held not only by individuals but even socially among groups of workers, for example, the fact that even social knowledge as such remains tacit and never readily "transparent" to be accessed by "any member of society", mitigates against "the possibility of an all-embracing collective plan", Hodgson declares. Innovation thus springs from "the striking of intuition upon the flintstone of tacit skills, rather than . . . rational deliberation". It is markets and private property rights, according to Hodgson, which enable "eccentric" inventors or the fabled "entrepreneur" to develop seemingly "far-fetched" ideas and then "test the demand for new innovations by bringing them to market". Second, given the "practice" oriented nature of knowledge, people "in any complex society . . . have no alternative to be specialists". Marx, Hodgson asserts, "gross[ly] underestimate[d] . . . the inevitability of a division of labour based on differentiated skills". Even democratic planning in the end will see the delegation of decisions to experts as the more "democratic" a decision-making process is, the more decisions individuals have to make. Should Adaman and Devine's model get off the ground it will gravitate toward bureaucratic command economy, Hodgson warns.[38] Third, there is the question of the configuring of modern technologies and consumption around an ever-expanding array of goods with similarly ever-expanding specificities and components. Hodgson takes Cockshott and Cottrell to task on this, arguing that even the more powerful computers will be unable to handle the details of today's complex demand structure. Hodgson suggests innovation now is increasingly driven by "process innovation" marked with an increasing quantum of tacit knowledge in the hands of "workers close to the production process" (something we may note lends support to Adaman and Devine's position, though is marshaled against Cockshott and Cottrell's centralized model).[39]

Adaman and Devine, to be sure, launch back, defending the ability of their participatory model to plug-in to the dispersed, contextual knowledge in society through its "negotiated coordination" predicated upon so-called market exchange. They see the representative *committee* in their model of "negotiated coordination", with its discrete operating procedure and direct experience in the economic activity under consideration, as precisely the kind of social institution in which tacit knowledge is embedded; with the added caveat of "self-reflexivity" in "application of reason to the decisions facing them".[40] Nevertheless, Pat Devine does find some common ground with Hodgson, Devine declares:

> [I]t is a mistake to imagine that detailed *ex ante* iterative coordination for the whole economy is possible in a complex modern economy. Much of the knowledge about people's needs is tacit – knowledge that is only gained through the practical experience of individuals and groups and cannot be codified or transferred, but can only be made use of by those who have had that experience. That is why it is impossible to centralize all relevant knowledge or attempt a series of *ex ante* iterations through a Walrasian auctioneer or computer equivalent. Socialist economic organization needs to . . . institutionalize learning processes through which people come to understand and empathize with other people's concerns as well as their own, and in the course of so doing negotiate an outcome that reconciles differences in a way that everyone accepts as reasonable.[41]

The Marxian economic redemption

As underscored by Japanese economist Makoto Itoh, it has in fact been a "mysterious lacuna" of the whole debate over the making of a successor socialist society that Marxian economic theory and the labor theory of value is *never* drawn upon by any of the protagonists.[42] The ramifications of such a lacuna are momentous and have stifled the sort of creative thinking about the future the present volume advocates. Let us conclude this chapter with a point by point dissection of the issues here.

First, in accordance with the schema of HM discussed in Chapter 3, because socialism was expected to build on "socializing" tendencies of capitalism, little attention was devoted by the Marxist profession to operational questions of socialist planning that would follow revolutionary prying of political power from the hands of the bourgeoisie. The advent of socialism in the Soviet Union and proclaimed commencement there of building socialism without a prefab model in hand of the successor society seemed only to corroborate the HM hypothesis. As we further note above, planning policies of Soviet socialism differed from models produced in the calculation debate. And, formative critical assessments and forecasts of early demise for the Soviet experiment by detractors such as von Mises and Hayek proved unfounded.[43] In this sense, the initial phase of the calculation debate occurred behind the back of the actual experience of building socialism in the Soviet Union as well as behind the back of Marxian political economy.

Hence, it is not just a question of historical interest that the calculation debate originated in the hands of scholars steeped in neoclassical price theory. The very fact that debate over the feasibility of socialism was posed in terms of "calculation" reflects the ideological hijacking of the debate by neoclassical economics and, whether it was to be "the market" or "the state" that was to do the "calculating", a vision of socialism that in effect remains a prisoner of capitalism. Remember, neoclassical economics purports to be studying such a thing as an "economy" without ever problematizing the historical conditions that render human material life "transparent" for theory to explore in the first place. And neoclassical economics never comes to grips with what makes it possible to even think about human socio-material relations in the abstract quantitative terms that are the metric of "calculation". Whether we have in mind the early Lange model of centralized state "calculation" or later participatory "iterative" model of Albert and Hahnel, or even participatory centralized "marketing algorithm" model of Cockshott and Cottrell, the wholesale enterprise of modeling socialism as a simulation of neoclassical equilibrium reduces socialism to an abstract, technical problem. What socialism is really about – human flourishing and socio-material betterment, extirpating of alienation and exploitation of the direct producers in society, reproducing human material life for the concrete purpose of satisfying human use value needs and so forth – is elided.

Second. So-called market socialism, counterposed to state centric socialist models as the means for resolving the calculation debate, is writ large symptomatic of the tendency to reduce socialism to an abstract, technical question. There is no better way of illustrating this than with the following quote from "market socialist" David Schweickart. He unabashedly asserts that what socialists really want is an economy that will "allow us to get on with our lives without having to worry so much about economic matters".[44] Presumably, Schweickart is addressing the requirement that as with various arrangements for public participation in decision making in the political sphere of human affairs in bourgeois society, so socialism calls for deepening and extending such participation to decision making related to human material reproduction. Under the spell of capitalist reification and neoclassical economics' blindness to its ramifications, humanity has been lulled into the false sense of security that across the sweep of human history there has always been such a thing as an "economy" that operates "on its own" akin to a natural force. Besides settling the historical question that what is referred to as "the market" in neoclassical speak is really the *capitalist* market. Dialectical economic theory demonstrates that reproduction of human economic life through integrated systems of self-regulating markets of the capitalist economy occurs *only* as a byproduct of value augmentation. And the *capitalist* market, as such, cannot be decoupled from capitalism. As I put it in the previous chapter, to abdicate human responsibility for managing economic life to the "extra-human" force of capitalist reification so as to "get on with our lives" is a deal with the devil. From another angle, whereas socialism is fundamentally about bringing "the prehistory of human society to a close" and obviating HM through superstructure management of the substructure rather than enslavement to it, Schweickart will see this prehistory persist in perpetuity.

Continuing with Schweickart, we can recall our point at the outset of this chapter that neoclassical economics switches the course of bourgeois economics away from the "messy" concern of classical economists like Adam Smith with the production of wealth to questions of distribution of resources among competing ends. This switch then turns the focus of "economics" away from production per se onto circulation forms of capital and the formation of relative prices in the capitalist market. Robert Albritton aptly captures what is at stake here:

> Price is at the same time both a nearly universal and superficial or lazy way of tying together and identifying those phenomena to be labeled "economic". As a category it almost immediately invites formalistic and mathematical thinking that tends to disconnect from anything historically specific. But if prices circulate titles to property, then it is crucial to understand what the structure of property relations is, how it is perpetuated, and how in general the circulation of titles and organization of production is shaped by this structure.[45]

We know, of course, that capitalist structuring of property relations revolves around the commodification of human labor power. And the "price mechanism" that Schweickart seeks to harness for his future society because it tells us "which production and marketing methods are the most efficient", hinges upon commodified labor power being made available in the market to be recruited in the production of *any* good according to shifting patterns of social demand and opportunities for profit-making. Of course, neoclassical economists like Schweickart simply cannot grasp the centrality of the commodification of labor power to the attributes of "the market" they worship.

Schweickart swallows the early value debate critique of Volume 3 of Marx's *Capital* on the basis of its undeveloped price theory and inability to show how "the price of a commodity [is] determined by the amount of labor it took to produce it".[46] But this makes nonsense of Marx's *Capital*. *Capital* advances a *labor theory of value* not price! Capitalist exploitation and alienation are intimately bound to the way surplus labor is extracted from the direct producers under capitalism and materialized as surplus value. It is the latter that is then "cut" by capitalist, landlord, and banker (as personifications of economic categories profit, rent, and interest). Workers are remunerated in the wage form that must be equivalent, at minimum, to the product of their necessary labor (that labor necessary and sufficient for intergenerational reproduction of the labor power of the direct producers). And wages are paid *prior* to the product of labor even being brought to the market and *irrespective* of whether capital in the throes of competition validates that expenditure of human labor power as socially necessary labor and bearing fruit in surplus value. The challenge for a genuine socialism here resides in the radical reconsideration of both the very question of surplus labor and, if surplus labor is performed by the direct producers, the transformation of its function as well as the relation of surplus labor to necessary labor (we will return to this in Chapter 6). This in turn directs socialist thinking toward transfiguring social relations of production and attendant social property relations rather than ameliorating an "ethical" slight in neoclassical economics fantasy "distribution" scenario.

Another way of approaching "the market" question is in terms of the claim by Adaman and Devine that "market exchange" can be decoupled from "market forces". Again, the debate with Hodgson over this plays out on the terrain of neoclassical economics and thus has little applicability to our interest in creative thinking about institutionally configuring a genuine socialism.[47] Hodgson's silly notion of prices in "market exchange" based upon "calculations by social agents concerning the future" (parroting a line from an introductory neoclassical textbook) would apply only to exchange of use values *not* commodities produced in the capitalist market as value objects the prices of which, as discussed above, are always backward facing.

But from the perspective of Marxian economics it is important to restate the fact emphasized by Marx (see also discussion in Chapters 3 and 4) that the gamut of *forms* – money, prices, wages, profits, and so forth – capital symbiotically weaves into its chrematistic of value augmentation, existed to various extents and in differing compositions in precapitalist societies *exogenous* to the interpersonal modalities of material economic reproduction in those societies. Impersonal "trade" or "exchange" is something that took place at the "borders" of societies under conditions where firewalls were maintained between impersonal trading *and* "exchange" as such imbricates in interpersonal material relations of precapitalist societies. At the dawn of the capitalist era marketization breaks down these firewalls as economic life is commodified and subsumed by the motion of value. The shape that "exchange" assumes here is M-C-M`. Adaman and Devine are not clear on whether they are talking about M-C-M`, C-M-C, or even C-C in their suggestion that "market exchange" can be decoupled from "market forces" and still operate as an ex post coordination mechanism. M-C-M`, of course, implies the commodification of labor power as this is the ground for a society of generalized impersonal commodity "exchange". And the economically (capitalistically) rational prices necessitate operation of "market forces".

Of course, given the exogenous origins of forms of value to the material reproducibility of human societies it is certainly the case that such forms may be utilized both strategically and benignly in achieving socialist goals. But it is not a question of simply "socializing" the market as Diane Elson, for example, argues.[48] Market forms may be utilized creatively in ways that combine elements of ex ante coordination with ex post. Socialism is not tied to choice between extremes of centrally fixed prices and "pure" capitalist market prices. Even in the current economic configuration prices are manipulated "ex ante" to stimulate politically structured seemingly "ex post" outcomes (such as in the state subsidizing of fossil fuel energy, to take a glaring example). However the distinction between "market exchange" and "market forces" is not a very good way of treating the range of socialist potentialities here. As we shall see in Chapter 6, the arbiters as per our ontology of socialism are *use value heterogeneity* and human *use value need*. The problem with the whole debate over market and planning is that the choice has been cast in either/or *society-wide* terms with wanton neglect of such questions. And the way economic forms including money, price, profits, and so forth may be democratically manipulated across economic sectors to satisfy human use value needs and realize socialist social and political goals.

Third, and related to the foregoing, debate over state and market also has its referent in the capitalist economy. Our earlier Marxian political economic discussion touched on the way light use value technological conditions of industrial capital were quite suited to capitalist marketization. On the other hand, the heavy steel and chemical technologies of the second industrial revolution would prove increasingly recalcitrant to the march of value and call forth an array of extra-economic, extra-capitalist supports for their capitalistic management. The stage structures of *consumerism* marking capital accumulation in the golden age period following WWII were even more dependent upon superstructure props. From social wage and social insurance to macroeconomic counter-cyclical intervention in business cycles the sheer extent of superstructure underwriting of "the market" provided grist to debate within the Uno approach to Marxian political economy, over whether the post-WWII golden age period actually constitutes a *stage* of capitalism or simply part of an open-ended world historic transition away from capitalism shaped by Cold War contingencies. In any case, the point here is that Marxian political economic study of capital shows the determinate role use value heterogeneity plays in the adoption of economic principles. Put differently, the debate over market and state arises in the context of shifting use value space in capitalist economies. It is then appropriated by early socialist theorizing of the purported socializing tendencies of capital inhering in the monopoly and oligopoly forms of emergent heavy industry from the late nineteenth century and the growing role played by state policy in support of capital.

To look closer at what is at stake here it is worth quoting Joseph Stiglitz from his book on socialism:

> ... Heavy industry was perhaps particularly well suited for the control mechanisms employed by the socialist system. The scope for individual discretion was limited, and accordingly so too was the scope for decision making ... [T]here may have been a short window of time, the period of heavy industry associated with steel, autos, coal, and so on, in which some variant of a socialism may have been able to work.[49]

Of course, so deeply steeped in bourgeois-think, Stiglitz has no inkling that Marxian political economy turns precisely this argument back on him with the fact of the capitalist era being clearly delimited by a narrow use value space conducive to capitalist market suppression of qualitative considerations in economic life in favor of quantitative ones. However, this is not our main point here. Rather, it is that creative thinking about the socialist future must incorporate institutional flexibility to be able to choose economic principles for particular categories of economic tasks based upon their use value nature. Stiglitz's argument unwittingly lends support to this as to the extent some large-scale, "heavy" repetitive production industries are required in future socialist societies there is no reason why organizational forms of economic planning cannot continue to be applied to them. We will return to this important question regarding the higher technology industries that Stiglitz claims are solely the prerogative of "the market". But framing of the debate in terms of "calculation", whether performed by market or state, occludes such creative thinking or debate from the outset.

Fourth, it is more than astonishing to read through hundreds of pages of debate over socialism only to see the studied attention given to the question of motivation for investment. Yet there is hardly a word to be found on the question of *motivation for work*! As we note in Chapter 3, debate over motivation in the context of the Soviet experiment swirls around that of material vs. moral incentives. Work, as in productive labor that furnishes the use values necessary for the very reproduction of human material existence, entails the giving by human beings of their life energy. Without this giving to furnish necessities of use value life, human society is impossible. Under conditions where labor power is commodified, and workers divested of access to means of production and livelihood are driven to sell their ability to perform productive labor in the capitalist market for a wage, the expenditure of life energy in work by human beings is a *disutility* and *alienating* to them. This is the case because no matter what the remuneration for expending their life energy is, it does not change the fact that their life energy is given *only* to secure *future* sustenance or enjoyment. The life energy itself workers make available in the market to capital is deployed *by capital* in producing *any* good according to shifting patterns of social demand and opportunities for profit-making. In this way, while capital "frees" workers from the interpersonal relations of domination and subordination and extra-economic compulsions characteristic of precapitalist economies, it nevertheless subjects labor to economic coercion. Soviet-style societies, on the other hand, did decommodify labor power, but they resubjected it to extra-economic compulsion that is an historical regression from capitalism as we explain in Chapter 3.

It is disconcerting to see recent discussion among socialists continuing to languish in the realm of material vs. moral or economic vs. extra-economic incentives as the only choice for the future. Cockshott and Cottrell, for example, slip towards a quasi-feudal arrangement, arguing for a "poll tax" that "establishes that all have the same *obligation* to work for the common good *before* they work for themselves".[50] In their iterative, participatory equilibrium simulating model,

Albert and Hahnel for their part advocate "peer pressure" as the compulsion to work.[51] This has rightly been criticized as "Orwellian".[52]

Hodgson, of course, would hardly see the issue of motivation for work as something to be addressed directly. But he does deal with it in a roundabout way in his emphasis upon the "inevitability of a division of labour based on differentiated skills". That this "inevitable" division of labor was constituted in the context of multifaceted process of capitalist disembedding, to take Karl Polanyi's term, escapes Hodgson. Step-by-step capital breaks down the rich multidimensionality of human skill as it fosters the separation of mental from manual labor, industry from agriculture, technology and energy from ecology, humanity from the natural environment, and science from humanity, all to build its regimented, one-dimensional world of value augmentation. Remnants of skill multidimensionality persist in Hodgson's "modern society" such as the millwright, with a skill set inclusive of engineering, design, metal work, mechanics, machine building and operation, and so forth. And there has always been the struggle, mounted with increasing intensity today given its necessity to an eco-sustainable future, to maintain multidimensional skilling in agriculture.[53] Though the tendency of capital hypertrophied in the surrogate economy of today, whether in slicing, dicing, and geospatially dispersing production or converting food provisioning into agrochemical industries, is always to disempower direct producers in favor of its centralized control mechanisms and foment the aforementioned multiplex disembeddings.

In the end, through economic motivation for work, the age of capital has fomented indifference among workers qua producers to use value in production along with disinterest among workers qua consumers to the modalities and outputs of production processes. Such leading to production processes and goods produced with the potential to destroy human life on this planet. The "differentiated skills" of the current division of labor is part and parcel of the social class, power, and property relations capital has visited upon the world. And that reinforces the indifference and disinterest among workers toward the material conditions of their existence. To hear the likes of Hodgson inveigh against the possibility of a social class upon the backs of the productive labor of which the possibility of human society rests empowered to bridge the gap between mental and manual labor by taking time to consider the most substantive questions relating to the expenditure of their life energy because it will interfere with their "leisure or consumption" (as if workers enjoy much of that in the current neoliberal morass in any case) reeks of bourgeois hypocrisy. In short, a genuine socialism of the future that ensures human socio-material betterment and extirpates capitalist alienation requires precisely an institutional and property reconfiguration that breaks down capitalist division of labor one-dimensionality and instates self-motivation as a paradigmatic form of social compulsion for work.

Fifth, it is still necessary to deal with motivation and economic knowledge in relation to innovation and discovery. To do this, we have to move beyond the bourgeois economic platitudes marking the debate, beginning with what Marxian economic theory teaches us about the capitalist business cycle. Long before neoclassical economics Marx pointed to "incessant equilibrations" of market competition and the market reaching a phase of "average activity".[54] However, Marx's work also helps us lay bare the root of capitalist "rivalrous competition" fixated upon by the so-called "Austrian" intervention.[55]

Let us reconstruct the argument as follows: The business cycle begins with capital investment in production-centered activity. The costliest component of this investment is that of fixed capital, the technology, equipment, factories upon which production takes place. New technologies that generally appear in clusters are adopted first by the most innovative firms. We will get to the question of the precise competitive conditions and specific point in the business cycle where the investment in new technologies is compelled. Here we can point out preliminarily that the motivation for incurring costs of the newest innovations is that innovating firms in each sector that first deploy new technologies will garner a rate of profit higher than the average or what Marx dubs a *surplus profit*. Early innovators then set the bar for competition that forces other firms in the same sector to adopt best practice or face potential extinction.

With capital accumulation in the upswing of the business cycle proceeding apace, competition tends to eliminate differences in profit rates among firms in given sectors as all businesses adopt best practice technologies that had provided leading innovators an edge, and surplus profit, at the outset of the cycle. Similarly, wide variations in pricing also recede as forces of supply and demand trend the economy toward relative price stability. For neoclassical economics, the fact of capitalist market forces trending the economy toward relative price stability is fixated on as the triumphal end of the matter because it confirms their quasi-religious faith in market "perfection". But, for Marx, the gravitation of the economy toward equilibrium constitutes *only* the *widening* or *prosperity phase* of the business cycle.

Capital accumulation, notwithstanding the high calculus of neoclassical artifice, does not stop here. Competition continues. Profits are made. And profits are reinvested. Businesses seek to expand in response to this or that market signal. Most importantly, however, given the expense of fixed capital its deployment entails a lengthy period of depreciation. Thus, business expansion in the course of the *prosperity phase* of the business cycle is based upon a given level of technological accouterment embodied in depreciating fixed capital investment. Put differently, even under conditions of relative price stability the economy still grows. And, as it grows, the economy begins to absorb the *industrial reserve army*. With investment and growth proceeding at a given level of technology, the industrial reserve army approaches a state of full employment. In this way, capitalism by its *own* internal dynamic fosters the overaccumulation or superabundance of capital in relation to the growth of the working population.

Remember, the purported efficiency of the capitalist economy resides in its ability to rapidly respond to price signals to allocate resources "optimally", simultaneously with profits being made (the latter is always the incentive for business to invest in this or that endeavor). If the price of machine tools, for example, rises, this signals to entrepreneurs that investment in that sector to supply growing demand will surely bear fruit in profits. But, with respect to human labor power, while capital does treat it like any other input into the production process, labor power is not just any commodity. That is, labor power, unlike machine tools, is not a capitalistically produced commodity. Thus it is impossible to adjust the *supply* of labor power to the demand for it as is the case with other commodities.

Capital, therefore, in viewing living workers one-dimensionally, as but another commodity input into the production process, is oblivious to the constraint the size of the working population places upon it. Until, of course, the industrial reserve army is completely absorbed and the continuing demand for labor power puts a strong upward pressure on wages and sends profits on a downward slide. When profits fall, businesses respond with their own private interests in mind and seek to grab market share from adversaries. While one or another firm may gain advantage from this strategy the tendency toward overaccumulation of capital in the economy as a whole is exacerbated. With profits in the production-centered economy now falling across the board, businesses begin to close and capital moves to other pursuits such as real estate or speculative activities. In response to the foregoing as well as growing perception of risk in lending, interest rates rise. However this only offers further inducement for capital to decamp from production-centered activity where profits have been plummeting and shift toward speculative endeavors. With businesses now closing en masse, more and more workers becoming unemployed and without ability to purchase goods, bloating inventories that even price slashing fails to alleviate add to the growing overall economic woes. At this point the capitalist interfirm discounting of bills seize up as do lines of credit both for short-term payments and turnover of commercial capital. Even the banking system is placed under duress. Finally, the economy spins into crisis and depression.

It is precisely in this *deepening* or *depression phase* of the business cycle, when capital has been devalued across the economy as a whole, that the stronger remaining businesses grab at the chance to scrap existing fixed capital and invest in deploying newer labor-saving technologies that have come available in clusters. To understand this we have only to put ourselves in the shoes of the rational capitalist. Even if new labor-saving technological accouterment had become available earlier in the business cycle it would hardly be rational for the capitalist to adopt it long before the expensive technology in use was depreciated and profit continuing to accrue to the business on the basis of it. In the midst of ongoing competition and growth predicated upon existing technology, each private business will come to the same rational conclusion to continue profitable expansion without incurring more huge fixed costs. With all businesses finding themselves in the same boat in the *depression phase* of the business cycle however, as stronger capitals lead the way making surplus profits to boot on the basis of new available technologies, other reviving businesses follow suit and so commences the recovery phase and another business cycle.

In the language of Marx's analysis, the technological accouterment of fixed capital is the *forces of production*. The capital/labor nexus at the heart of the process of capital wealth augmentation is the *relations of production*. It is the capitalist relations of production within the ambit of which labor power is maintained as a commodity that are threatened in the throes of the *depression phase* of the business cycle. To reconstitute the capital/labor relation, and capitalism, capital is forced to incur the increased cost of investment in new technological accouterment and revolutionize the forces of production so as to renew capital accumulation. In this alternation of capitalist business cycles between *widening* and *deepening* or *prosperity* and *depression phases* dialectical economic theory demonstrates how, in the maelstrom of economic crisis and *general disequilibrium*, the contradiction between value and use value in the very maintenance of capitalist social relations of production compels capital to revolutionize the forces of production, restructuring its technology complex at a "higher level" of development. Sekine summarizes:

> ... Economic theory consists of two parts, the micro-equilibrium part and the macro-dynamic part, and each comes from the nature of capitalism itself. Marx's *Capital* contains elements of both ... According to the dialectic, even in the "pure" space in which capital is supposed to have full control over all producible use-values, labour-power can still get out of hand and can give rise to a so-called "fundamental disequilibrium" in the system. When this occurs, the market logic is powerless to remedy it; *an element of use-value space itself (technology) must change* in order to ensure the system's survival. This is a reminder of the imperfect subsumption of the use-value space under the logic of capital, i.e., the reminder of the historical transience of capitalism.[56]

To look back in the light of the foregoing at Hodgson's arguments, his chants for "the market", read capitalism, forever fail to grasp the fact of the exogenous nature of technological innovation in capitalist economies. That is, as per our general norms of economic life (see Chapter 2) capital drives to expand the reproduction process of society faster than the natural growth of the working population given its extra-human goal of value augmentation. To resolve the crisis convulsions that befall it capital is forced to search outside itself and its market operations for a technological fix (we will return to this point below). Thus, notwithstanding the conditions of dispersed, "un-thought-of" knowledge in society, innovations sparked by Hodgson's "striking of intuition upon the flintstone of tacit skills" that are then "discovered" by his heroic entrepreneur will *always* be delimited to those believed to contribute to the efficiency of abstract mercantile wealth augmentation and the maintenance of capitalist social relations of production to that effect. Use value possibilities springing from the mind of Hodgson's "eccentric inventor", that are deemed solely to further human use value need, are certain to rot in abeyance. Indeed, Hodgson belabors the notion of "the market" resolving "conflicting plans" for innovation. This, however, brings us to the heart of bourgeois ideology. Capital does "free" human beings from the web of interpersonal extra-economic compulsions that ensnared them in precapitalist economies. But it subjects their "free" self-seeking economic proclivities like a Stalinist dictator to its single-minded chrematistic of abstract mercantile wealth augmentation to the detriment of any other use value "plan" unsuited to its reifying logic.

Further, Hodgson intimates that even should some political/organizational formula be devised for "institutionalization" of "learning processes" in ways that tap into tacit knowledge held by individuals and groups who utilize such knowledge experientially, as Adaman and Devine see things, socialist democratic "committee" transmission mechanisms would delay the efficient economic application of that knowledge. Again, this is nonsense. Even in the assumption by dialectical economic theory of neutralized use value space for capitalist accumulation, innovations in technology and fixed capital stock that appear in clusters through the course of business cycles are largely "tested" only under conditions of generalized crisis in the *depression phase* of the cycle. And the cyclical oscillations around replacement of fixed capital have always been at least decadal affairs.

Of course, it goes without saying that socialism seeks to extirpate the contradictory and anarchical process of innovation and change characteristic of the capitalist commodity economy. In fact, as briefly discussed in Chapter 1, capital itself tries to escape from the crisis and generalized devaluation of capital it is wracked by as market competition plays out in the course of its business cycles. This is particularly the case as capital becomes increasingly "bulky" or heavy and complex and fixed investment costs exorbitant. During the post-WWII golden age, oligopolistic MNCs eschewed the price competition that neoclassical economics modeling peddles to students as reflective of "really existing" economic goings-on and to which Hodgson clings to as the deal breaker for socialism. And, oligopolistic power and extended geospatial reach of MNCs allowed them to innovate at the end of the *prosperity phase* of the business cycle to avoid tightening of labor markets. As well, MNC behemoths were empowered to innovate selectively, maintaining less efficient technologies alongside best practice ones according to competitive conditions they faced in different locales of their operation. Moreover, despite organizational structures akin to a Soviet command economy and operating in oligopolistic market conditions that erected formidable barriers against new market entrants, MNCs nevertheless managed to solve Nove's decision-making challenge of dynamic allocation of inputs across production processes;[57] as well as von Mises's challenge of motivation to innovate in the absence of market price competition and where managerial functionaries, as in the case of Japanese *Keiretsu* to take a clear example, were not remunerated through share ownership.[58]

Bracketing here for further discussion in Chapter 6 my point on deploying select economic principles creatively in relation to particular types of use value production or use value "sectors", and the questions raised by Greens for economies of environmental sanctity, we need to make four points. One, there is simply no reason why in future socialist management of material-goods-producing industries (either producer or consumer industries) under varying conditions of public (including worker, cooperative, community/associational, and so forth) ownership, that there cannot be competition among a few firms in a sector to spur innovation where necessary. Two, that given self-motivation as the paradigmatic form of compulsion for work, a socialist economic incentive system drawing upon the way surplus profit accrues to innovating firms in the commodity economy cannot be devised to benefit the workers and communities of the publicly owned socialist firms that successfully innovate in socially responsible ways. Three, pace Nove, why ICT à la Cockshott and Cottrell cannot be utilized (whether as bar code, card chip reader, point of sale technology) to transmit information in the context of dynamic industrial processes with tight coupling of tasks and numerous diverse components across socialist enterprises in real time? Four, ICTs facilitate the tapping into tacit knowledge for innovation from dispersed, experiential communities on a global scale unimaginable only decades ago.[59] And this process will only be enhanced as e-firewalls separating private MNCs' R&D are broken down by socialist commonwealths.

Sixth, now we have arrived at the crux of our argument on innovation. In Marx's *Capital* and dialectical economic theory, the sort of innovation treated in analysis of business cycle oscillations is limited to industrial technologies that increase the organic composition of capital yet are still amenable to the chrematistic operation of the capitalist market. The epochal transmutations of capital that materialize world historic stages of capitalism are another question altogether. This is the case because the technological changes involved in the shift of capital accumulation from "light" technologies of textile production to "heavy" technologies of steel and industrial chemical production, for example, entail far more than simple increases in the organic composition of capital. Rather, their development into the early twentieth century was made possible by significant transformation of business financing, the structuring of the firm, the role of the state, the international dimension of capital, and so on. Further, while some of the key technologies such as the Bessemer process in steel manufacturing were "discovered" by 1860, their efficient widespread adoption awaited decades and occurred in tandem with other major socio-economic changes and not even in Britain where the "discovery" took place, but in Germany and the US.

The form accumulation assumes in the capitalist stage of *consumerism* is an even more glaring case in point. Much of the technological accouterment of the stage, petroleum energy, the internal combustion engine, semiautomatic assembly line production, had appeared by the beginning of the twentieth century. Yet, while the auto industry carved a presence for itself out of the early twentieth-century economic landscape in the US in particular, it was not until after WWII that the automobile society characterized by mass consumption of automobiles and consumer durables along with infrastructure of highway networks and private family suburban homes took shape. And to make such a society the basis for a sustained period of capital accumulation required sweeping socio-economic, socio-political, and even ideological change that reverberated across business structures, the state, the superstructure, and social relations generally, as well as the international political economy.[60] In short, "the market", "entrepreneurial discovery", even "economics" has little to offer in explaining the emergence of a new stage of capitalism here.

Further, historical periods of transition between world historic stages of capitalism have been punctuated by sustained economic depressions, political upheaval, and/or war. And at each juncture there has *never* been a guarantee that capital accumulation could successfully spring from such episodes of crises. The changes in use value space or technologies exogenous to capitalist market operations that allow the recuperation of capital accumulation from *depression phases* of business cycles constitute qualitatively different phenomenon from these major historical periods of transition. Punctuating the period separating the capitalist stage of *imperialism* and *consumerism* were two world wars, a global depression, and political revolution that brought the Soviet Union into being.

But the real question that brings us back to Marx's fundamental insight into the fact of capitalism as an historically constituted and historically delimited society is whether there exists a use value space on the horizon that is operable according to the capitalist economic principle of abstract value augmentation; and this even assuming Herculean superstructure support akin to that of the golden age? We answer this question in this book with a resounding *no*. I have also made the extended case elsewhere.[61] To be sure, there exist a slew of use values and innovative, environmentally friendly technologies along with eco-sustainable choices on our energy matrix that beckon humanity from the horizon of the future but their utilization defies capitalist operation. Yet we are conditioned to think otherwise. It is worth quoting Richard Heinberg at length on this:

> . . . True, the field of home entertainment has seen some amazing technical advances over the past five decades – digital audio and video; the use of lasers to read from and record on CDs and DVDs; flat screen, HD and now $_3$D television; and the move from physical recorded media to distribution of MP$_3$ and other digital recording formats over the Internet. Yet when it comes to how we get our food, water, and power, and how we transport ourselves and our goods, relatively little has changed in any truly fundamental way . . .
>
> The nearly miraculous development in semiconductor technologies that have revolutionized computing, communications, and home entertainment during the past few decades have led us to think we're making much more "progress" that we really are . . . The slowest-moving areas of technology are, understandably, the ones that involve massive infrastructure that is expensive to build and replace. But these are the technologies on which the functioning of our civilization depends.[62]

There are four points to be made here: First, the process of conception and evolution in ICTs owes little to Hodgson's "market", "eccentric inventor", or "entrepreneur", but military planning with massive state R&D funding and, to the end of the Cold War, often largely carried out secretively with potential cross-fertilization with civilian applications forestalled.[63] Second, the application of ICTs to "innovating" largely the same complex of goods marking the golden age economy, automobiles, television, telephones, stereo entertainment, has discombobulated capitalist market pricing because of the ever-growing component of indirect "knowledge work" costs factoring into ICT pricing. This has seen income flows increasingly skew to unproductive knowledge workers and patent holders as technological rent even as remuneration for productive work plummets with the global transplanting of Hodgson's division of labor to low wage, proto-capitalist production locales like China. In this sense, the evolution of technologies that Stiglitz asserts Marx never foresaw and thus supposedly "doomed" socialism, in the end have proved recalcitrant and unmanageable for capital.[64] Third, the way ICT innovation has piggybacked on the early/mid-twentieth-century use value complex is one of the more environmentally unsustainable aspects of current consumption patterns given its generation of rapid product and even production system obsolescence (along with "obsolescence" of labor forces employed in its production processes) and in turn, mountain after mountain of toxic e-waste.

Fourth, the important point Heinberg makes for our purpose is that the possible application of the raft of new available technologies beckoning humanity to the transformation of our energy, production, transportation, residential, leisure, and so forth infrastructure in ways that conserve the earth's resources and promote eco-sanctity for future generations necessarily requires once-and-for-all installations that in turn lend support to satisfaction of human use value wants predicated upon qualitative considerations in economic life rather than quantitative ones. However this is the diametrical opposite of a society the social goal of which remains the augmentation of abstract, quantitative mercantile wealth.

Finally, Hodgson's ultimatum over purported "inexplicit" foundations of *all* knowledge and subsequent "danger" of subjecting "*all* human affairs to open reason and discussion" reflects the totalitarian tendencies inhering in neoliberal idolatry of "the market" buttressed in his writing by constructivist philosophy of science. As Roy Bhaskar so compellingly argues in his groundbreaking oeuvre to CR philosophy of science, the constructivist position on knowledge constitutes a case of the "epistemic fallacy" that claims that in answering the epistemological question of "how" we can know, the ontological question of "what" there is to be known is simultaneously answered.[65] And Bhaskar further maintains that seeking to evade the task of explicitly problematizing ontology "merely results in the passive secretion of an *implicit* one".[66] The problematization of ontology as we have seen in Chapter 2 carries weighty implications for knowledge and theory construction that we ignore at our peril. While we cannot make a necessitarian claim about "all" knowledge or "all" human affairs (a certain *je ne sais quoi* is sure to remain in my marriage), the unique reificatory ontology of capital does provide a foundation for knowledge of capitalism as captured in dialectical economic theory. In turn, in demonstrating how capital satisfies the general norms of economic life to reproduce a human society as a byproduct of abstract value augmentation, dialectical economic theory simultaneously confirms the possibility of socialism – a society in which those same general norms are satisfied by conscious decision making by associations of free human beings for concrete human purposes. Marxian economic theory does in this way provide a robust foundation for reasoned discussion about organizing human material life. And those like Hodgson who claim otherwise and direct us to surrender human power to make our economic lives to the "extra-human force" of capitalist reification are dead wrong.

Notes

1 See Michael C. Howard and John E. King, *A History of Marxian Economics Volume 1* (Princeton, NJ: Princeton University Press, 1989) pp. 11–13, 16–18, 21ff.
2 See, for example, the excellent study by A. K. Dasgupta, *Epochs of Economic Theory* (New York: Basil Blackwell, 1987).
3 Howard and King, *A History of Marxian Economics: Volume 1*, pp. 42 ff.
4 Mark Blaug, "The Formalist Revolution of the 1950s", *Journal of the History of Economic Thought*, 25, 2 (2003) pp. 147–8.
5 Howard and King, *A History of Marxian Economics: Volume 1*, p. 61; also Howard and King, *A History of Marxian Economics: Volume 2*, pp. 227 ff.
6 Westra, *Political Economy and Globalization*, Chapter 3.
7 Blackburn, "Fin de Siècle: Socialism after the Crash", pp. 17–18.
8 Itoh, *Political Economy for Socialism*, pp. 83–98.
9 Ibid., p. 89.
10 Ibid., pp. 103–5.
11 Howard and King, *A History of Marxian Economics: Volume 1*, p. 288.
12 Geoffrey M. Hodgson, "Socialism against Markets? A Critique of Two Recent Proposals", *Economy and Society*, 27, 4 (1998) pp. 409–10.
13 Hudis, *Marx's Concept of the Alternative to Capitalism*, pp. 183–7.
14 Alec Nove, *The Economics of Feasible Socialism* (London: Allen and Unwin, 1983).
15 Alec Nove, "Markets and Socialism", *New Left Review* I/161 (1987) pp. 100–1.
16 Ibid., p. 102.
17 Itoh, *Political Economy for Socialism*, pp. 113–14.
18 David Schweickart, *After Capitalism* (Lanham, MD: Rowman & Littlefield, 2002).
19 Ibid., pp. 24–31.
20 Ibid., p. 49.
21 Ibid., pp. 24–31.
22 Ibid., pp. 50–5.
23 Michael Albert and Robin Hahnel, *The Political Economy of Participatory Economics* (Princeton: Princeton University Press, 1991); idem, *Looking Forward: Participatory Economics for the Twentieth Century* (Boston: South End Press, 1991); idem, "Socialism As It Was Always Meant to Be", *Review of Radical Political Economics*, 24, 3/4 (1992).
24 W. Paul Cockshott and Allin Cottrell, *Towards a New Socialism* (Philadelphia, PA: Coronet Books, 1993).
25 Fikret Adaman and Pat Devine, "The Economic Calculation Debate: Lessons for Socialists", *Cambridge Journal of Economics*, 20 (1996); idem "On the Economic Theory of Socialism", *New Left Review*, I/221 (1997).
26 Cockshott and Cottrell, *Towards a New Socialism*, p.104.
27 W. Paul Cockshott and Allin Cottrell, "Question 2: Feasibility and Coordination", *Science & Society*, Special Issue, Designing Socialism: Visions, Projections, Models, Guest Editor: Al Campbell, 76, 2 (2012) pp. 195–8.
28 Ibid., p. 198.
29 Adaman and Devine, "The Economic Calculation Debate", pp. 533–4.
30 Itoh, *Political Economy for Socialism*, pp. 89, 91–3, 98–9.
31 Israel M. Kirzner, "Entrepreneurial Discovery and the Competitive Market Process: An Austrian Approach", *Journal of Economic Literature*, 35 (1997) p. 72.
32 Geoffrey M. Hodgson, *Economics and Utopia: Why the Learning Economy Is Not the End of History* (London: Routledge, 1999) pp. 38–40.

33 Hodgson, "Socialism against Markets?" p. 413.
34 Ibid., pp. 413–15.
35 Ibid., p. 414.
36 Geoffrey M. Hodgson, "The Limits to Participatory Planning: A Reply to Adaman and Devine", *Economy and Society*, 34, 1 (2005) p. 143.
37 Hodgson, "Socialism against Markets?" pp. 417–18.
38 Ibid., pp. 419–20.
39 Ibid., pp. 425–6.
40 Fikret Adaman and Pat Devine, "Participatory Planning As a Deliberative Democratic Process: A Response to Hodgson's Critique", *Economy and Society*, 30, 2 (2001) pp. 236–7.
41 Pat Devine, "Question 2: Feasibility and Coordination", *Science & Society*, Special Issue, Designing Socialism, pp. 175–6.
42 Itoh, *Political Economy for Socialism*, p. 129.
43 Ibid., pp. 88–9, 92–3.
44 David Schweickart, "Market Socialism: A Defense", in Bertell Ollman (ed.), *Market Socialism: The Debate among Socialists* (London: Routledge, 1998) p. 19.
45 Albritton, *Economics Transformed*, pp. 60–1.
46 Schweickart, *After Capitalism*, p. 25.
47 The interested reader may refer to Adaman and Devine, "Participatory Planning", pp. 231–2; Hodgson, *Economics and Utopia*, pp. 42ff.
48 Diane Elson, "Market Socialism or Socialization of the Market?" *New Left Review*, I/172 (1988).
49 Joseph E. Stiglitz, *Whither Socialism* (Cambridge, MA: MIT Press, 1994).
50 W. Paul Cockshott and Allin Cottrell, "Value, Markets and Socialism", *Science and Society*, 61, 3 (1997) p. 345, *emphasis added*.
51 Albert and Hahnel, "Socialism As It Was Always Meant to Be", p. 62.
52 Hillel H. Ticktin, "The Problem Is Market Socialism", in Ollman (ed.), *Market Socialism*, p. 75.
53 See the discussion, for example, in Jan Douwe van der Ploeg, *The New Peasantries: Struggles for Autonomy and Sustainability in an Era of Empire and Globalization* (London: Earthscan, 2009).
54 See Karl Marx, *Capital*, V III, http://www.marxists.org/archive/marx/works/1894-c3/index.htm, Chapters 10 and 50.
55 Points that Marx touches on in *Capital* V I, Chapter 25 and in *Capital* V III, Chapter 10, are woven into a more coherent dialectical narrative which is treated in both the *doctrine of production* and *doctrine of distribution* in Sekine, *Outline of the Dialectic of Capital* Volume 1, pp. 219–20, 224–6; Volume 2, pp. 51–9.
56 Thomas Sekine, "General Equilibrium and the Dialectic of Capital", in Bell (ed.), *Towards a Critique of Bourgeois Economics*, pp. 193–6.
57 Berger, "How Finance Gutted Manufacturing".
58 Itoh, *Political Economy for Socialism*, p. 72.
59 Berger, "How Finance Gutted Manufacturing".
60 See Westra, *Evil Axis of Finance*, Chapter 1.
61 Westra, *Political Economy and Globalization*, Chapter 4.
62 Heinberg, *The End of Growth*, pp. 179–80.
63 See for example Carlos Aguiar de Medeiros, "The Post-war American Technological Development As a Military Enterprise", *Contributions to Political Economy*, 22, 1 (2003); Fred Block, "Swimming against the Current: The Rise of a Hidden Developmental State in the United States", *Politics and Society*, 36, 2 (2008).

64 Stiglitz, *Whither Socialism?* p. 205.
65 Bhaskar, *A Realist Theory of Science*. In later work, Roy Bhaskar, *Dialectic: The Pulse of Freedom* (London: Verso, 1993) p. 206, Bhaskar claims the *"linguistic fallacy"*, collapsing questions about being into "our discourse about being", represents the epistemic fallacy in a modern guise.
66 Bhaskar, *Dialectic*, p. 205.

6 The institutional matrix of heterogeneous economic life

In Chapter 2 it is argued that much of the confusion swirling around Marxism since Marx's passing is tied to the misapprehension of the *cognitive sequence* at the heart of his work. That is, the scientificity of Marxism had been largely claimed to reside in HM as an overarching theory of historical directionality. It was then the "few rough structural principles" of historical directionality, to paraphrase Eric Hobsbawm quoted in Chapter 3, coupled with Marx's revolutionary statements at the close of Volume 1 of *Capital* on the historical process of "socialization" compelled by capital (the "inevitabilities" of both that revolutionaries expected to ride the wave of), that guided early socialists as they set in motion the first socialist experiments beginning with the Soviet Union in 1917. Notwithstanding the best intentions and struggles of many of those who wholeheartedly believed in a socialist future and gave their lives on the front lines of its attempted construction, we should not be surprised as we look back from our current vista that the Soviet-style experiments fell so far short of both expectations and the depictions of a socialist future scattered across Marx's various writings. After all, given the equation of Marxism with HM as a master theory of historical directionality and fossilization of Marxist thinking about the future in this vein, transformatory actors had little in the way of substantive knowledge of human material life to draw upon in their revolutionary socialist constructive endeavors.

However, as the present book makes clear, the locus of scientificity in Marx's corpus is Marx's project in his monumental *Capital* refined and completed as dialectical economic theory. Marxian economics' claim to scientificity resides *not* in abstruse dictums of historical directionality as emanate from HM. *Nor* does it reside in grafting high calculus of physics onto the yoga of individual "rational choice" as in neoclassical economics. Rather, the scientificity of Marxian economics resides in what constitutes the ultimate meaning of *science* – the pursuit of objective knowledge or capital-T truth of the world and all its furniture. Indeed, science without this aspiration, as Nicholas Rescher bluntly states, would be "nonsensical".[1]

The possibility of pursuing objective knowledge in the social world is intimately bound to the peculiar ontology of one social scientific object of study – *capital*. To recapitulate, this is the case given how capital uniquely reifies human social relations of production rendering them "transparent" for the first time in history for theory to explore. The pursuit of objective knowledge in Marxian economic theory is foregrounded by the ontologically significant fact of commodity economic subsumption of material life abstracting from the sensuous qualitative nature of use value life to differentiate among its constituents in the capitalist market in quantitative terms. Theory construction is thus "reality assisted" in the sense that it is predicated upon the *real* "force of abstraction" of the commodity economy as adverted to by Marx. The dialectic is the "special purpose" and "content specific" method for producing knowledge of an object of thought with the unique "Absolute-like" ontological properties – self-abstracting, self-reifying, self-infinitizing, and so forth – of capital. Dialectical economic theory therefore effectuates the important demand of science that a correspondence exist "between the *causal structure* of those objects or events to be explained and the *logical structure* of the theory that purports to explain them", as Christopher Norris, cited in Chapter 2, puts it. And, in extrapolating the deep structural tendencies of capital to logical conclusion in a self-contained thought experiment, the dialectic of capital produces the definitive theory of the economic substructure of society; a theory that then provides keys to the economic anatomy of other historical societies. Finally, in capturing the way capital meets the general norms of material life to wield an entire society as a byproduct of its abstract, quantitative chrematistic of value augmentation, dialectical economic theory simultaneously confirms the possibility of socialism, a society where those same general norms are met by free associations of free human beings reproducing their economic lives for the concrete purpose of human flourishing.

In sum, while we have emphasized at several points in this book the fact the socialism brings the "prehistory" of human society to a close in obviating HM as it builds a progressive future where the superstructure manages the economic substructure of society, socialism like all other human societies necessarily retains an economic substructure. And, as a scientific theory of the economic substructure of society, dialectical economic theory produces indispensible knowledge of material life for the building of socialism. It is for this reason that Marx admonished utopian socialists of his day who set about drawing up blueprints of the future without knowledge in hand of the capitalist economy. The most important knowledge dialectical economic theory furnishes for socialist construction is that of the general norms of economic life. The innate viability or material reproducibility of a socialist society whatever institutional choices are made to ensure it meets progressive social goals hinges upon the socialist society of the future satisfying the general norms of economic life. A close second in importance are the ontological principles of socialism I have sketched out. That is, as *Capital* reconstructed as dialectical economic theory *defines* what capital *is* in its most fundamental incarnation, so the ontology of socialism provides a "definition" of socialism as the diametrical opposite or antithesis of capitalism. That is socialism begins with creative thinking about de-reifying human economic life or turning it "right-side up" by reproducing human material existence for the concrete purpose of human flourishing. Of momentous significance in the ontology of socialism is the insight into the question of motivation in socialist society. Soviet-style societies had decommodified labor power but subjected it to extra-economic compulsion; a historical regression from capitalism that had already "freed" work from the interpersonal relations of domination and subordination it had been subjected to across precapitalist history. A genuine socialism of the future that offers an historical advance over capitalism must craft its institutions and patterns of production and property relations to instate self-motivation as the paradigmatic compulsion for work that, to paraphrase Marx, is to become "life's prime want". The issue of the qualitative heterogeneity of use value life, to take another example, carries the weightiest ramifications for environmental sustainability as we shall see.

But, the flow of knowledge from Marx's work to inform construction of socialism does not end with specification of the general norms of economic life and elaboration of an ontology of socialism. In fact while HM conceived as a master theory of historical directionality offered little to socialists beyond misguided sense of inevitability, HM as a comparative approach to material life across the sweep of human history contains invaluable insights for socialists. Without HM as such, for example, it would not be possible to build our typology of forms of economic compulsion and alienation so as to differentiate capitalist economic compulsion and alienation from the forms of extra-economic compulsion and alienation deriving from direct producers ensnared in interpersonal relations of domination and subordination characteristic of precapitalist societies. HM and Marxian economic theory working in tandem further help us grasp the fact of economic forms such as money, prices, wages, profits, commodities, and so forth being exogenous to the key modalities or principles of economic reproduction of precapitalist societies. This allows us to think creatively about how such forms may be utilized benignly by socialists as part of the superstructure management of economic life.

Marxian political economy as a whole that includes *dialectical economic theory*, *stage theory*, and *historical analysis* of capitalism also contributes in important ways to future-directed thinking. In part because it helps us zero in on what must be *undone* in our economic lives at the current conjuncture to rid them of all disabling residues of the commodity economy. And given the insights stage theory and historical analysis offer into how capital accumulation moves asymptotically away from its ideal image in the stages of *imperialism* and particularly *consumerism*, socialists are provided with working evidence on ways economic life may be organized by extra-economic, extra-capitalist superstructure interventions. This sort of knowledge interfaces with our understanding of the heterogeneity of use value life because it shows how the recalcitrance or pull of use value on value and capital leads to particular institutional outcomes. In any case, this is but a snapshot of the rich field of knowledge Marxian analysis offers for future directed transformatory action. Though, again, all revolutionary knowledge in Marxism emanates from Marxian economic theory that is the repository of scientificity in Marx's corpus.

Economic principles of a heterogeneous socialist future

At numerous points throughout this book I have used the terms economic *principles* or economic *forms*. In previous work, I have also referred to economic principles as "modes of socio-material communication" to highlight all the varied potential communicative interactions human beings have engaged in to reproduce their material existence.[2] These range from primitive hunting-gathering activities of early humans to so-called symbolic, "silent trade" between separated societies, through the impersonal cash nexus of the capitalist market and even virtual socio-material communications with crypto-currencies in cyberspace. But when we consider human history in toto it emerges that economic principles or forms fall into three major genres or broad types. It is through these *key economic principles* that the general norms of economic life are met in major historical epochs of human society. Of course, in no human society is material economic life reproduced solely according to a single key principle. Yet one has always tended to be dominant and crucial for ensuring that demand for basic goods in society is met with no chronic misallocation of resources. And in class societies, the principles operate to meet the general norms of economic life within the context of the prevailing social class relations of production. As explained by Marx in the *Grundrisse*:

> In all forms of society there is one specific kind of production which predominates over the rest, whose relations thus assign rank and influence to the others. It is a general illumination which bathes all the other colours and modifies their particularity. It is a particular ether which determines the specific gravity of every being which has materialized within it.[3]

However, the key principles of human material reproduction are not unlimited. Nor can they be simply conjured up ex nihilo. In what follows I will collate important work of economic historian Karl Polanyi and anthropologist David Graeber with that of Karl Marx to display the key principles of material reproduction. The purpose of this exercise is to set the stage for discussion of how socialists may deploy particular principles to materially reproduce their society while simultaneously meeting socialist future directed progressive transformatory goals such as those of human flourishing, extirpating human alienation, and eco-sustainability.

Drawing upon his exhaustive historical studies of actually existing precapitalist economies Karl Polanyi dubs the "economistic fallacy" the classical and neoclassical economics "error" of "equating the human economy in general with its market form".[4] Polanyi's notion here corresponds to some extent to Marx's understanding of economic life as the transhistorical foundation of human society: and capitalism as simply the historically delimited or transient "software" that manages economic life for the century and a half or so of its existence, on the basis of a given complex of use value life.[5] If for Polanyi, then, the self-regulating market characteristic of the commodity economy is but one way material life has been organized, how was human material life reproduced across the other millenniums of its existence? As alluded to above, in precapitalist economies Polanyi had argued, economic life always embedded in an array of social relationships or practices – thaumaturgy, religion, culture, politics, ideology, and so on – and was indistinguishable from them. He defines economic relations as they imbricate with this broad spectrum of social practices in terms of two key principles of economy, *reciprocity* and *redistribution*. *Reciprocity* for Polanyi encompasses a wide gamut of practices engaged in by the most primitive societies involving some variant or degree of *sharing* or *cooperation*, including things like "gift" giving and "give-and-take" in the context of kinship relations or customary/communal practices, along with what may be referred to as small-m markets that involve the sorts of one-off use value "exchanges" captured in terms of C-C. Polanyi, however, is not very clear on this point – where *reciprocity* ends and capitalist market "exchange" of commodities or value objects begins. *Redistribution*, on the other hand, occurs in more advanced, geospatially larger-scale precapitalist societies and entails the movement of goods, tribute, taxes, tithes, and so forth toward the "center" and their reallocation according to interpersonal relations of domination and subordination of various kinds and the "status" of varying social sectors (see Figure 6.1).

Polanyi's reciprocity basically corresponds to what Marx refers to as *primitive communism* within the schema of HM. Looking at *reciprocity/primitive communism* in terms of their modality of meeting the general norms of economic life, it is clear firstly that most members of society will constitute the direct producers in one way or another. This includes the most rudimentary divisions of labor in the "family" and or "clan". As Marx described it:

> The more deeply we go back into history, the more does the individual, and hence also the producing individual, appear as dependent, as belonging to a greater whole: in a still quite natural way in the family and in the family expanded into the clan . . . then later in the various forms of communal society . . .[6]

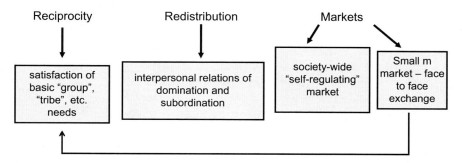

Figure 6.1 Karl Polanyi on economic principles

In this way, the norm of direct producers receiving at minimum the product of their necessary labor is hardly problematic. While there certainly were status distinctions in the societies that fit within the *primitive communism/reciprocity* mode of material reproduction there was little in the way of social class divisions marking the relations of production. On the other hand, early human history is littered with examples of societies that would have struggled to reproduce their material existence through the *reciprocity* principle, but "collapsed" given their inability to meet social demand for *basic goods* though, more often than not, this stemmed from constrictions placed upon early material reproductive life by natural forces.

It is instructive that the politico-economic and philosophical tradition of *anarchism* has always tended to hark back to "reciprocity" of sorts in its vision of the future. As underscored by Sekine,

> [I]n the loud controversy over socialism versus capitalism the anarchists' voice has always been drowned out and has remained hardly audible, even though the anarchists and the socialists were close siblings to start with. They rallied together against the tyranny of capital, as it was about to establish its hegemony. But the anarchists rejected the idea of empowering the state to control the capitalist market, and, rather, looked for the activation of the natural impulse of people to prefer mutual aid, reciprocity, cooperation, and sharing in order to integrate the economy at a *human-to-human* level. This understandably alienated socialists, who were determined to seize the power of the state and to use it to their advantage . . . Despite these circumstances the anarchists' view of society could not be wholly suppressed. For no society would have survived had it been organized exclusively in terms of the anonymity of the market and the technocracy of the state . . . In the living world of flesh-and-blood human beings the concrete-specific principle of reciprocity could in no case be dispensed with.[7]

When we add to anarchist antipathy to "the state" with its rule/law based systems of control of people over people as an artifact of human domination demanding immediate abolition, its views of industrial technologies as embodiments of domination and hierarchy, we can see how anarchist advocating of self-organizational forms of production and distribution such as mutual aid associations, cooperatives, communes, and so on renders anarchism an attractive position in debates over eco-sustainable futures. Anarchism also draws questions of shrinking geospatial scale and cultivating of the "local" economy to the fore.[8] But the flipside to Sekine's point above is that simply reducing economic scale and engaging forms of *reciprocity* to manage the metabolic interchange between human beings and nature do not *in themselves* guarantee viable material reproduction of human society nor its eco-sanctity. Anarchism itself confronts this dilemma as it seeks to deal with questions of how to bring *some* technology back in to the social future under conditions where the anti-human, anti-democratic, anti-environmental thrusts of technology are contained.[9] We will return to this.

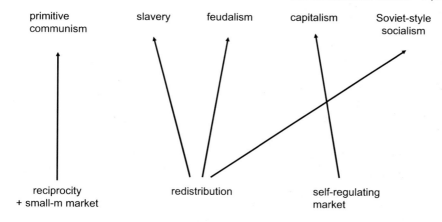

Figure 6.2 Karl Marx – Polanyi correspondence

Redistribution, on the other hand, corresponds to the kinds of interpersonal production relations of domination and subordination characterizing epochs of *slavery* and *feudalism* as outlined in Marx's schema of modes of production in HM. And, while Polanyi does not make the connection himself (and nor could Marx possibly make it given his temporal emplacement in history), arguably, *redistribution* corresponds to the principle of economic planning as deployed by the state in Soviet-style economies. To a certain degree, it is also relevant to state macroeconomic programming as undertaken during the golden age when social democratic tendencies among major economies were at their height (see Figure 6.2). Let us stay on the issue of *redistribution* as the principle of economic management in Soviet-style societies, however. We have already discussed how through the decommodification of labor power in Soviet-style societies and the socializing of consumption the general norm of economic life of direct producers receiving at minimum the product of their necessary labor is met. Where Soviet-style societies miscarried with regard to their long-term viability is over the general norm of allocating basic goods to meet social demand with a minimum waste of social resources. The most precipitous consequence of this failing, which brought Soviet-style planning face-to-face with its anarchist antithesis, was the experience of Soviet-style policies in agriculture. James C. Scott paints the following picture:

> The rural society that the Soviet state inherited (and for a time encouraged) was one in which the allies of the czarist state, the great landlords and aristocratic officeholders, had been swept away and been replaced by small-holding and middle peasants, artisans, private traders, and all sorts of . . . lumpen elements . . . They created, in place of what they inherited, a new landscape of large, hierarchical, state-managed farms whose cropping patterns and procurement quotas were centrally mandated and whose population was, by law, immobile. The system thus devised served for nearly sixty years as a

mechanism for procurement and control at a massive cost in stagnation, waste, demoralization, and ecological failure.

That collectivized agriculture persisted for sixty years was a tribute less to the plan of the state than to the improvisations, gray markets, bartering and ingenuity that partly compensated for its failures . . . so did a set of informal practices lying outside the formal command economy – and often outside Soviet law as well – arise to circumvent some of the colossal waste and inefficiencies built into the system.[10]

Again, as Marx correctly emphasizes, there is in general always one key economic principle that plays the central part in a mode of production. In the case of capitalism, in particular, the most advanced economy in the *prehistory* of human society, the deep causal inner logic of capital does asymptotically impel economic life toward its ideal image up to a point in actual history, divesting material life of non-economic, non-capitalist encumbrances to increasingly reify it, reproducing human economic life as a byproduct of value augmentation. Without this tendency economic theory would be impossible: as would knowledge of the material substructure of society and formulation of concepts such as "mode of production". And we would have no robust grasp of the infrastructure or general norms of economic life on which to base creative thinking about future socialist societies of human flourishing. Marxian economic theory is therefore the zero of social change.

However, the deep causal inner logic of capital never completely purifies its historical use value environment of non-economic and non-capitalist interferences. And, as discussed at various points in this book, as capital asymptotically shifts away from its ideal image with the production of heavy and complex use values in the stages of *imperialism* and *consumerism*, it comes to rely ever more upon *redistribution* or the planning principle of the state. Finally, we have stressed in Chapter 1 of this book the extent to which neoliberal ideology of "the market" constitutes a façade behind which the planning principle of the state as "big government" with its "big bank" and commanding heights "big MNCs" operates as an expropriation machine preying on *real* economic activities wherever these remain. Elsewhere I have elaborated upon the fact that as capital abdicated its production-centered economy for what I refer to here as the "Merchant of Venice" surrogate economy of rent seeking and casino games, it places the satisfying of general norms of economic life to materially reproduce human society into a kind of twilight zone.[11] Those plugged in to the planning principle of the state that, as discussed in Chapter 1, through its fiat money creation, its rule/legal backstopping of OTD banking and leverage play have battened on the expropriation. At the other end of the social spectrum, and I am bracketing for discussion in Chapter 7 whether the trends here are in any way "revolutionary" or simply act as subsidies for neoliberalism, the recent proliferation of co-ops, community currencies, local employment and trading systems (LETS), and so forth, are indicative of how as the market principle of capital has loosened its grip on economic life, forms of *reciprocity* are surging to meet human needs. We will return to questions of these forms in the following section.

Anthropologist David Graeber has recently offered up a nuanced view of historical patterns of material life in terms of what he sees as three "moral grounds" for differentiating principles of economy. The first is what he dubs "baseline communism". In his view we are all essentially communists at a fundamental level whether it entails offering a stranger a light for a cigarette without expecting anything in return; or something more taxing, like helping people in the immediate aftermath of a natural disaster. Graeber maintains to the extent people do not perceive themselves as enemies, Marx's principle of socialist distribution set out in the *Critique of the Gotha Program* – "from each according to their abilities, to each according to their needs" – exists as a foundational norm of human sociality. The same logic that holds among individuals, according to Graeber, may be extended within groups: and from there, to the management of common resources. Graeber sees "baseline communism" diverging from *reciprocity* (though he qualifies this with the comment except for "reciprocity in the broadest sense") on the point that there is no compulsion that the communistic "giving" will be reciprocated. In the end, he argues for "baseline communism" as a moral principle rather than a form of property or ownership.[12]

Graeber then moves to principles he calls "exchange" of which there are two species in his account. What we may refer to as "exchange 1" is the sort of exchange Graeber notes imbricates in interpersonal relations such as gift giving where comparing the "value" of goods exchanged does not occur. Then there is "exchange 2" or "commercial exchange" as Graeber puts it, which is impersonal. Though, in either case, for Graeber, "exchange" is concerned with "equivalence": equivalence between the parties as well as between the goods. Although, for Graeber, non-commercial exchange, gift giving, tit-for-tat "games", and so on grey into barter in a fashion somewhat akin to Polanyi's notion of a small-m market activity.

Finally, there are relations of "hierarchy" involving unequal parties. Charting this on a continuum, Graeber sees plunder and theft at one end, selfless charity at the other. Graeber argues that "hierarchy" often crystallizes in social relations of superiority and inferiority that are regulated through webs of custom or habit.[13]

In Graeber's typology, "baseline communism" corresponds to Marx's *primitive communism* and Marx's vision of human behavior in a genuine socialist society as Marx states in the *Critique of the Gotha Program*, which Graeber approvingly

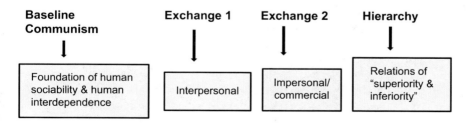

Figure 6.3 David Graeber on "moral principles" upon which economic principles founded

quotes. "Hierarchy", would describe social relations in class societies, particularly as these imbricate human material production and distribution in interpersonal relations or webs of custom and habit as Graeber puts it. But "hierarchy" can also be extended to capitalism as a class society even though capital seeks to cover this with a veneer of formal equality.

In fact, one of the major weaknesses of Graeber's analysis (and to some extent Polanyi's) is that it occludes *class* as a working category. While it is true, as argued in Chapters 2 and 3, that class is only an objective category in the context of dialectical economic theory where it is the personification of an economic category. Nevertheless, the use of class in HM that draws upon understanding of its role demonstrated in Marxian economics as the central relation of production in class society provides insight into how something like interpersonal "hierarchy" enmeshes with historically specific social class relations to mediate the metabolic interchange between human beings and nature as the substantive foundation of human existence. The schema of HM also allows us to grasp possibilities of the operation of "hierarchy" of one type or another in the *absence* of class structures. After all, the societies depicted in Marx's *primitive communism* and Polanyi's *reciprocity* evidenced "hierarchy" in terms of "status" distinctions, but where specifically social class relations of production do not emerge. Then there is the question of hierarchy in a non-class socialist society. As Marxist David Harvey correctly points out, though radical chic sees hierarchy as anathema, scale issues force reconsideration of it. While the local "commons" might be "governed" through horizontal human social relations, Harvey suggests this is not possible when confronting intercommunity or even global problems in a progressive future. In fact, even the much-vaunted (in radical accounts of non-hierarchical social existence) Zapatista movement sees decision making occur democratically through delegates and officers, Harvey maintains.[14] In this sense, "baseline communism" and "hierarchy" do not *necessarily* conflict as two divergent "moral principles".

Another glaring problem with Graeber's work is his seeking to depict what is ostensibly capitalism under the rubric "exchange", even "commercial exchange". Polanyi at least attempts to come to grips with the ontological peculiarity of capital with his reference to the "self-regulating market" and metaphor of the capitalist market disembedding from the social. Graeber declares:

> Markets aren't real. They are mathematical models, created by imagining a self-contained world where everyone has exactly the same motivation and the same knowledge and is engaged in the same self-interested calculating exchange. Economists are aware . . . that to come up with a mathematical model, one always has to make the world into a bit of a cartoon. There's nothing wrong with this.[15]

But there *is* something egregiously "wrong with this"! Neoclassical models are cartoonish precisely because they derive from a bourgeois imaginary mesmerized by reification that strives to obfuscate rather than expose the workings of the capitalist commodity economy. We have already belabored the point that capitalist exchange is always the exchange of value objects or commodities as part of the value augmentation process. And to understand capitalism and *its* exchange process theory must start from the perspective of the *seller* (not "everyone") whose "motivation" and "self-interested calculation" is tied to the abstract-general, quantitative value of the commodity being sold *not* to its sensuous, material concrete-specific use value characteristics as is the consumer. Graeber continues, noting how "principles get tangled up in each other and it's thus often difficult to tell which predominates in a given situation – one reason that it's ridiculous to pretend we could reduce human behavior . . . to a mathematical formula".[16] On the latter point, Graeber is, of course, right. But that is not what capitalism *is* about nor is it how scientific knowledge of capital is produced. Capital, as per the so-called "calculation debate" proceeding as its prisoner (reviewed in Chapter 5), *does* seek to reduce human material life to an abstract mathematical calculus of surplus value realization and value augmentation. And it allocates resources to "viably" reproduce a human society only as a byproduct of that "mathematical formula" of value augmentation. Therefore there *is* something very *real* about capital and its systems of self-regulating markets. In fact, if this was not the case, we would not even be discussing something like "economic life" and its forms because prior to the dawn of the capitalist era of reified "thing-to-thing" economic relations, material life was always enmeshed with other social practices as Polanyi saw it and inseparable from them.

Further, "commercial exchange" as the "exchange" of "equivalences" does not adequately capture the role the commodification of labor power plays in the capitalist chrematistic of value augmentation. Commodified labor power does not "exchange" its capacity for productive work for a wage. Rather, the wage is the price set in the market for use of commodified labor power as an input into the production and value augmentation process of capital. As such the wage must constitute what is necessary and sufficient for the reproduction of labor power or, put differently, be equal to the product of the worker's necessary labor. But, if in the course of the working day, the time of which is set by capital, the worker did not perform surplus labor, there would be no surplus value and no capital or capitalism. In this fashion, what seems like an "exchange" of equivalences when capitalism is viewed as an "exchange", barter, or "trading" society, as with the yoga of neoclassical economics, is exploded by Marxian economic theory as it probes deep into the inner sanctum of capital where it uncovers the exploitation of human labor power in the way capital subsumes the wellspring of human wealth creation to turn it into a means of abstract value augmentation.

Finally, Graeber is quite simply wrong in claiming it is "often difficult to tell which [principle] predominates in a given situation". On the one hand, this would render all modes of human economy indistinguishable from each other; something that, in a sense, classical and neoclassical economics does by naturalizing capitalism through its spurious physics-like "science" of human behavior. Again, we need not get into debates over human nature here. Neoclassical artifice is rooted in its argument for "economics" (after all its self-styled naming of its discipline already contains within it a transhistorical statement) as the analysis of price movements.

146 *The institutional matrix*

In early history, few things were priced, today almost everything has a price, but human behavior is constant. Voila, science . . . .change society only if you uncover evidence of change in human behavior. And so goes the Nobel Prize to leaders in the study of "neuroeconomics"![17] But we know this is nonsense. For the study of "price" itself, as Albritton put it previously in Chapter 5, constitutes a "lazy" way of thinking about "economic" phenomenon. For behind "price" is always a social division of labor and historically specific set of property relations. And it is these that bestow upon "price", however it appears, whatever substantive historical meaning it has. The fact that a society is able to organize its economic life around "objective" quantitative, ex post price signals in a way that effectuates an allocation of resources, *not* "optimal", of course, as capitalism is a class society, but in a "viable" fashion that meets the general norms of economic life, hinges on the commodification of labor power that allows capital to shift to the production of *any* good as per changing patterns of social demand and opportunities for profit-making. Thus, for capitalism, this *market principle* of capital undergirded by the sine qua non – the commodification of labor power – *must* "predominate" in every "situation" where it has existed historically as a *kind* of human society. Indeed, why Graeber likely does not see this, which also shows his regression from Polanyi's more astute analysis, is that his approach to the anatomy of human material life is based not on uncovering *economic principles* but on so-called "moral" principles that he largely formulates ad hoc. Indeed, Marx's overarching contribution to economic knowledge garnered from his economic theory of capital is precisely the fact that lurking in the often pale background of the hum and buzz of history and webs of complex interpersonal relations of "hierarchy" and the like, are economic principles the predominating of one which ensures the material reproduction of human life. Graeber's copious anthropological studies have examined every tree, but they missed the wood.

Yet, on the other hand, this brings us back to what is, in reality, the revolutionary edge of Marxism that much Left brouhaha unfortunately serves to blunt. Dialectical economic theory scientifically proves that which Polanyi asserts.

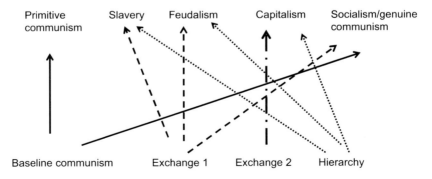

Figure 6.4 The Karl Marx/David Graeber correspondence

That the metabolic interchange between human beings and nature is the substantive transhistorical foundation or "hardware" of human material existence. The principles of capitalist commodity economy constitute the historically transient operating system that subsumes human material life to reproduce it as a byproduct of value augmentation. Marxian economic theory accomplishes its task by demonstrating that the historical possibility of capitalism necessitates the surmounting by abstract-general value of all concrete-specific use value obstacles or "contradictions". But this demands the assumption of an easily neutralized or tamable use value space. By assuming tamable use values and allowing capital in theory to have its way with the world, and in so establishing how the *market principle* of capital organizes the economic substructure of a human society, Marxian economics simultaneously confirms the possibility of other economic principles satisfying the general norms of economic life to materially reproduce a human society. The *planning principle of the state* or, what Polanyi's historical studies elaborate as *redistribution*, is established by Marxian political economy at the level of stage theory, which displays how the superstructure mediates the causal force of capital in world historic stages of capitalism. In the contexts of first *imperialism* and later *consumerism*, the *planning principle of the state* evolved from a mediating role to one of Herculean support of the dominant forms of heavy and complex capitalist industrial production. The economic principle of *reciprocity* or what Graeber dubs "baseline communism" while never "predominant" in any but the most historically rudimentary societies, has nevertheless remained irrepressible into the modern era particularly at times of social decomposition. However, its cooperative, human-to-human sharing thrust makes it an *economic principle* in the strong sense of the concept and socialists neglect this at the future's peril.

To sum up, in collating work of Marx, Polanyi, and Graeber we can say that there exist three broad proven *principles of economy* that have predominated at various historical junctures and operated to meet the general norms of economic life to materially reproduce human societies. Instructively, each principle corresponds to economic views at the core of one of the major global ideological traditions. Let us now take the capitalist *market principle*, the socialist *planning principle of the state*, and the anarchist *principle of reciprocity* or "baseline communism" and see how they might be utilized in building a model of a socialist society as guided in its basic incarnation by our ontology of socialism and tested in terms of both its viability in meeting the general norms of economic life *and* in meeting Green necessity for a future of eco-sanctity. We should also keep in mind our discussion in Chapter 5. That hitherto debate amongst socialists along with operations of actually existing socialist experiments revolved around one particular principle, not only without a clear grasp of the implications of that principle for reproducing substantive economic life, but with little creative thought about how in relation to managing a specified, delimited category of use value life a given principle may effectively be recruited to serve socialist designs for human flourishing. As we shall see, one of the areas where the thickest blinders exist is on the question of the exogenous nature of forms of the commodity economy to substantive economic

Ecosocialist interventions

As environmentalism emerged as a rallying point for mass publics, cutting across social class divides in calls for social and political change to realize an eco-sustainable future, a brave new Green Left of *ecosocialism* took shape in the hope of channeling Green interests back in line with traditional socialist demands for social equity.[18] Ecosocialism or eco-Marxism has taken giant strides in linking calls for eco-sustainability to critiques of capitalism in contrast to so much, simply Green, environmentalist, work that as we have seen in Chapter 4 either blithely assumes that capitalism can be greened or has unwittingly secreted elements of capitalism into its purported eco-sustainable models. The latter malady in effect only reinforcing the truth inhering in Marx's admonishment to the utopian socialists of his day; that being, not to spin models of the future without objective economic knowledge in hand of the workings of the capitalist commodity economy and understanding of substantive economic life that flows from that. But, besides internecine debate, recognized by eco-Marxists themselves, over the Marxist theoretical foundations of ecosocialism, ecosocialism has not been forthcoming with compelling so-called "red-green" institutional alternatives.[19]

Eco-Marxist Joel Kovel, for example, correctly talks about enshrining the provision of use value in human economic reproduction. As to how this might be done, Kovel suggests "shifting the coefficient uv/xv [use value/exchange value] in the direction of the numerator in order to build anti-capitalist intentions". Thus "exchange is negated through a withdrawal from capitalist values".[20] Kovel then proceeds to discuss how empowering the direct producers in democratic "ensembles" as a type of ecosocialist community could be the basis for wider change. In later writing, he adds to the "uv/xv" transition the "I-V" factor to depict the "intrinsic value" of nature, which he then argues is a concept differentiating "ecosocialism from the various socialisms of the 19th and 20th centuries". Kovel further specifies his notion of "ensembles" recasting it as a "Commons"; in effect the "collectively owned and organized spaces, originating in the primordial communistic productive zone whose enclosure is a hallmark of capitalism". He continues: "Once appropriated ecosocialistically, the horizons/zones of Commoning converge and become capable of being integrated with each other. Thus occurs a widening process toward ecosocialist transformation". To further explicate what he has in mind, Kovel adds: "Simple reflection tells us as a general rule that the earlier the social structure, the less estranged from nature . . . [thus] indigeneity serves as an important index of ecosocialist potential".[21]

In an impressive tome that, from a Marxist perspective, unearths and elaborates upon the root and mechanisms of environmental destruction in capitalism, John Bellamy Foster et al. turn to the question of what must be done. They argue for "social control over the metabolic order of reproduction, encompassing all realms of productive life". This then entails "an elementary triangle of socialism":

(1) social ownership, (2) social production organized by workers, and (3) satisfaction of communal needs. Social control serves as the root basis for this transformation to a socialist metabolic order.

The elementary triangle of socialism, it is claimed, "is dialectically interconnected at a more fundamental level" with an "elementary triangle of ecology":

> (1) social use, not ownership, of nature, (2) rational regulation by the associated producers of the metabolism between human beings and nature, and (3) the satisfaction of communal needs – not only of present but future generations.[22]

Chris Williams, with another devastating critique of innate eco-bankruptcy of capitalism, also begins to stutter when the time comes for putting forward an alternative. "I don't want to engage in grand utopian schemes for what exactly will be done after private property on earth is abolished" Williams declares. He then turns to the raft of changes ecosocialists along with many environmentalists believe must occur:

> Every single facet of industrial life – energy production most urgently, but also transportation, housing, trade, agriculture, manufacture of commodities, and waste production treatment – all require gigantic systemic change and complete structural reorganization. It will be nothing short of totally remodeling the world on a social, political technological, cultural, and infrastructural level.[23]

Williams importantly discusses the need to reembed urban life in agriculture and remake farming practices in the both larger- and smaller-scale farming organizations that preceded the agrochemical takeover. There will no longer be "the right to privately own pieces of the earth for . . . private gain. There would be a rational plan for its sustainable use", he continues. As well, "artificial lines on maps we call borders" will be abolished as ipso facto, the nation-state.[24]

While I am certainly on the same socialist page with these authors in my desire for a progressive, eco-sustainable socialist future of human flourishing the dire environmental picture their writings paint of the rapidly disappearing possibility of any livable human future (as with my own writings elsewhere and in this book) stands in sharp contrast to the hesitancy and truncated response to what is being cried out for now: a model or plan of the successor socialist society of the future that indicates its viability or material reproducibility, socialist pedigree as far as meeting socialist social goals, and long-term eco-sanctity. Simply fomenting "anti-capitalist intentions", to paraphrase Kovel, does not cut it. Let us do some house cleaning here as we proceed to make our first major institutional point.

First, and this needs to be made crisply clear because I am seeing more and more of this hackneyed reference in socialist writings, "exchange value" is *price* or value *form* and *not* to be conflated with *value* the substance of which is socially necessary labor (see Box 6.1). Yes, Marx uses the term exchange value in his early writings up to the *Grundrisse*. But in Chapter 1 of Volume 1 of *Capital* as his dialectical elaboration upon *forms* of value unfolds, Marx is unambiguous:

> When, at the beginning of this chapter, we said, in common parlance, that a commodity is both a use value and an exchange value, we were, accurately speaking, wrong. A commodity is a use value or object of utility, and a value.[25]

And from that juncture Marx never looks back. It is not a small semantic issue as I have emphasized in other contexts in this book because fundamental to Marx's analysis of capitalism as well as his understanding of economies of precapitalist societies, is that markets, prices, money, and other economic forms that capital symbiotically draws together in its chrematistic of mercantile wealth augmentation as it subsumes human material life, existed *endogenously* to the modalities of precapitalist material reproduction. As such prices, money, markets of sorts may exist benignly and external to the core principle or principles of material reproduction in socialist societies; though, of course, there is also no necessity that these forms be utilized. Moreover, what is "wrong" with capitalism is not simply that goods are bought and sold in markets for prices. It is that capitalism is an "upside-down", "alien" society in which human material existence is reproduced as a byproduct of value augmentation.

Box 6.1

In the *doctrine of circulation* in dialectical economic theory, the formative elaboration upon the social commensurability of commodities or their "moneyness" necessitates *only* an initial demonstration of the possible *expression* of value in the use value of another commodity, and then the eventual *measuring* of the value of a commodity in terms of money with the establishment of a "normal price" for it. That is, the "exchange" of commodities C – C` in a capitalist market is never direct but occurs as C – M (denoting commodity and money) and M – C`. Of course, the presupposition is always the capitalist commodity economy as a whole, only at this point in the theory the dialectic must necessarily hold implicit both the modalities and conditions through which such a normal price is actually arrived at in the market and the specific *determination* or *substance* of the value of a commodity.

To stay with Kovel, I am not exactly sure what he means by "primordial communistic zones" that capital "encloses". What capital *did* enclose as its historical process of subsuming economic life ramped up in seventeenth-century Britain was the *feudal* commons, which was an integral part of the story of the commodification of labor power. Nevertheless, in reading Kovel I sense that what he is suggesting is a variant of a point made by Marx that ended up misleading Marx's followers in their early endeavors at socialist construction. That is, when the capitalist "integument" is stripped away, one "finds" ("primordial communistic zones") read socialism. His simple formula for socialism of shifting economic life to the "uv" numerator encapsulates that wrongheaded view. It was that misconstrued position that lulled transformatory actors into the belief, for example, that decommodifying labor power was a sufficient move in building a progressive future. As we saw, however, simple decommodification of labor power led to the reinstating of extra-economic compulsion for work that is an historical regression from capitalism. The notion of "Commoning" rings similar to the growing Left chorus of calls during the neoliberal era for decommodifying economic life and reinstating "public goods" of the golden age welfare state. But we have to be careful here. Money, in the neoliberal era, has been decommodified. Yet its "commoned" issuance by "big government" and "big bank" is politically directed toward facilitating debt-fuelled, leveraged casino play and wealth expropriation of real economic activities. "Commoning" has to be infused with details of its socialist substance rather than being simply used as a buzzword with a radical ring counterposed to neoliberal "privatizing", for example.

Approached from another angle, Kovel's "primordial communistic zones" resonates with Foster et al.'s notion of socialists reexerting "social control" over "the metabolic order of reproduction". As argued above, the metabolic interchange between human beings and nature through which humankind labors to furnish the use value basis of its social existence *is* the ultimate, substantive foundation of all human life. *But* that is the transhistorical "hardware", so to speak, which still requires an operating system or "software" of a particular *kind*. To belabor the point above, when we uninstall the capitalist "software" of the commodity economy of value augmentation with its forms of property and social relations of production the "hardware" of the metabolic interchange between human beings and nature, of course, remains. However socialists must install their own operating system, which means creatively thinking about the *economic principles* that will realize socialist goals. Put another way, without some economic principle to give it shape, the "social control" Foster et al. argue for is but an empty slogan. Even Kovel's harking back to "indigeneity" for its "ecosocialist potential" does not obviate this question. Whether we use Marx's *primitive communism*, Polanyi's *reciprocity*, or Graeber's "baseline communism" in relation to "indigeneity", we are still talking about an *economic principle* entailing cooperation, sharing, mutual aid, and so forth, through which indigenous societies reproduce their material existence. And, as pointed out above, history is littered with "indigenous" societies that "collapsed" for reasons certainly tied to their inability to operationalize an economic principle in a fashion that satisfied general norms of economic life to materially reproduce their societies.

Finally, Williams's reference to "remodeling" the world at multiplex levels is indeed what human civilization requires. However, when one calls for "remodeling" the world the call should be accompanied by some design or at least rudimentary detailed sketch of what that remodeled "model" will look like. Indeed, terms like "rational plan" or those like "rational regulation by the associated producers of the metabolism between human beings and nature", in the case of Foster et al. do *not* a "model" make. Similarly, socialists have been bandying about notions for some time of "social ownership", "social organization of production", and so on, but there exist huge potential institutional variations within the ambit of such open-ended categories. And these variations bring us back again to questions of *economic principles* through which socialist goals will be realized and that will inform institutional choices.

To be sure, ecosocialists such as David Pepper have begun setting out institutional options based on really existing conditions and trends. Pepper's work dovetails with eco-anarchist writing drawing to the fore that which is often held implicit in ecosocialist use of terms such as "indigeneity", "satisfaction of communal needs", and so on; that is the problem of *scale* and reinvigorating *local* and community material life ravaged by the forces euphemized as globalization. It also shares common ground with progressive Greens like McKibben who advocate clearly for "splitting things up" because current scale "is out of whack with our needs", as quoted in Chapter 4. On the institutional list are of course community-based agriculture, local renewable energy, producer and consumer co-ops, local exchange/employment and trading systems (LETS), community currencies, local finance/"public banks". Pepper, of course, acknowledges that the "really existing" exemplars of cooperatives, LETS, community currencies, and so forth he points to are not "'pure' ecosocialist experiments, isolated from the capitalist context". But, he maintains, neither are they simply "local retreats" from globalization and capitalism.[26]

Heterogeneous use value sectors and socio-economic organization

In earlier work I have talked about building on ecosocialist and eco-anarchist calls for rethinking questions of scale as part of the creative thinking about institutional options and choosing among economic principles as adverted to in numerous places in this book.[27] The attractiveness of small-scale, local economies for socialists is easy to understand on several levels. This is the case particularly as articulating socialist views today continues to struggle under the nightmarish weight of failure, on human, material reproductive and environmental grounds, of "large-scale", centrally planned Soviet-style experiments. On the other hand, as I make clear in Chapter 4, small scale/large scale, local/regional/global, and so forth are simply geospatial categories that in themselves tell us nothing about the material economic reproducibility or "viability" of the society and economy, nor its modalities of eco-sanctity. But let us now place questions of scale more firmly in the context of specific socialist goals, ontological foundations, and discussion of *economic principles* and the way these operate to satisfy the general norms of economic life.

First, let us think about socialism in terms of ontological principle one, purging human material life of constituents of the abstract, quantitative chrematistic of value augmentation to remake it for the concrete, qualitative purpose of human flourishing: and principle four, which calls for the reembedding of human material existence in the qualitative heterogeneity of use value life. Then there is a case to be made that economic scale reductions called for by ecosocialists will foster those socialist ontological ends through the *reembedding* of mental in manual labor, industry in agriculture, technology in ecology, humanity in the natural environment, and science in humanity; all which capital impelled the sundering and disembedding of to build its regimented, one-dimensional world of value augmentation. As Jan Douwe van der Ploeg puts it in his discussion of "repeasantization" in global agriculture, for example:

> [P]easant . . . *craftsmanship* . . . travels to the design of . . . skill-oriented technologies . . . that critically depend upon the centrality of labour and associated skills. . . . Thus, skill is all about . . . building on the specificities of different elements of the social and natural world. It is . . . in this latter aspect that the main difference between skill-oriented and mechanical technologies resides . . . mechanical technologies . . . cannot deal with specificity or variation. Specificity is . . . a threat . . .[28]

Or:

> There is an almost "natural" co-evolution of . . . science and Empire. Science constructs the patterns of regularity . . . Empire increasingly standardizes the world . . . Science mainly studies what is thought to be possible and relevant . . . with the order imposed by Empire . . .
>
> Science is, of course, Janus faced in that alongside its focus on the regular and similar, it *also* focuses on the exceptional, the dissimilar and the seemingly impossible. In fact, it even *produces* these in its own "locales" . . .
>
> Thus, attention to deviations, the unexpected and the local is . . . an indispensable part of science.[29]

Second, small-scale communities – meaning social divisions of around 150,000 people, depending upon the population of the region, country, and so on where the social change is taking place, though somewhat larger or smaller scale is also feasible in the plan here for certain areas – opens the possibility for operationalizing *reciprocity* as the core economic principle of human material reproduction: where *reciprocity* entails some combination of community currency, LETS, small-m markets, mutual aid organizations, cooperatives, barter or personal "exchange" specifically of services. To operationalize *reciprocity* with regards to satisfying the general norm of economic life that calls for meeting social demand for basic goods while avoiding any chronic misallocation of social resources, particularly the allocation of human labor, necessarily requires some community agreement on what constitute basic goods and ex ante consideration of social resources earmarked for their production. This in turn essentially means that, at least where community provisioning of basic goods is concerned, careful, transparent accounting of labor

154 *The institutional matrix*

time society devotes to the production of basic goods is made. That then suggests that small-scale socialist communities necessarily avail themselves of some sort of network of direct democratic assemblies and administrative system that functions on behalf of the assemblies, as articulated by eco-anarchist Murray Bookchin for example (we will return to the question of socialist political structure below).[30]

There exist a range of possibilities for the organizing of intracommunity property relationships. One method is that of the socialist/anarchist Spanish village Marinaleda where the family and single family house (leaving to practice and specific socio-political norms what is understood by "family") is the basic living unit but land itself is owned by the village cooperative as a whole.[31] Though, that model does not preclude residents from essentially constructing houses in the manner they like or, for example, using the land allotments for service provision such as bars or restaurants. In Marinaleda, the cooperative, the main agricultural crop, which happens to be olive oil (the production of which, instructively, is referred to in the first of the two van der Ploeg quotes above), pays all employees in whatever role the same wage, distributes no profits, rather investing them in creating employment or diversifying into other agricultural produce. The cooperative also runs a cultural center, medical facilities, schools, parks, sports facilities, swimming pool, free Wi-Fi for all homes, internet café at the cultural center, and we are talking about a village of 3,000 inhabitants here. Again, Marinaleda is a "local" example of cooperative, socialist economy in the current ex-capitalist economic morass. This means that it remains linked in several ways to the wider European Union/Spanish economy in terms of the Euro currency, sourcing of building materials, sales of the products of its cooperative, and so on. I draw upon its experience here, however, *not* to argue how "local" struggles might be transformed into broader initiatives of change or to enter into debate over whether "local" cooperative, environmental initiatives in the end subsidize or support the current economy. But simply to focus attention to the possibility, in really existing economic conditions, of the Marinaleda model as one way (though not the *only* way, of course) of *internally* organizing the small-scale communities under discussion as part of an ongoing socialist transition: thus subdividing the proposed small-scale community economy of around 150,000 people into democratic cooperatives similar in size to Marinaleda village.

Getting back to the question of the general norm of economic life that social demand for basic goods be satisfied without chronic misallocation of social resources, the possibility exists of utilizing labor time directly both for allocating means of production and distributing the limited range of basic goods for consumption amongst individuals, families, and the cooperatives. Of course, as Peter Hudis observes, in Marx's discussion of the transparent measure of *actual labor time* by freely associated producers in socialist societies to allocate resources, Marx is *not* talking about "socially necessary labor" as the substance of value. Hudis notes how utopian socialists of Marx's day had been roundly criticized by Marx for conflating the two, a misconception that at bottom related to the fact that, along with classical economists such as David Ricardo, they never came to grips with the *kind* of labor that creates value.[32] Cockshott and Cottrell, we may recall from Chapter 5, also advocate direct calculation of labor time. They maintain that modern ICT has the ability to calculate sets of simultaneous equations involved in determining labor time embodied in goods notwithstanding multiple inputs into their production. In the current context, as we shall see momentarily, the use value dimension of economic life in the small-scale communities proposed here is far less complex than envisioned by Cockshott and Cottrell with their model of simulated *society-wide* market equilibrium. And, as Itoh opines, this still does not necessarily preclude the use of some kind of accounting unit independent of labor time for communities to periodically assess changes in the community product as a whole in order to make comparisons, for example, among such socialist communities in a socialist commonwealth.[33]

Again, however, the use of actual labor time is being proposed solely as a way of organizing production and distribution of basic goods. Throughout the entire small-scale community, a community currency utilized in the function of money as means of exchange will provide a way of mediating interpersonal "exchanges" of an array of other non-basic goods or services alongside other microarrangements whether LETS, mutual aid, "gift" arrangements, and so-forth within the ambit of forms of *reciprocity*.[34] Though, we would assume, that socialists will want to socialize most services from energy and water to health care to education to transportation. This will reduce the scope of small-m market activities but will certainly never exclude them. The small-scale community model advanced here also provides a working way of annexing market "exchange" (of the *interpersonal* type) from capitalist (impersonal) "market forces" as proposed by Adaman and Devine as reviewed in Chapter 5. However, some kind of "negotiated coordination", among democratic "committees" as Adaman and Devine put it, would apply only to actual labor time accounting for basic goods leaving various modalities of community, cooperative, and individual *reciprocity* to facilitate richness and diversity in community material economic life.

The reference in the heading of this section to economic *sectors* follows up on previous work that considers the fourth proposition in the ontology of socialism that socialists entrench the heterogeneous use value dimension of material existence in each and every aspect of socialist economic and institutional configuring. It is thus felicitous to label the small communities as set out here, *qualitative use value sectors* of a socialist economy. The reason for this is that the use value complex the production of which is managed by such communities lends itself to the predominating of qualitative considerations in material reproductive life. These community qualitative use value sectors essentially produce final consumption goods or use values largely for themselves. In the developed world the challenge is to forge qualitative use value sector communities from potentially arable lands and "non-built" areas (erstwhile farmland, for example, "rezoned" for "monster home" suburbs for the wealthy) adjacent to major urban centers, as well as around smaller towns and rural districts. Depending on local conditions goods to be produced will include food staples as well as any other food crops for which there is community demand and supportive soil conditions. Of course, aquaculture, hydroponics, greenhouse gardening, and so on expand the potential array of products beyond that circumscribed by climate zone. All in all, agriculture must shift away from its current agrochemical structure toward sustainable *agroecology* that "mimics nature and integrates crops and livestock with the environment".[35] Much building construction material, furniture, apparel, household sundries, bicycles, children's toys, innumerable varied purpose crafts, and so on are also produced in the qualitative use value sector community. Such scaled communities will be responsible for their energy needs as well waste recycling.

Across the non-developed world combinations of villages in which a semblance of community culture persists will constitute the geospatial site of the qualitative use value sector communities. Though the challenges here are even more daunting compared to developed countries. This is particularly the case given how the so-called Washington Consensus forced much of the non-developed world to orient its prime agricultural land to servicing wealthy country demand. The poverty and hunger in the non-developed world requires an immediate delinking from global markets that have fostered production of globally traded goods to the detriment of locally consumed staples. Vegetables, for example, now "luxury" for non-developed country poor placed under the gun of Washington Consensus policies, flourish in soil across the non-developed world and can easily grow again in sustainable, non-agrochemical industrial fashions in the here and now:[36] Such insights have already been given rudimentary mass transformatory expression in third-world agriculture reclamation movements like La Via Campesina and through what Joan Martinez-Alier dubs "the environmentalism of the poor".[37] Indeed, Cuba is a poster economy for socialist agricultural development as such, following the collapse of the Soviet Union and under ruthless embargo by the US. The "agricultural techniques" Cuba developed to deal with the dearth of "chemical inputs and limited fuel, electricity and machinery . . . included organic fertilizers, animal traction . . . mixed cropping, and biological pest control", which along with "urban gardens and farms yielded a major increase in domestic fruit and vegetable production".[38] Early critical socialist voices from the third world, such as Clive Thomas, for example, unfortunately, little heeded in the heady early days of Soviet-style experiments, had also urged that huge potential for employment, poverty reduction, and fruitful interchange with local agriculture resided in the local sourcing and production of a range of similar goods as proposed for our qualitative use value sector communities.[39]

Something to consider in the non-developed world, however, is that the transition to socialism will take place from often quasi-feudal property and landholding structures, and hence, for rural populations with scant historical experience of their own, freehold farms, enabling the latter is a catalytic revolutionary force. A really existing historical example of this, paradoxically, is the initial decommunization process in the early post-Mao Zedong era of China's "reform". The "household responsibility" system, as it was called, allotted socialist land previously held and worked in common by the giant Great People's Communes (GPCs) to individual families. And, on the basis of land quality and extended family size mandated a minimum quota of in-kind deliveries of basic grains to the state. But, beyond that "responsibility", permitted peasant families to engage in producing whatever they wanted with no restriction. Not only did this system spawn a network of town and village enterprises (TVEs) producing precisely that range of "local" goods and farming supports discussed in the context of our qualitative use value sector communities here and adverted to by third-world critics of Soviet-style socialism like Clive Thomas. But agricultural productivity and crop diversity exploded, surprising even Communist Party members themselves, and rendered China self-sufficient in food in ways virtually unrivalled across centuries of China's history.[40]

What is certainly the sine qua non of a progressive, socialist future is the decommodifying of human labor power and extirpating of both precapitalist and capitalist forms of alienation. As argued in Chapter 3, labor power regimented by capital in the service of value augmentation renders the worker *indifferent* to *use value* in production as it engenders *disinterest* amongst workers qua "consumers" to the wherewithal and modalities of the production process itself. The later, in particular, facilitating the production of use values with the potential to destroy human life itself on the planet. Therefore work, the metabolic interchange between human beings and nature as that elemental human activity upon which the existence of human society rests, is destined to remain for direct producers in capitalist society a *disutility* or *alienated*. That is, no matter how high wages paid to workers are, remuneration is simply a means for workers to secure only *future* sustenance or enjoyment. However, simply decommodifying human labor power as occurred in Soviet-style societies, does not in itself surmount *all* forms of human alienation as it opens the door to reinstating modes of alienation akin to those existing in precapitalist economies where work imbricates in webs of interpersonal relations of domination and subordination. Soviet-style socialism, with its reversion to forms of extra-economic compulsion for work, rooted very congenially in third-world societies given the redistributive and egalitarian changes it promised. Third-world societies had scant experience of capitalist social relations of production that historically "freed" work from extra-economic compulsions subjecting it instead, paradigmatically at least, to economic coercion alone. Soviet-style socialism proved unattractive to those in advanced capitalist economies with the historical experience of economic compulsion where workers felt themselves "free to lose".[41] For this reason, a definitive ontological principle of a genuine socialism is that to constitute an advance over capitalism work, even work in its most arduous forms, must become self-motivated. That is, the compulsion for work cannot be extra-economic or economic. Work in a genuine socialism, as Marx himself put it in *Critique of the Gotha Program*, must become "life's prime want".

How to engender self-motivation as the paradigmatic compulsion for work in socialist society and extirpate all forms of alienation is certainly a task that can be addressed in a relatively uncomplicated fashion under the proposed institutional conditions of collective or cooperative property relations in the small-scale qualitative use value sector communities in developed societies. Alternatively, in third-world economies, self-motivation may be promoted through some institutional community tweaking of the "responsibility" system; though where basic goods are not commandeered by the state but supplied to the community under participatory democratic conditions. Unproblematic cultivating of self-motivation is possible given the core material reproductive concentration of the communities upon essentially producing final consumption goods and supportive use values largely for the community itself and its individual inhabitants themselves. This fact, which bridges the sundering of production and consumption in capitalist economies, helps reverse both worker indifference to use value in production as well as disinterest amongst workers qua consumers to the wherewithal and modalities of the production process itself. Indeed, even in the cooperative island of Marinaleda still crashing in the waves of Spain's ghastly financial and unemployment crisis, Dan Hancox notes, "The lament about work being boring, tiring or unstimulating was always followed by a 'but': but at least we have it *here*. But at least we have it *now*. But at least we have it *together*. But at least we fought and won it *for ourselves*".[42]

However, the fact of having work as such is really just the beginning for socialist qualitative use value communities. The potentialities for building new socialisms in the twenty-first century in the design advocated here include what Kate Soper terms an "alternative hedonism" where "enjoyment and personal fulfillment are indissolubly linked to methods of production and modes of consumption that are socially just and environmentally protective". Soper rejects views that pigeonhole ecosocialism as harking back to some idealized, "puritanical" or "simple" existence. She concurs with what we have suggested above that agroecology or organic agriculture along with "skill oriented technologies" in Ploeg's conception of repeasantization will increase the labor intensity of food production somewhat, for example. Yet, within the frame of "alternative hedonism", at the outset in the developed world, of course, such "reversions . . . would be motivated . . . by considerations of their hedonist gains and compensations . . . [They] would take place within a new context of thinking about work and leisure, need and pleasure".[43]

This brings us to a related question of institutionalizing self-motivation as the paradigmatic compulsion for work. In his iconic section of *Capital* Volume I on the fetishism of commodities, Marx declares that Robinson Crusoe (who classical economists favor weaving their tales around),

> knows that his labour, whatever its form, is but the activity of one and the same Robinson, and consequently, that it consists of nothing but different modes of human labour. Necessity itself compels him to apportion his time accurately between his different kinds of work. . .All the relations between Robinson and the objects that form this wealth of his own creation, are here so simple and clear as to be intelligible without exertion . . .
>
> Let us now picture to ourselves, by way of change, a community of free individuals, carrying on their work with the means of production in common, in which the labour power of all the different individuals is consciously applied as the combined labour power of the community. All the characteristics of Robinson's labour are here repeated, but with this difference, that they are social, instead of individual . . . The total product of our community is a social product. One portion serves as fresh means of production and

remains social. But another portion is consumed by the members as means of subsistence. A distribution of this portion amongst them is consequently necessary. The mode of this distribution will vary with the productive organisation of the community, and the degree of historical development attained by the producers.[44]

It is true as Marx explains that even should Robinson Crusoe, alone on his island, work each day to either put some things away for future "rainy days" or, as stated in the foregoing, take time during a working day to refurbish means of production, the labor time Robinson devotes to such tasks over and above what Robinson requires in terms of food, drink, shelter, clothes, and so forth, to reproduce his ability to work productively, all constitutes Robinson's *necessary labor*. The only conditions that might see Robinson engage in *surplus labor* in this understanding would be a gang of armed pirates stumbling upon Robinson and, liking his set up but not wanting to work themselves, compelled Robinson to work to support them as well. We may extrapolate precisely the same conditions for the performance of necessary and surplus labor from Robinson to Marx's and *our* qualitative use value sector community of freely associated individuals.

Of course in our qualitative use value sector communities there will be a large cross-section of the community that does not take part in productive labor per se but either engages in some kind of service provisioning including administrative work for this or that productive activity, educators, medical professionals, artists, entertainers, ICT professionals, and so forth, and a range of social dependents including the young, the aged, the infirm, temporarily unemployed, and both lists go on. In our progressive socialist community we expect the gendered division of labor to be eliminated. Thus socialized child care services in each cooperative will liberate women who choose childbearing roles to choose or continue vocations as they please. In fact, the apportioning of the working day can easily account for circumstances where childbearing occurs within a "family", and each partner works part of the day, leaving childcare services to situations where there is just the one doing the childbearing who chooses to remain/engage in a particular vocation. As well, the reembedding of mental in manual labor, science in humanity, and humanity in the natural environment socialists seek to cultivate, will help erode the excrescences of today where up to 80 percent of a population batten on "services" upon backs of the 10 percent of able-bodied producers of use value sustenance. Nevertheless, for Marx, according to the quote above, there would still be *no* surplus labor performed in socialist society as all deductions would be tabulated as being made from labor necessary to reproduce the livelihood of the direct producers at a democratically decided level of comfort and amenities.

On the other hand, in *Capital* Volume III, section 3 of Chapter 48, Marx declares:

> Surplus-labour in general, as labour performed over and above the given requirements, must always remain. In the capitalist as well as in the slave system, etc., it merely assumes an antagonistic form and is supplemented by

complete idleness of a stratum of society. A definite quantity of surplus-labour is required as insurance against accidents, and by the necessary and progressive expansion of the process of reproduction in keeping with the development of the needs and the growth of population. . . . In fact, the realm of freedom actually begins only where labour which is determined by necessity . . . ceases; thus in the very nature of things it lies beyond the sphere of actual material production. Just as the savage must wrestle with Nature to satisfy his wants, to maintain and reproduce life, so must civilised man, and he must do so in all social formations and under all possible modes of production. . . . Freedom in this field can only consist in socialised man, the associated producers. . . . But it nonetheless still remains a realm of necessity. Beyond it begins that development of human energy which is an end in itself, the true realm of freedom, which, however, can blossom forth only with this realm of necessity as its basis. The shortening of the working-day is its basic prerequisite.[45]

While in this account Marx suggests that distinguishing between necessary labor and surplus labor will continue to play a role in the socialist kingdom of freedom this still leaves the door open to creative apprehension and organizing of both which radically alters what relations exist between the two components of the working day from that characteristic of class societies including capitalism. After all, within the context of the qualitative use value sector communities proposed here, and in what are envisioned here as genuine socialist economies generally, for that matter, labor time directed toward satisfying community and cooperative needs or supporting socialized consumption of use values and services will continue to form part of necessary labor. To go back to the Marinaleda exemplar where no profits are distributed but reinvested, to the extent cooperative or communal enterprises utilize the proceeds of that surplus labor which exceeds labor time expended in individual and community consumption for expanding or diversifying production and consumption according to democratically decided goals of cooperative member assemblies (as is the case in Marinaleda), then what antagonism marks the division between necessary and surplus labor in class societies is thereby obliterated. Indeed, under conditions of socialist common ownership and democratic decision making where direct producers along with other members of cooperatives participate in the allocation of social resources to satisfy concrete human needs toward human flourishing, then the distinction between Marx's two positions on necessary labor and surplus labor largely evaporates. In fact, Itoh importantly notes that the dearth of popular participation of any significance over the use of social funds in Soviet-style societies factored into the growing sense of alienation that overcame such societies and fueled arguments about the class nature of those economies as visited in Chapter 3 of this book.[46]

To be sure, Marxist critiques of ecosocialism abound. Canadian Marxist Greg Albo, to take one example, mounts a vigorous one of what he dubs "eco-localist" projects. The projects Albo has in mind are the sort of Green visions à la

McKibben where "the market", read capitalist market, is uncritically assumed to be transplantable as a mechanism of Green autarkic, local community "exchange". We have already dealt with how notions, as such, of "the market" in Green writing, miscarry through their conflating two kinds of "exchange" (that of use values *and* the process of capitalist "exchange" of commodities or value objects); something that in turn springs from the narcotizing of Greens by classical and neoclassical economics. Thus we need not revisit the issue at this juncture. But, while Albo does not aim his remarks at ecosocialists like Kovel or Foster et al. directly, some broader points he makes can nevertheless be placed within the context of even the argument here of qualitative sector use value communities as the bedrock of a new genuine eco-sustainable socialism. Hence it is worth our dialoguing with him as we cover the remaining bases in this chapter of our model for a progressive, eco-sustainable future of socialist human flourishing. On the one hand, then, Albo maintains that in the developed world, much of current spatiality is marked by urban space. These urban spaces, where populations routinely exceed one million inhabitants, bring to bear enormous challenges for maintaining infrastructure, power, equitable social distribution of use values, and so forth, he warns. On the other hand, Albo declares:

> The question of economic coordination is also compounded when different cities are considered, each having differentiated specializations and social and ecological capacities. Even if the idealism of the most utopian social ecology perspective – such as is entailed in imagining semi-autarchic cities – were to be granted, the coordination of exchanges, distribution and regulatory relations between such cities (via the market, or via planning?) would still require considerable attention and deliberation. Confronting the contradictions of economic coordination produced by capitalism within and between territorial scales, concentrated as they are at the level of local socio-ecologies, is fundamental to the success of any strategy . . . .[47]

To this important point we may also add that, whether in terms of communication systems, ICTs, medical equipment and devices, transportation equipment and infrastructure, certain construction materials, heavy construction equipment, standardized tools and implements, scientific laboratories, and this list can easily be added to, it will not be feasible or even possible, except in the most extremely favorable circumstances for qualitative use value communities of around 150,000 people, to offer *all* of what have come to be accepted as rudiments of human civilization and human flourishing. Even assuming socialist devotion to eco-sustainability realized through scale reduction as integral to the new visions of civilization and flourishing. In fact, the sustainable energy matrix itself, alluded to in Chapter 4, the wind turbines, solar power plants, panels, accoutrement of solar PV, transmission lines even within the context of the miniaturized power generation and microgrids that environmentalists argue constitute real-world alternatives, already adopted within certain locales, outstrips the possibility of production supply by every individual small-scale community alone.[48]

Further, thinking about the heterogeneous use value characteristics of the aforementioned technologies, goods, and infrastructures, it is the case on the one hand that their production entails precision standardized production methods along with a relatively complex and diverse spectrum of material and technological inputs. Second, the production requirements demand more often than not what may be defined as medium-sized enterprises with a relatively sophisticated technological accouterment. This holds for production of the goods themselves, the production of their means of production, as well as for many of their inputs. Therefore, taking account of the foregoing with regards to the specific use values under discussion, meeting the general norm of economic life that the right goods be produced to the correct specifications and in the right quantities to meet demand without incurring chronic misallocations of social resources, *reciprocity* in whatever configuration is clearly not a viable economic principle for managing their production and distribution. This leaves the *market principle* of capital or *redistribution*, the planning principle of the state, as the two options. But, on the one hand, because the pricing of these goods will be laden with a host of social and environmental costs and, on the other hand, the products, certainly those related to mass public transportation and infrastructure, will be once-and-for-all type installations (in fact even goods such as tools or electronics destined for individual or cooperative consumption will be designed in ways that reverse the treadmill of obsolescence characteristic of current economic life), the usefulness of the market principle is diminished. This suggests that some variant of *redistribution* in the form of democratic participatory planning will be required to mange this component of socialist use value production.

Crucially, for the progressive socialist pedigree of production, attention must also be devoted to the nature of the labor process for the use values under discussion. Remember, a fundamental ontological principle of socialism is the instatement of self-motivation as the paradigmatic compulsion for work. We argued previously that under conditions of qualitative use value communities, where work revolved around goods destined for consumption or direct support of consumption, tendencies of both worker indifference to use value in production as well as disinterest amongst workers qua consumers to the wherewithal and modalities of the production process itself (which the age of capital engendered) would be reversed, and self-motivation for even arduous work, cultivated. In the production process under consideration here, the labor process is considerably distanced from final consumption and, to the extent some technical division between mental and manual labor persists, potential worker alienation arising along with indifference to the what and how of production will necessarily have to be institutionally guarded against.

Once more, following up on previous work cited above, it is suggested that the model of the socialist economy be divided into *three economic sectors*. The first, as already discussed, is the qualitative use value sector communities. The second is what may felicitously be referred to as a *quantitative use value sector* or "heavy/complex" industry sector where inhering in the products of labor is the requirement that a modicum of potentially alienating quantitative considerations in material reproduction remain, even though socialist property and institutional structures will operate to ensure concrete, qualitative factors guide decision making. The third is the urban or *state*, "administrative" sector.

Let us open the discussion by starting to address Albo's point that "confronting the contradictions of economic coordination produced by capitalism within and between territorial scales is fundamental to the success of any strategy". In fact, if we conceive "economic coordination" broadly to account for accumulation and property relations of capital, we can immediately see how the commodification of labor power by capital went hand-in-glove with its multiplex disembeddings, which in turn saw social wealth siphoned off to commanding heights industries concentrating in and around select urban zones. This process is then consummated even in agriculture with the advent of agrochemical industries. The commodification of labor power as the sine qua non of capital is fundamentally about the "freeing" of productive workers from the means of production and land, economically coercing them to sell their labor power to capital as the basic condition of their livelihood and material reproduction as individuals, families, and class. The importance of the bedrock qualitative use value community as the foundation of the broader socialist project is that it definitively undoes the capitalist separating of direct producers from the means of production and land, particularly where the provision of basic goods required for human survival is concerned.

As well, as argued in Chapter 1, the current neoliberal "Merchant of Venice" surrogate economy of casino games, rent seeking, and expropriation of production-centered activities worldwide is politically orchestrated through action of "big government", "big bank", and "big MNC". To exorcize this excrescence and the pathologies it has saddled human material life with, the proposal here is to institutionally reverse its patterns beginning with the vesting of ownership and management of the quantitative use value sector in the hands the qualitative use value sector communities it services. This can be accommodated through networks of shareholding and democratic decision making that bind the quantitative use value sector to satisfying the use value needs of its qualitative use value community "owners". Quite simply, elements of the quantitative use value sector productive infrastructure may be carved out of that currently controlled by existing corporations and major capitalist business to the greatest extent possible during the initial socialist transition. Though part of it will have to be created anew, particularly given considerations of eco-sanctity, which means shifting away from the petroleum and coal energy-based infrastructure currently in play, and depending on the way the socialist societies come into being along with the state of material and energy resources available at the time and place. Ultimately the geospatial scale and locale of the quantitative use value sector will be decided by its shareholding owners, residents, and cooperatives of the qualitative use value communities.

In dealing with the kinds of use value production and production methods of the quantitative use value sector, general norm of economic life three – stating that if the productive technology of a society remains constant, its reproduction process cannot expand faster than the natural rate of growth of the working population – looms large. In capitalist economies, regimented according to the abstract dictates of value augmentation, and where labor power is commodified and essentially viewed by capital as but another input into its quantitative chrematistic, the absorption of the industrial reserve army during the prosperity phase of the business cycle propels the overaccumulation of capital in relation to the size of the working population, which in turn is the root of anarchic oscillations of prosperity and depression inherent to capitalism. In Soviet-style societies, the relentless compulsion of state planners on state enterprises to fulfill or exceed central plan growth targets under conditions of the decommodification of labor power produced the perverse effect of enterprise "hunger" for resources and workers, which in its own way fomented a chronic misallocation of resources as it fostered social alienation and division.

To forestall such dissonance emerging between the socialist relations of production and forces of production as occurs in capitalist economies and the Soviet-style experiments the production of quantitative sector goods will need to be carefully tailored to social demand of the qualitative sector communities and state "administrative" sector. This "tailoring" requires democratic participatory planning at several levels. One level is the operational need to always maintain a modicum of "slack" in utilization of stocks of means of production and inputs as well as unused capacity in each industry to enable production units to flexibly adjust to potential shifts in patterns of community demand and need. Under conditions of the planning principle of the state there was little attention devoted to this potential problem in Soviet-style societies spawning their infamous "economies of shortage".[49] While I see the utilization of sophisticated computer programs as advocated by Cockshott and Cottrell to simulate total *society-wide* market allocation of all resources and goods as a misguided vision of socialism held prisoner by modalities of capitalism, given the specific use value characteristics of the goods produced by the quantitative goods sector and the fact that end demand emanates from qualitative goods communities, and is democratically negotiated, adopting ICT to perform the calculations necessary to ensure coordination of economic processes and distribution of inputs intrinsic to the sector will be both feasible and contributory to socialist goals of meeting use value need. While labor time forms the basis for assessing productivity as Cockshott and Cottrell see it, the possibility nevertheless remains for adopting some type of "shadow" price calculation method for these use values the production of which lends itself to a certain extent to a quantitative calculus. We have already discussed in Chapter 5 the socialist potential for competition among socialist firms with fruits of innovation flowing to workers, management staff, and ultimate "owners", the qualitative use value communities.

Anarchists like Ben Brucato, cited previously, have evinced concerns over the ultimate control and hierarchical implications of technologies.[50] And, as we have noted, under the conditions of production of the sort of use values to be produced in the quantitative use value sector as well as the fact that production of these goods is distanced from final consumption of the direct producers, the potential for alienation of the direct producers in work arises. Potential work alienation in the quantitative use value sector may be partially offset by automation. But, as discussed in Chapter 4, so-called high-tech Green visions come up against material and resource limitations and accessibility as well challenges of environmental sanctity, not to mention energy availability. Though, I believe with parsimony in resource and energy utilization under conditions of far-reaching socialist change advocated here, along with careful democratic participatory planning by qualitative sector communities of social needs to be satisfied by quantitative sector operations, as well as adoption of ICTs to streamline communication among units and eliminate waste, the possibility of a socialist future of eco-sustainable flourishing is within human reach. In fact, for the more demanding energy requirements of quantitative use value sectors the centralized, larger-scale facilities of solar thermal energy is what will likely be settled upon.[51] But this will *not* be an automobile/consumer society. To believe otherwise is delusional (we will return to this). In any case, the vesting of ownership of the quantitative goods sector in qualitative use value communities will also help offset the kinds of technological domination that worry anarchists as well as the potential alienation of the direct producers from the products of their own hands as occurs in capitalism. Further, a system of democratic rotation of labor forces from bedrock qualitative sector communities it services along with the urban state administrative sector linked to it may be established.[52] Such democratic rotation of labor forces contributes to the breaking down of the skewed class division of labor bequeathed by capital and the fostering of skill multidimensionality as Marx envisioned. Finally, given the fact that the goods emanating from the qualitative use value sector are destined to meet qualitative use value community and urban state sector (we will treat the place of the latter in the whole edifice momentarily) need, satisfying the general norm of economic life that the direct producers receive at minimum the product of their necessary labor, the proposed rotating labor forces of the quantitative sector will partake in the sharing of the social product on the same grounds as that existing in qualitative goods communities whether the product is categorized in toto as necessary labor or divided into necessary and surplus labor components for accounting purposes. And, to the extent education and training for production and services is socialized as part of the necessary labor of society, it is also possible to bring individual consumption funds into line with Marx's measure of socialism paraphrased from *Critique of the Gotha Program* by Graeber, "from each according to their abilities, to each according to their needs". Though, again, LETS and varying shades of operation of *reciprocity* within qualitative use value sector socialist communities will certainly give rise to individual richness and variances in consumption "style" but without unraveling socialist relations of production or undermining socialist property configurations (we will revisit this below).

Let us, however, return to questions of "economic coordination between territorial scales", to paraphrase Albo. What we are considering here in this proposed model or broad design scheme is a process of socialist transformation guided by our ontology of socialism and cognizant of constraints placed upon socialist designs by the need to satisfy the general norms of economic life and meet tests of environmental sustainability. And, we are talking about socialist projects beginning in the here and now under really existing real-world conditions. In terms of Marx's iconic phrase from his *Critique of the Gotha Program*, the new socialist society will come into this world "still stamped with the birthmarks of the old society from whose womb it emerges". The "birthmarks", approached in geospatial terms, as alluded to at various points across the pages of this book, entail a broad brush constructed edifice of giant urban agglomerations supported by globalized agrochemical chemical industry that push the limits of four major planetary boundaries – biodiversity, hydrological cycle, land system change, biogeochemical cycles of nitrogen and phosphorous – we discuss in Chapter 4.

Cities, of course, even in the relatively recent past, as Lewis Mumford explains, more often than not were built by bringing together townships, municipalities, boroughs, districts, towns, villages, and so forth, all which had seen urban development embedded to some extent in agricultural and natural support systems. Even as cities grew in size and enclosed green spaces within their cores, this was accompanied by a parallel movement of suburbanization to remake in the surrounding countryside "the life-maintaining agencies, gardening and farming, recreation and games, health sanatoria and retreats" as Mumford describes it.[53] The socialist future that seeks to remold material economic, social, ecological, and democratic life for human flourishing simply cannot co-opt urban agglomerations as per the status quo. Yet, it has to be recognized, to repeat Albo's point, that really existing advanced economies are highly urbanized. For that reason it was argued above that it is desirable to the greatest extent possible to see parts of cities, particularly where suburban/urban sprawl for the über rich in the developed world and impoverished dispossessed in the third world has usurped potential prime agricultural lands, to be reshaped into qualitative use value sector communities. And that for the immediate socialist transformatory future city centers will remain seats of politics, administration, and culture. Though for administrative purposes the city-state sector will still subdivide into the boroughs, districts, townships, municipalities, and so forth upon which cities were founded at the outset.

Yet even within the cores of cities not partitioned as qualitative use value sector communities or with industrial segments that may form part of the quantitative use value economic sectors it is still expected that socialist change will bring about new balances in sustainability. Already in both the advanced world and third-world urban agriculture, for example, has emerged as an important site of change. One estimate suggests "'as many as 800 million urban farmers produce about 15% of the world's food".[54] In the US, urban community-based agriculture flourished during periods of wartime rationing and also became part of the emergency response to the Great Depression. Today, urban agriculture not only supplements diets of the poor but is a conduit to resuscitating urban community life and development and fosters new norms of community cooperation.[55] To take an example from the third world, in Cuba, where the collapse of Soviet-style experiments forced a rapid constitution of a local food production regime. Urban agriculture provided a huge boost to this effort as 8,000 gardens cultivated by over 30,000 people sprang up in Havana between the collapse of the Soviet Union and 1998. The Ministry of Agriculture in Havana in fact replaced its front lawn with a garden operated by its employees and provided lettuce, bananas, and beans for the Ministry lunch-room.[56]

Cities must also be the vanguard of change in the social energy matrix. We have already pointed to the adoption of microgrids powered by solar thermal plants or potentially hydroelectric plants where these are already emplaced. Wind power is also a possibility. In fact, already in the Netherlands planning is underway to shift *all* electricity generation for passenger train transportation to wind turbine power by 2018.[57] Solar heating, of course, is another much-touted staple of future urban sustainability particularly for individual buildings. This would be paired with solar PV for single-building electricity. Intermittency is an issue for solar PV, however, and storage battery production comes up against the resource and material barriers alluded to in Chapter 4. On the other hand, a study completed in the US in 2009 found that "off-the-shelf" retrofitting of even existing buildings countrywide in terms of things like lighting, insulation, heating/cooling equipment, building system controls, and so forth would reduce total US energy consumption by 23 percent.[58]

But the heart of any genuine transition of urban spaces toward eco-sanctity, which is an integral plank in socialisms of the future, is necessarily de-automobilization. As outlined in Chapter 4, road transport accounts for 75 percent of the almost one-quarter of total global CO_2 emissions contributed to by transportation. If Marxists like Albo are serious about "strategies" that genuinely challenge the interfacing of territorial scale and "socio-ecologies" of neoliberalism and abstract mercantile wealth augmentation as the social goal, well . . . the automobile is the poster commodity for the post-WWII era in those regards. Daniel Newman, in an artful unpacking of the key questions here, notes first, how mass automobilization in the post-WWII era undermined community cohesion and fostered social atomization as it allowed for the shifting of many elements of community life from work, to accessing basic sustenance, education, and the list goes on, great distances from human residences and communities. The automobile industry is also the single largest manufacturing sector in the world and has been on the frontline of superstructure support for capital. States have showered road building and related infrastructure with funds to the dearth of numerous other mobility options and public transportation. Indeed, from our really existing exemplar above there is no reason wind cannot be constituted as the source of electricity for broader transcontinental railway transportation across the environmentally sustainable socialist world. That is possible however only by undoing the gross misallocation of social resources devoted to the automobile. But Newman argues there is instead a concerted emphasis upon so-called "green" cars. This is a manifestation of the importance of automobile society to current power structures. Notably for its propagandistic value, Newman maintains. Automobiles are the "incentive to carry on conforming . . . to own a little slice of the world" beyond one's home.[59]

It is time to bring this chapter to a close with treatment of the two vital "coordination" problems of socialist organization based upon models of reduced scale as put forward here. First, drawing upon work by Nobel Laureate Elinor Ostrom as well as writings by eco-anarchist Murray Bookchin, Marxist David Harvey delves into questions of governance and political forms. Harvey begins with the notion of the commons or "Commoning" to take Kovel's term, and points to the city or urban commons as an optimal setting for fleshing out its contradictions. Traditionally, Harvey explains, common resource provision in cities from water and waste to parks and recreation is something generally handled at meso-metropolitan or even macroregional governmental scales. Harvey points to Nobel Laureate Ostrom's writing however, which studied delivery of public goods in urban agglomerations to show that managing public provisioning in fact proved more effective and efficient where there was "strong participation of local inhabitants in smaller jurisdictions". Evidence, as such, for Harvey, bolsters cases of eco-socialists and eco-anarchists for going small scale to manage commoned goods.[60]

But, for Harvey, in such schemes of participatory localism, the devil lurks in the details of how potentially autonomous communities, as would be the case with the qualitative use value communities argued for here, will relate to each other. A problem, Harvey maintains, exacerbated by potential wealth asymmetries among local communities. Harvey points to real-world examples of "local" governance miscarrying such as the EU. And he reminds us that neoliberalism favors "local" administration as part of its abdicating of government provision of public goods. Harvey then lays down the gauntlet:

> How can radical decentralization – surely a worthwhile objective – work without constituting some higher-order hierarchical authority? It is simply naïve to believe that polycentrism [Ostrom] or any other form of decentralization can work without hierarchical constraints and active enforcement. Much of the radical left – particularly of an anarchist and autonomist persuasion – has no answer to this problem . . . Instead there is the vague and naïve hope that social groups who have organized their relations to their local commons satisfactorily will do the right thing or converge on some satisfactory inter-group practices through negotiation and interaction.[61]

This, then, brings Harvey to Bookchin.

Bookchin develops his arguments on local democracy through his nuanced grasp of the political development of the city in ancient Greece, particularly the experience from which abiding ideas of Plato and Aristotle were drawn. The lessons of the Athenian *polis* for getting scale right, according to Bookchin, were that to yield the good political life the structure had to be large enough to guarantee most material sustenance but not too big to negate public face-to-face decision making by assemblies. Such assemblies operating at the level of towns or municipalities would then be linked to each other through forms of confederalism. Bookchin declares: "The anarchic vision of decentralized communities, united in free confederations or networks for coordinating communities of a region, reflects the traditional ideals of a participatory democracy in a modern radical context".[62] For Harvey, then, the bottom-up directional flow of decision making from municipal to confederal assemblies advocated by Bookchin, with delegates to the confederal assemblies being "recallable and answerable" to the municipal assemblies, "is by far the most sophisticated radical proposal to deal with the creation and collective use of the commons across a variety of scales".[63]

In basic outline, the broader participatory democratic polity of the tri-sector socialist society will operate akin to such a confederal system with power running from bedrock qualitative use value sector communities through the political edifice (see Figure 6.5). However, urban administration, particularly as relating to the

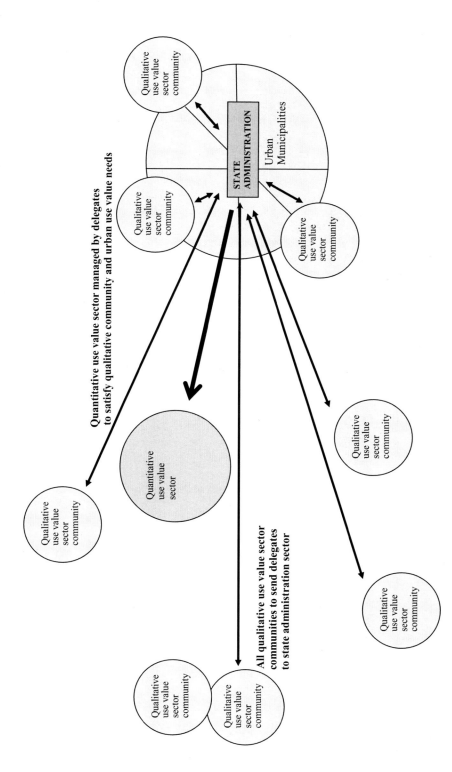

Figure 6.5 Directional flow chart of political power in tri-sector community socialist economy

democratic divisions of municipalities, boroughs, townships, and so forth of large cities that are not melded into qualitative use value sectors in their own right, will add another layer of participatory complexity to the design. Though I agree with Bookchin that "[d]ecentralization of large cities into humanly scaled communities is . . . *indispensible* to an ecologically sound society".[64]

But there is a glaring elision in both Bookchin's work, concerned as it is with anarchistic decentralized popular power, and in Harvey's argument in support of Bookchin focused on governance between scales. And that is the central question of the *kind* of economy or economic principles that will operate in each sector or "scale", their economic synchronicity or propensity for coordinating productive activities to guarantee the material reproducibility of society with satisfaction of the general norms of economic life, the socialist pedigree of the principle(s) regarding our ontology of socialism along with their ability to deliver on long-standing socialist goals such as wealth redistribution, their eco-sanctity, and, of course, the flexibility they convey to superstructure management of the economic substructure so that human flourishing in all areas of human life may be fostered. Again, we are bracketing the transition scenario. Chapter 7 will delve into the actual strategic choices available now. Though, most, unfortunately, are suboptimal to put it gently. But here, to emphasize the feasibility or "viability" of the design we are supposing that the socialist transition follows what may be deemed an enlightened path where, for example, socialist governments accede to power in nation-states and begin the process of dismantling existing economic structures with the plan to construct a socialist economy according to this model.[65] Such a transformatory process possibly entails the breaking up of nation-states themselves, replacing them with a socialist commonwealth of sorts.

We have touched on the participatory governance issue but what remains are the aforementioned questions beginning with that of superstructure coordinating or management of intrasocialist "region", "state" intersector economic relations. Keeping in mind our earlier strictures that the new socialist society must ultimately expunge the "birthmarks" of the old society, particularly at the outset regarding the relations of production, wealth divisions, and property relations of the old society, I believe this can be greatly facilitated by the use of a multicurrency system where a state currency will coordinate material and service flows between sectors as well as factoring in to global economic relations among socialist units in a global socialist commonwealth. But, and this "but" is vital, what we advert to in Chapter 4, the Dejima, or "protruding island" principle from the Tokugawa Shogunate that creates a firewall separating qualitative use value sector community economies as well as urban municipality economic life with *its* potential LETS and community currencies from state macrocoordination with the state currency, must be applied.

In this fashion, within the qualitative use value sector communities basic needs of the direct producers in society are satisfied under conditions of some variant of collective, cooperative, property (with the possibility of even elements of "private" community property for residential needs). While modes of *reciprocity* or "baseline communism" along with use of community currencies will create an invigorated environment for human flourishing, to the extent community "money" circulates, and "markets" of sorts persist, community currency money only plays the part of money as means of exchange. As "exchange" transactions will largely be either of services or of goods for their use value utilities, the role of money as measure of value will be suppressed. And community currencies have no efficacy as store of value or idle M. In short, though there will certainly be room for some divergence of incomes and alternate lifestyles, qualitative use value sector communities offer zero conduits for capital accumulation or gaping wealth/property asymmetries. And, as already noted, following up on studies such as completed by Nobel Laureate Elinor Ostrom, the management of socialist "commoned" or public provisioning is also optimized in settings where community forms of direct participatory decision making are the rule. In fact, governance of material reproduction in subdivided urban boroughs, municipalities, and so forth, may also strive to emulate qualitative use value sector community arrangements with some potential forms of barter or intermunicipality/qualitative use value sector community reciprocity to ensure basic goods provisioning, specifically food. And with participatory democratic assemblies from every qualitative use value community and urban municipality sending delegates to the state administrative sector, this confederal polity will be able to exercise socialist and environmental quality control over participating communities.

The purpose of the state currency is to coordinate transactions or "trade" among qualitative use value sector communities and urban municipalities as well as between these communities/municipalities and the quantitative use value sector. State currency will also be used to manage intercommunity, intersocialist "region/state" travel. State currencies will need to be exchangeable at varying rates for local community currencies given that administrative, service, and productive tasks performed outside qualitative use value community sectors or urban townships must be remunerated with those receiving such enabled to partake of potential consumption opportunities beyond ex ante coordinated supply of basic goods in their originating or other community (state currencies will also be a way of mediating resettlement of people among communities). As well, state currencies may be rendered "exchangeable" for trading purposes among socialist "states" or "regions" in the global socialist commonwealth. State currency here plays each of the three roles of money to some extent. It may even be issued by the state administrative sector "bank". Nevertheless, state money, as state money today, is and remains fiat money. And, as is the case today, state fiat money is issued under a political mandate for a particular social purpose. Unlike today, however, state currency is *not* issued to foment casino money games, rent seeking, and "Merchant of Venice"-like expropriations of productive wealth and sustenance of humanity as is the case today. Rather state money issuance in socialist societies is predicated upon the furnishing of use values and services for human flourishing. Because, the state administrative sector itself will be a creation of the qualitative use value sector communities and urban townships or municipalities where cooperative/communal property is held, and these communities maintain Dejima-like firewalls between their social economies and community currencies (meaning no state currency circulation *within* them and above mentioned exchanges of state currency for local currency occurs on community entry), there will exist no possibility for state currencies to be used in the service of some renewed efforts at financial accumulation by state administration personnel.

Further, the locus of capital accumulation historically, of course, has been the production of standardized material goods that lend themselves to quantitative considerations in economic life and the suppression of qualitative considerations. But, because ownership of the quantitative use value sector (in effect, the "industrial" sector of the tri-sector socialist economy) is vested in the qualitative goods sector communities the needs of which it services with its use value production capacities, it also offers no avenue for renewed capital accumulation. (While urban municipalities play a part in quantitative use value sector governance, to reverse the wealth extractive modalities of the current economy, their "ownership" rights over quantitative goods sector "property" will be restricted). The participatory, democratically recallable state administration that interfaces with the planning delegates of the quantitative use value sector to operationalize participatory planning goals is also dependent upon the qualitative use value sector communities for satisfying its use value sustenance needs. And again, command of state currency in the hands of state administrative sector delegates or "planners" does not confer upon them any kind of power beyond executing their delegated tasks, as property and social use value wealth, as emphasized, is largely held behind the Dejima-like firewalls of qualitative communities. Finally, with labor power decommodified and self-motivated to rotate through quantitative use value sectors to furnish use values for their qualitative communities, there exists no foundation for class domination, exploitation of workers, or accumulation of capital in the meeting of social demand for quantitative sector goods (see Figure 6.6).

While the coordination functions of the state administrative sector are expected to be large at the outset of the socialist transformatory process, as the participatory democratic activities of managing the progressive, redistributive, eco-sustainable socialist society of human flourishing become regularized, the state as such will "wither away" as forecast by Marx.

To sum up, Marx's admonition to utopian socialists not to draw up blueprints of the future was based on Marx's view, on the one hand, of the necessity for in-depth knowledge of precisely what capitalism is for the obvious reason that if the future society is to offer a progressive historical advance over capitalism, without a grasp of what precisely capitalism is, transformatory actors would have no way of knowing whether their efforts would genuinely result in the human material betterment they sought. On the other hand, Marx understood the role his *Capital* played in exposing the deep causal inner logic of capital in simultaneously elucidating the economic substructure of human society, as human anatomy offered the key to the anatomy of the ape. And that the knowledge of the substructure of human society derived from dialectical economic theory would provide a scientific foundation for our thinking about socialism. In short, Marx never instructed us not to think creatively about economic configuring of a future socialist society. But rather to wait until we had a solid basis in dialectical economic theory for

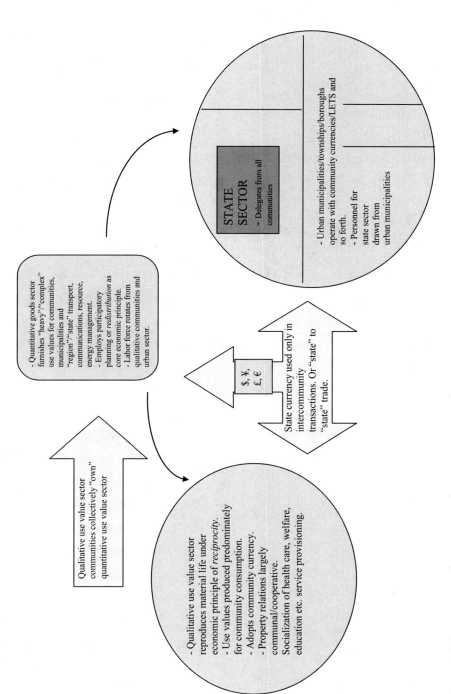

Figure 6.6 Economic coordination across heterogeneous use value sectors

doing so. What this chapter has done is to take state-of-the-art knowledge of human material life derived from Marx's economic theory and historical studies and supplement it with cutting-edge insights from the best of economic history and anthropology to produce a design for the socialist future of human flourishing. Though, as a scholar, I have certainly gone out on a limb here in striving to fill in institutional blanks of grand phrases such as "rational regulation by the associated producers of the metabolism between human beings and nature", pace Foster et al. Yet, in the end, we still have but a model or template, delineating the material reproductive "viability" and socialist and eco-sustainable pedigree, but the final blueprint is to be worked out in direct revolutionary practice.

Notes

1. Nicholas Rescher, *Scientific Realism: A Critical Reappraisal* (Dordrecht: D. Reidel Publishing Company, 1987) p. 42.
2. Richard Westra, "Socio-material Communication, Community, and Eco-sustainability in the Global Era", in Carl A. Maida, (ed.), *Sustainability and Communities of Place*. Series on Environmental Anthropology, Roy Ellen, Editor. (Oxford: Berghahn Books, 2007).
3. Karl Marx, *Grundrisse*, http://www.marxists.org/archive/marx/works/1857/grundrisse/ch01.htm.
4. Polanyi, *The Livelihood of Man*, p. 6.
5. Thomas T. Sekine, in private discussion and unpublished writings that I have been privy to, began using this ICT metaphor.
6. Marx, *Grundrisse*.
7. Thomas T. Sekine, "Socialism beyond Market and Productivism", in Albritton, Bell, Bell, and Westra (eds.), *New Socialisms*, pp. 236–7.
8. David Pepper, *Eco-socialism: From Deep Ecology to Social Justice* (London: Routledge, 1993) pp. 152ff.
9. See for example the discussion in Ben Brucato, "Toward a Peak Everything: Postanarchism and a Technology Evaluation Schema for Communities in Crisis", *Anarchist Studies*, 21, 1 (2013).
10. James C. Scott, *Seeing Like a State: How Certain Schemes to Improve the Human Condition Have Failed* (New Haven, CT: Yale University Press, 1998) pp. 203–4.
11. Westra, *Political Economy and Globalization*, Chapter 4.
12. Graeber, *Debt*, pp. 94–102.
13. Ibid., pp. 102–13.
14. David Harvey, *Rebel Cities: From the Right to the City to the Urban Revolution* (London: Verso, 2012) pp. 68–70, 125.
15. Graeber, *Debt*, pp. 114–15.
16. Ibid., p. 115.
17. Robert Shiller, "The Neuroeconomics Revolution", *Aljazeera*, 25 November 2011, http://www.aljazeera.com/indepth/opinion/2011/11/20111122155856959773.html.
18. See, for example, Derek Wall, *The Rise of the Green Left: Inside the Worldwide Ecosocialist Movement* (London: Pluto, 2010).
19. See the discussion in Qingzhi Huan, "Eco-socialism in an Era of Capitalist Globalization: Bridging the West and the East", in Qingzhi Huan (ed.), *Eco-socialism as Politics: Rebuilding the Basis of Our Modern Civilization* (Dordrecht: Springer, 2010) p. 4.

20 Joel Kovel, *The Enemy of Nature: The End of Capitalism or the End of the World* (London: Zed Books, 2002) p. 214.
21 Joel Kovel, "Ecosocialism as a Human Phenomenon", *Ecosocialist Horizons*, 3 August 2013, http://ecosocialisthorizons.com/2013/08/ecosocialism-as-a-human-phenomenon/.
22 John Bellamy Foster, Brett Clark, and Richard York, *The Ecological Rift: Capitalism's War on the Earth* (New York: Monthly Review Press, 2010) pp. 416–7.
23 Williams, *Ecology and Socialism*, pp. 216–17.
24 Ibid., pp. 220–5.
25 Marx, *Capital*, V1, Chapter 1 (first paragraph in the section "The Elementary Form of Value Considered as a Whole").
26 David Pepper, "On Contemporary Eco-socialism", in Huan (ed.), *Eco-socialism as Politics: Rebuilding the Basis of Our Modern Civilization*, pp. 38–9.
27 This takes in Thomas T. Sekine, "Socialism as a Living Idea", in Henryk Flakiersk and Thomas T. Sekine (eds.), *Socialist Dilemmas, East and West* (New York: M. E. Sharp, 1990); Sekine, "Socialism beyond Market and Productivism"; Westra, "Socio-material Communication, Community, and Eco-sustainability in the Global Era"; idem, "Green Marxism and the Institutional Structure of a Global Socialist Future" in Robert Albritton, Bob Jessop, and Richard Westra (eds.), *Political Economy and Global Capitalism: The 21st Century Present and Future* (London: Anthem, 2007); idem, "Renewing Socialist Development in the Third World", *Journal of Contemporary Asia*, 41, 4 (2011).
28 van der Ploeg, *The New Peasantries*, pp. 170–2.
29 Ibid., pp. 220–1.
30 See Murray Bookchin, *Remaking Society: Pathways to a Green Future* (Boston, MA: South End Press, 1990) pp. 174ff.
31 What follows draws upon the excellent discussion in Dan Hancox, *The Village Against the World* (London: Verso, 2013).
32 Hudis, *Marx's Concept of the Alternative to Capitalism*, pp. 155–60.
33 The discussion in Itoh, *Political Economy for Socialism*, treats a Soviet-style scale economy, yet is relevant to our discussion here.
34 An expanding variety of potential add-ons that fall within *reciprocity* or "baseline communism" broadly conceived have been put forward. See the accounts, for example, in Anitra Nelson and Frans Timmerman, *Life Without Money: Building Fair and Sustainable Economies* (London: Pluto Press, 2011). Or that in Gwendolyn Hallsmith and Bernard Lietaer, *Creating Wealth: Growing Local Economies with Local Currencies* (Gabriola Island, BC: New Society Publishers, 2011).
35 Danielle Nierenberg, "Agriculture: Growing Food – and Solutions", *State of the World 2013*, p. 194.
36 Ibid., p. 195.
37 See for example Joan Martinez-Alier, "The Environmentalism of the Poor", United Nations Research Institute for Social Development (UNRISD) and University of Witwatersrand, paper presented to conference on *The Political Economy of Sustainable Development: Environmental Conflict, Participation and Movements*, 30 August 2002, http://www.unrisd.org/80256B3C005BCCF9/%28httpAuxPages%29/5EB03FFBDD19EA90C1257664004831BD/$file/MartinezAlier.pdf.
38 Pat Murphy and Faith Morgan, "Cuba: Lessons from a Forced Decline", *State of the World 2013*, p. 334.
39 See for example Clive Y. Thomas, *Dependence and Transformation: The Economics of the Transition to Socialism* (London: Monthly Review Press, 1976).

40 Barry Naughton, *The Chinese Economy: Transitions and Growth* (Cambridge, MA: MIT Press, 2007) pp. 88–90.
41 So-called rational choice Marxist John Roemer entitling his book, *Free to Lose: An Introduction to Marxist Economic Philosophy* parodied the title of Milton and Rose Friedman's book, *Free to Choose: A Personal Statement*. While Roemer never addresses this question, the "freedom to lose" as embodied in the way capital "frees" work from extra-economic compulsion to subject it solely to economic coercion is a powerful liberating force in the course of human history.
42 Hancox, *The Village Against the World*, p. 118.
43 Kate Soper, "Hedonist Revisionism", in Albritton, Bell, Bell, and Westra (eds.), *New Socialisms*, pp. 129–30.
44 Marx, *Capital* VI IV, "The Fetishism of Commodities and the Secret Thereof".
45 Marx, *Capital*, V III, Chapter 48, "The Trinity Formula".
46 Itoh, *Political Economy for Socialism*, pp. 65–6.
47 Greg Albo, "The Limits of Eco-Localism: Scale, Strategy, Socialism", *Socialist Register 2007: Coming to Terms with Nature*, 43, http://socialistregister.com/index.php/srv/issue/view/444#.U3QU57HDDIU.
48 On "microgrids", see McKibben, *Eaarth*, pp. 186ff.
49 Itoh, *Political Economy for Socialism*, p. 71.
50 Brucato, "Toward a Peak Everything".
51 See the discussion in T. W. Murphy, Jr., "Beyond Fossil Fuels: Assessing Energy Alternatives", *State of the World 2013*, Chapter 15.
52 Instructively, eco-anarchist Murray Bookchin also advocates some form of workforce rotation "between town and country". See Bookchin, *Remaking Society*, p. 195.
53 Lewis Mumford, *The City in History: Its Origins, Its transformations, and Its Prospects* (London: Secker & Warburg, 1961) pp. 333–5, 421ff, 484.
54 See Luc J. A. Mougeot, *Growing Better Cities: Urban Agriculture for Sustainable Development* (Ottawa: International Development Center, 2006) p. 6.
55 Thomas A. Lyson, *Civic Agriculture: Reconnecting Farm, Food, and Community* (Medford, MA: Tufts University Press, 2004) pp. 95–6.
56 Norberg-Hodge et al., *Bringing the Food Economy Home: Local Alternatives to Global Agribusiness*, pp. 110–12.
57 Railway Technology Market & Customer Insight, "Eneco to Power Electric Trains with Green Energy in Netherlands", 19 May 2014, http://www.railway-technology.com/news/newseneco-to-power-electric-trains-with-green-energy-in-netherlands-4269898. I am grateful to Nina Somera for bringing this article to my attention.
58 Phillip Saieg, "Energy Efficiency in the Built Environment", *State of the World 2013*, p. 185.
59 Daniel Newman, "Cars and Consumption", *Capital & Class*, 37, 3 (2013) pp. 458, 467, 469–70.
60 Harvey, *Rebel Cities*, pp. 80–1.
61 Ibid., pp. 83–4.
62 Bookchin, *Remaking Society*, pp. 179–82.
63 Harvey, *Rebel Cities*, pp. 84–5.
64 Bookchin, *Remaking Society*, p. 187.
65 Thomas T. Sekine, "Fiat Money and How to Combat Debt deflation", unpublished.

7 Conclusion
A road to the eco-kingdom of freedom

To put in context the question of what is to be done along with that of popular constituencies that will, or might potentially support the kind of sweeping social change this book argues is necessary to achieve a progressive, redistributive, material economically reproducible, eco-sustainable society of human flourishing, we need to reinforce one point.

The Marxist profession, largely fixated upon Marxism qua HM as a master theory of historical directionality, has devoted much of its attention to Marx's contributions to exposing the exploitative, alienating, asymmetric wealth distributive bents of capitalism. The reason for Marxist foci as such is the fit of the foregoing with the HM scheme of working-class revolution that harnesses the historical tendencies of capitalism that purportedly set the stage for a socialism that ameliorates the above ills. But Marxists for the most part paid scant attention to a more fundamental question. One that only Marxian economic theory answers. And, which, at first blush, seems to run counter to their revolutionary élan. That is, how is it possible for an economy manifesting such an array of ills, and effectively wielding an entire human society for the abstract purpose of value augmentation, to reproduce human material life as a byproduct of this chrematistic in the first place? Put differently, exploitation, as it is often construed in Left parlance in terms of workers getting their fair share ("market socialist" David Schweickart, for example) or empowered to "manage" the enterprises they work in (see recent writing by US Marxist Richard Wolff[1]), along with asymmetric wealth distribution or "inequality" (a recent "hot" topic), and alienation viewed as paucity of "meaning" or "satisfaction" in work, are ills that bourgeois state and social policies also seek to redress. Of course, while Left support for bourgeois ameliorative policies, as such, has been an important plank in the deepening of these initiatives beyond the piecemeal, particularly during the post-WWII "golden age" period, in the end, policy per se in capitalist economies is all about maintaining capitalism or making it work "better" and, supporting that goal, is a comprador strategy for those genuinely interested in fundamental social change.

For Marx, as captured by dialectical economic theory, capitalism is not *just* an exploitative, alienating, asymmetric wealth distributive society, but an "upside-down", "alien" society that reproduces human economic life for the "extra-human" purpose of quantitative mercantile wealth self-expansion. Looked at from another angle, what dialectical economic theory displays is that while capital is nevertheless preoccupied with exploiting, alienating human beings, asymmetrically distributing wealth, to exist as an historical society it must, as a byproduct of its self-aggrandizing chrematistic of value augmentation that fosters the above ills, meet the general norms of economic life. Yes, its resource allocative process operates under constraints of its social class relations of production. Yes, it revolutionizes the forces of production through anarchic convulsions of business cycle oscillations that absorb and reconstitute the industrial reserve army (that, of course, when capital is working "well", otherwise it potentially falls into extended periods of depression often punctuated by wars, and from which it can *only* reemerge if a use value space tamable by its logic is available). Yes, it ensures the direct producers, at minimum, receive the product of their necessary labor through the wage form (which, during the "golden age", gave rise to a "middle class" life style in advanced bourgeois democracies, though in other periods really only offered workers little more than bare sustenance to reproduce their labor power as a class). But it *did* those things required of it to guarantee its material reproducibility as an historical society for roughly the century and a half of its existence.

Drawing upon Marxian economic theory, what I argue at length in earlier work, and in condensed fashion in Chapter 1 of the present book, is something bourgeois economics in any of its past or contemporary orthodox/heterodox incarnations, along with Marxists bound to Marxism qua HM as a master theory of historical directionality, simply cannot fathom. That is, what is euphemized as "globalization" or even, "financialization", in current parlance, is emphatically *not* as shrill neoliberal ideological chanting proclaims – the epiphany of "the market" (read a "pure" capitalism of sorts)! But, what in my book *Political Economy and Globalization* I argue is, in fact, a retreat of capital to whence it originated, that dubbed by Marx, the "interstices" of the world. To review material from previous chapters, Marx's notion of the antediluvian existence of capital in the "interstices" of the ancient world draws upon his grasp of the fact that *forms* of capital such as money, wages, profits, even "markets" of a kind, existed at various points across the sweep of human history, external to the modalities of material reproduction characterizing past historical societies. Their capitalist substance originates in the unique symbiosis – predicated upon the commodification of human labor power – that capital weaves with such forms as it subsumes the metabolic interchange between human beings and nature to wield human society as a byproduct of its chrematistic of abstract mercantile wealth augmentation.

Again, the claim that capital has loosened its grip on human economic life is based on a raft of factors. The increasing knowledge-intensive economy of "brain work" saddles capitalist market operations with an ever-growing quantum of *indirect costs* that subvert the price mechanism. Remember, the capitalist market is attuned to *direct costs* of commodified labor power and material inputs. The *direct costs* computed by the capitalist market underpin its capitalist "rational" or "objective" pricing upon which, in turn, resources are allocated so as to ensure the material economic reproducibility of capitalism as an historical society. With pricing in current economies an increasingly subjective affair due to the weight of *indirect costs*, workings of the market principle of capital can only but produce skewed allocative outcomes. And, if an historical society cannot allocate resources except in a haphazard fashion, its demise is nigh.

Further, the disinternalizing of production by commanding heights industries in advanced economies along with the slicing, dicing, and disarticulation of production-centered activities across low wage often proto-capitalist locales means that the idiosyncratic capitalist activity of profit-making and reinvestment of profits in the "real" economy is no longer central to major economies like the US. These so-called advanced economies, as is the case with the US where the "service sector" constitutes near 80 percent of total employment, can hardly be called capitalist given the fact that service work is not in any way an economic activity specific to capitalism. And, for service work there is no way to gauge in any capitalist market "rational" or "objective" fashion whether remuneration workers receive is sufficient to reproduce their livelihood as is the case for commodified labor power receiving the product of its necessary labor. Of course, at the exclusive top tier of the bifurcated service sector, the "1 percent", livelihoods are hardly endangered by the subjective remuneration calculus. But at the swollen bottom tier, the "99 percent", as recent protest movements have it, they certainly are. It is true that in capitalist production-centered economies income remuneration of services has a comparative metric in wages of commodified labor power. Yet with production-centered activities in the US sliced, diced, and disarticulated to the likes of China well . . . we can certainly see how "inequality" has emerged as even an "in" bourgeois topic. Finally, the predatory ravages of idle M, as finance became unhinged from capitalist production-centered activities that had circumscribed it through the capitalist era to the end of the "golden age", have beset humanity with a "Merchant of Venice" dynamic of wealth extraction. Money that makes money or M-M existed in the past in the activities of merchant capital and antediluvian "loan capital" or usury. The current regime of casino games played with idle M is a modern reincarnation of the latter.

We make this point, that the current "surrogate" economic excrescence can hardly be labeled as capitalist, not for its own sake, however. Rather, to gather the threads of the argument above, the point is made to emphasize that if the general norms of economic life are *not* being met largely by the market principle of capital, then, for human society to exist for any length of time, some *other* principle or principles *must* be operationalized. To be sure, as discussed in Chapter 1, from the early twentieth century capital accumulation moved asymptotically away from its "pure" image as the scope of superstructure support for the market principle of capital steadily enlarged. In this way, though the predominating principle of economic reproduction remained the market principle of capital (otherwise we would have no basis for referring to the society as capitalist), the planning principle of the state was recruited to perform promethean functions by the "golden age" period to support accumulation.

The chimera of the neoliberal era, and its secreted ideology that has been swallowed hook, line, and sinker by much of the Left along with the (to be expected) Right, is that it is a period where "the market", read capitalism, has been reloaded. This position built on the neoliberal attack on the specific accouterment of the post-WWII welfare state and public goods provisioning. Nothing, however, could be further from the truth. Neoliberalism drew heavily upon superstructure support of "big government" to enact and enforce (domestically and globally) a raft of rule and legal changes, many well under the political radar, ostensibly to "free" capital from its "golden age" tethers. However, the surreptitious legal shifts only "freed" bloating pools of idle M – that had *no possibility of ever* being converted into *real capital* for investment in production-centered activities – to commence their predatory ravages expropriating "pounds of flesh" from the bones of humanity. As Richard Duncan, cited in Chapter 1, explains, the next step here for "big government" with its "big bank" was an orgy of money creation and "monetarist" policy manipulation of the value of money. This orgy facilitated the growth of US and other major economies' total credit market debt to outer galactic expanses. Such out-of-this-world credit explosion, then, underwriting the bloating asset bubbles of neoliberal "growth", along with securitization and leveraged casino games played around these. And it engendered the consumption fete amongst those plugged into the bubble upside. Duncan, as we may recall, dubs this excrescence "creditism". But the "ism", in a fashion probably unintended by Duncan, confers on this "surrogate economy" an aura of coherence when its "Merchant of Venice"-like force has none. The proof of this is that after each casino game bubble burst, the mess created only gets bigger, pulling the state in to mop as much of it as it can get under the public mat as evidenced by the ratcheting up of "big government" spending as a proportion of GDP across the neoliberal decades. In short, the ultimate paradox, and in fact perversity here, is that the planning principle of the state is deployed for the benefit of a caste of über rich, capitalists without capitalism in a way that is predatorily destroying humanity rather than contributing to its material reproduction.

Then we have the proliferation of new alter-economic institutional forms, most based on modalities of *reciprocity*, as adverted to in Chapter 6. These include: producer and consumer co-ops, local exchange/employment and trading systems (LETS), community currencies, local finance, and so forth. We will have the chance momentarily to take up the case whether or not these amount to, or potentially may spur, some broader transformatory initiative. Here I simply want to point out that it is no accident that these forms of *reciprocity* have spawned across the neoliberal decades and most recently, following the meltdown of 2008–2009. Spain, for example, has witnessed the rise of a so-called "parallel" economy of barter. And we are talking about barter "exchange" of everything from dog-walking services to automobiles and even real estate![2] The German city of Oberhausen, rendered bankrupt from the financial crisis, to take another example, has introduced a new "Schwarzbank" or black bank currency of "coals" that residents earn for tasks performed for the community, with the "coals" then useable for purchases of goods from the many participating businesses.³ But, such ad hoc community responses to the loosened grip of capital on human material reproduction, as with the narrowly focused role of state planning upon backstopping a "surrogate economy" of casino play, are hardly sufficient replacements for the market principle of capital in reproducing the material life of human societies. In the case of the barter economy in Spain or "Schwarzbank" in Oberhausen, these projects were launched simply for *local* human survival purposes.

However what must be drilled home given the stupefying spell this casts over not only creative thinking about the institutional configuring of a socialist future of human flourishing but strategic thinking on what is to be done along with potential constituencies organizing to do it is this: capitalism is an historically delimited society centered on the production of an historically constituted complex of material goods. Marx captures the historical delimitation of capitalism in terms of *the* fundamental *contradiction* of capital, that between value and use value. Value is the abstract, quantitative, historically delimited principle of capital. Use value is the transhistorical foundation of human existence. While all sorts of nonsense over "contradiction" is being peddled on Left conference circuits, the ultimate contradiction in the sense of the exhaustion of capitalism as an historical way of managing human material affairs is posed by the use value space that confronts capital. Capitalism comes into being around the standardized manufacturing of a light use value complex that lends itself to production by commodified labor power and the suppression of qualitative economic considerations in favor of a quantitative calculus. The final *stage* of capitalism, the stage of *consumerism* or period of the post-WWII "golden age", is marked by mass production of consumer durables, represented by the leading automobile sector, as the use value space managed by capital (though with the Herculean superstructure support we note). But, with the disarticulation and ultimate abdication of the production-centered economy of consumer durables followed by the "surrogate economy" of casino play, capital so clearly reveals the exhaustion of its historical role. Neoliberalism could trash the public goods provisioning and welfare state accouterment of the "golden age" superstructure because the substructure of consumer durable production was also gutted. Remnants of the edifice of consumer durable production continue to operate in the US, of course, but neither it nor another use value complex exists to sustain another period of capital accumulation. Major economies like Germany and Japan have desperately fought to retain bigger slices of their consumer durable production-centered economy. And, they also maintain elements of the superstructure support that goes with it. Though year by year, they are shedding more of both.

To put it succinctly, there will *never* be the heroic showdown between capitalism and socialism because capitalism in any *substantive* sense *is gone*. Quite simply, capitalism has been historically outpaced by a use value space that it is unable to manage according to its market principle and the emergence of new use value possibilities that now beckon humanity from the horizon of the future. Yes, significant residues of capital persist, particularly in the realm of the superstructure. These include the ideological fixation on abstract, quantitative mercantile wealth expansion as the social goal along with political policy exhortations to wring quantitative "growth" at any cost to society and the earth's biosphere from a decayed and depleted economic and resource substructure (even though such "growth" has been decoupled from the development, industrialization, and creation of real material wealth that came with the age of capital). And, the lingering superstructure manifestations of capital, including the view that capitalism is forever, are now the greatest dangers to humanity.

There must be some way out of here

Eric Olin Wright, in an opus that gathers together ideas put forward in what he refers to as The Real Utopias Project,[4] offers up a useful framework for addressing our question here. As a quick aside, I should note that the bulk of Wright's work on "real utopias" proves singularly uninteresting, and hardly a tract on "utopias". In fact, at the center of each "utopia" model Wright advances, there is this thing he blithely calls "the economy", without in any way seeing the need to problematize the *kind* of economy and economic principles he has in mind, or in our earlier analogy, the specific configuring of software that will operate the material substructure of society for socialist ends.[5] Thus, I have not engaged with that part of the book, given how for us, the *kind* of economy or economic substructure that will be managed by the superstructure to viably reproduce human economic life for concrete, progressive, use value need, eco-sustainable purposes of human flourishing is *the* question.

But, in the final section of the book, Wright interestingly breaks the transformatory trajectory question into three broad potential strategy types. These are: "ruptural", "interstitial metamorphosis", and "symbiotic metamorphosis".[6] Let us take up his third strategy first. The notion of "symbiotic metamorphosis" involves the abiding question, first broached within the famous "Revisionist Controversy" of the early twentieth century,[7] of working *within* the really existing economic and bourgeois democratic political structure in a "bottom up" fashion to enact progressive reforms.[8] Wright, of course, reads this in the light of a "utopia" of capitalism. Participants in the "Revisionist Controversy", even Eduard Bernstein who held the "symbiotic metamorphosis" position, did have grander ideas for the end game. In any case, as I have emphasized across the pages of this book, the old devil we know, capitalism, is no more and, contrary to neoliberal ideological chanting, cannot be resurrected. But, as with our formative discussion of Green alternatives in Chapter 4, let us for the sake of brief engagement, rather than dismissing the enterprise out of hand, bracket the capitalism or not capitalism issue and focus on "symbiotic metamorphosis" as simply an approach to current economic conditions. Greg Albo surveys what are accepted as "credible" ways to deal with our economic ills along such lines. These largely revolve around the "policy matrix by which to transform a neoliberal state back into a Keynesian welfare state".[9] In Chapter 1 I suggested that much of the Marxist Left is in fact closeted Keynesian in their fatalistic grasp of capital as the only game in town. This Marxist position finding support, as I explain in the chapter, in Marxism apprehended as HM, a master theory of historical directionality. The position then further buttressed by the nightmarish weight of Soviet collapse in the minds of many erstwhile Marxists. So, if not socialism, to them, there must be capitalism.

In any case, Albo reviews arguments espoused by Nobel Laureate Paul Krugman on pumping up the volume of stimulus and pairing that move with a spreading of stimulus dollar relief beyond commanding heights "big bank" and "big MNC" to cover the ordinary person on the street debtor. With mortgages and credit card debt under some control, voila . . . the onset of a renewed bout of demand-driven growth. Albo rightly finds this policy proposal wanting due to the fact that it leaves the financial architecture at the root of the recent meltdown and lingering recession intact (we will return to this). From there, Albo moves on to consider responses to the crisis by social democratic states. While he shows that groups and organizations within these states have developed specific policy initiatives to deal with troublesome, "footloose" elements in the workings of finance, in the end social democratic states have been going with the program of "competitive austerity" in line with dictates of global financial interests that hold their debt.[10]

However, there is a deeper structural problem with any strategy of "symbiotic metamorphosis" today that seeks to "transform a neoliberal state back into a Keynesian welfare state", and/or beyond. Here, stage theory as a level of analysis in Marxian political economy as a whole proves invaluable. In Chapter 1, as well as in Chapter 2, Box 2.4, discussion of stage theorizing of *consumerism* as the post-WWII stage of capitalism, it was explained that the partial decommodifying of labor power with a social wage topped up by "big government" macroeconomic countercyclical demand programming, was the necessary superstructure accompaniment for a capitalist economic substructure of consumer durable mass production.[11] The exorbitant cost of fixed capital in core "golden age" industries like autos, plus the high throughput requirements of profit-making, rendered devaluations of capital, weakened demand, and work stoppages anathema. The key supportive task of the superstructure thus was to put a floor under wage diminutions in the depression phase of the business cycle that in turn forestalled potentially destructive price competition among large oligopolistic MNCs. Rather, business cycle oscillations were characterized by MNC alternations between full capacity utilization followed by contractions of output and maintenance of overcapacity where price levels in key consumer durable industries fluctuated minimally. Paradoxically, therefore, the partial decommodifying of labor power during the "golden age" was insurance for capital that labor power would remain a commodity and capital accumulation continue.

With the demise of the golden age and disinternalization of MNC production-centered activities leading to the slicing, dicing, and disarticulating of production across value chains running through key low wage proto-capitalist third-world locales, there simply was no reason for capitalists without capitalism operating commanding heights "branded" MNCs that no longer make anything, to retain a commodified labor force. To add some numbers to the picture, already by 1987, contract suppliers in the US auto industry employed more workers than the big three auto MNCs. By 1994, the "temp" agency Manpower surpassed General Motors to become the single largest US employer. By 2003, retailer Wal-Mart would dwarf Manpower as the paramount US employer.[12]

But this is only a part of the story. The spate of ICT investments at the close of the twentieth century paralleled by an overall trajectory of fixed capital disaccumulation from the demise of the "golden age" transformed what remained of the paradigmatic use value production space of *consumerism*. To repeat what was said in Chapter 1, and alluded to previously, the increased dimension of knowledge intensity factoring into costs has seen MNC revenues stream toward technological rent and a cohort of ICT patent holders, engineers, software and gadget designers, and so forth with precious little flowing to profit for reinvestment in the production-centered activities that employed the "golden age" labor force. Remember, much of the work of making things is undertaken not by commodified labor power as occurred in "golden age" advanced economies but under proto-capitalist conditions in places like China where productive workers do *not* receive remuneration equivalent to their necessary labor (see Box 7.1).

When we add into this unseemly mix the "Merchant of Venice" dynamic of predatory casino money games through OTD banking that has seen MNCs become arbitragers in their own right, buying and selling their own debt with the perverse impact of such on income flows, and real economy business cycles replaced by rotating bubbles and bursts, it becomes clear that even if person-on-the-street debts were paid down à la Krugman, the simultaneous bailing out of the "surrogate economy" of FIRE would continue to exacerbate the economic malignancies of wealth flows to rents and casino games.[13] And the sheer magnitude of costs of a social wage and welfare state that would inflate incomes of McJobs proportionate to "golden age" levels would "crowd out" all other funding commitments in the US budget. Nor would there be any "rational" economic purpose for a reconstituted "golden age" welfare state into the future. The "golden age" economic substructure will *not* magically reappear with the raised incomes and devaluation of the dollar, for example. We are where we are precisely because the capitalist integument of the stage of *consumerism* has been outstripped by morphing of the use value space and technological change. Or, put in Marx's language in HM, the forces of production can no longer be managed according to capitalist social relations. And we have not even got into the potentially destructive environmental consequences of seeking to maintain the carbon-based, automobile-centered consumer durable economy.[14] No, if "big government" has any "big" investment plans for the future as shaped by current, really existing, economic conditions it is to manage the fallout of the current malaise with a prison/security/military industrial complex in a fashion that protects "green zone" islands of prosperity for über rich from the looming economic and climate change induced chaos as per journalist Naomi Klein's dystopian scenario.[15]

Box 7.1

The notion of proto-capitalist, proto-industrial production derived historically from analysis of what were dubbed the "sweated trades" (garment industries) and involved particular forms of contracting out of work that marked the dawn of the capitalist era. In the capitalist stage of *mercantilism* the stage specific form assumed by capital, *merchant capital*, idiosyncratic to wool production, was characterized by the proto-industrial production system of putting-out manufacturing. As touched on in Chapter 2, Marx referred to the putting-out system of wool production in his manuscript fragment, "Results of the Direct Production Process", as the formal subsumption of the labor and production process by capital. The reason Marx distinguished formal subsumption from what he dubbed the "real" subsumption of labor by capital was because the former existed in modes of production other than capitalism where capital operated in the interstices of the world in its antediluvian forms. The basis on which Marx made determinations over the formal subsuming of labor processes in capitalist and non-capitalist society or, put differently, the commodification or non-commodification of labor power is as follows: First, Marx points to the issue of the compulsion for work. Precapitalist economies are marked by extra-economic coercion as opposed to capitalism in which the paradigmatic form in which surplus labor is performed derives from the "free" sale of labor power by workers to capital in the capitalist market; thus the compulsion for work is solely economic. Second, there is the question of "time"; whether the manufacturing activity that is drawn into the circuit of merchant capital or even "usurer's", money lending capital is supplementary to the means by which the material reproduction of the direct producing class is ensured. And, third, there is the question of the scale of the operation (Marx notes that whether the tools or raw materials are supplied to producers is less of a determinant here).

The argument I make in my two previous books, *Political Economy and Globalization* (pp. 179ff.), and *The Evil Axis of Finance* (pp. 161ff.), is that in the case of the third world as a whole in which agrarian relations of various sorts form the basis of sustenance for around 60 percent of populations, and provide for flows of casual labor into urban agglomerations that constitute the work force for global value chains, Marx's second point is crucial in that the reproduction of this labor force is not ensured by wages and must be supplemented by total family incomes from agrarian social relations of production and other casual endeavors. In the specific case of China, with its authoritarian residence permit system, the mobility question and "free" sale of labor power characteristic of capitalist commodification of labor power also emerges as something that must be considered in assessing whether in Marx's definition, labor power is commodified. After all, why have global value chains cut through this part of the world in the first place? This is part and parcel of the retreat of capital to its antediluvian forms in its process of disintegration.

Yet, notwithstanding the writing on the wall flowing from current global trends, the strong belief in even Marxist circles that capitalism is the only game in town continues to have a powerful impact on drawing Left thinking back in tow with the "symbiotic metamorphosis" line. As Luke Cooper and Simon Hardy put it, "In a sense, despite claims of the revolutionary left, Eduard Bernstein's perspective of slow gradual change to the system won out – even if actual social democratic reformism seems to be in decline".[16]

Let us now turn to Eric Olin Wright's notion of a "ruptural" strategy. Rupture is essentially what is presaged in the radical commentary of trending Left gurus cited in the opening pages of Chapter 1. In this sense, as Wright correctly states, the idea of heroic confrontation with despised structures of power is particularly appealing to the growing cohort of young activists most incensed by the stealing of their futures by the current economic excrescence.[17] It also plays an important part in the socialist imaginary of the past where Marx's own words are often brought to bear upon the idea of socialism as consummating heroic working-class struggles against the bastion of bourgeois political power, the state. Though, as I note in Chapter 1, Marx's words also evidence caution on the question of whether a modern militarized bourgeois state can be frontally assaulted and brought down. Marx's insights here hold even more true for the present in that so-called law enforcement agencies have multiplied astronomically as have their paramilitary arsenals become more sophisticated in the deadliest fashions.

The "ruptural" strategy also brings us face-to-face with the agency question. Answers to this question by Marxism have often been framed in terms of Marx's oft repeated line from *Capital* Volume I cited in Chapter 3 in this book on how centralizing the means of production and concomitant socialization of labor would "burst" the capitalist integument, with the "expropriators then being expropriated". That is, revolutionary rupture will come at the hands of the revolutionary working class as per their concentration and socialization in the factory. As Marxist David Harvey observes, even in actual historical "ruptural" struggles of the past, however, from the Paris Commune through Leningrad 1917 to the Seattle general strike of 1918, and even Paris 1968, the revolutionary movements tended to be "broadly urban" rather than "narrowly" factory, working class.[18] But even with expanded criteria at hand on potential radical workers and urbanites and others, to what extent can we expect sustained anti-systemic "ruptural" action from such a group? And who would we include in such a group?

One approach to the above question is through the understanding of current reconfiguring of class structures alluded to in Chapter 1. In his influential book Guy Standing argues that world economic forces operating essentially from the period we identify with the neoliberal decades have engendered a new "*class-in-the-making*, if not yet a *class-for-itself*, in the Marxian sense" – the "precariat".[19] This "precariat" is differentiated from remnants of the "old" working class of the "golden age" with company tenure of sorts and reduced but remaining social entitlements. And it differs from the so-called "wretched of the earth" or lumpenproletariat in Marx's terminology. Rather, for Standing, despite its internal diversity, the "precariat" is paradigmatically subject to a welter of work and life insecurities relating to the flexible, contingent, informalized, casualized, and ultimate precariousness of work.

What is instructive is that while Standing does not adopt the terminology of this book, his descriptions of the economic changes at the root of the "precariat" phenomenon synch with what has been discussed above as the disinternalization of MNC and advanced economy production operations along with their slicing, dicing, and disarticulation across the globe. In particular, is Standing's reference to the hundreds of millions of contingent and casual workers drawn from China's rural areas to its urban workshops to produce for global value chains; they "are the engine of the global precariat" declares Standing.[20] For what I have argued is that as capital has been beating its retreat to the interstices of the world across the neoliberal decades the need for maintaining labor power as a commodity also diminishes. This is why crisp clarity over *forms* of value is so important. As commodified labor power is not *just* about working for a wage. Commodification of labor power demands that wages be sufficient to reproduce the livelihood of workers as a class under given historical conditions. But, among third-world labor forces recruited in the service of global value chains, that test is not being met as after the youth of workers has been sapped they are jettisoned back to the rural villages that partially supported them ensuring that they *never* reproduce themselves as an industrial working class. Standing's discussion of the depths of precariousness generated by growing casualization and informalization of work suggests a similar experience taking place around the world in advanced countries, though minus the third-world rural village fallback option. However, if a social group or class in the making is unable to reproduce its livelihood it will never be "made" into a *class*; especially not one empowered to act "for-itself". Arguably, this was one of the reasons for the disarticulation of global production systems in the first place!

We may also note that the existence of a "precariat" as such has had an important impact on the role of unions in major economies. Unions, of course, have been the traditional organizational conduits for workers over the course of the twentieth century, and did stage many significant confrontations with capital to the benefit of all working people. But, through the neoliberal decades, as Luke Cooper and Simon Hardy explain, a peculiar bifurcation in union structure set in. At the "bottom" of the structure it is not just a question of industrial systems where unions congregated being disarticulated, leading to plummeting membership or that wages have stagnated at best, dropped at worst, and with the hungry precariat loitering outside, provoking little sustained discontent. Instead, on the one hand, a feeling of worker "impotence" pervades due to the increase in workplace stratification that erodes workplace solidarity, rendering workers "more like associated individuals, rather than collective social actors". On the other hand, Cooper and Hardy suggest unions have become ever more "distant" from rank and file. At the "top" end, however, while unions of the post-WWII period had been bureaucratized, the neoliberal decades witnessed the strengthening of managerialism within unions underpinned by the exorbitant salaries of union leaders that not only exceeds pay of average members but confers on union leaders lifestyles more in line with the 1 percent than the rest.[21]

David Harvey casts an even wider net in an effort to situate social groups with anti-systemic intentions. Harvey had argued in earlier work that the neoliberal decades are marked by what he dubs "accumulation by dispossession".[22] Harvey teases that concept out of Marx's arguments in *Capital* Volume 1 on "primitive accumulation" of capital. Quite simply, Marx sought to dispel bourgeois myths of strife-less origins of capital in market "exchange" and expanding division of labor à la Adam Smith. For Marx, capital was born in pillage, slavery colonialism, and other unholy acts of "dispossession". However, Marx was clear, that as wealth extracted from the world by those means streamed into the West European and British heartland of early capital accumulation, it contributed to a new form of "possession". And when the "possession" of means of production in bourgeois hands ultimately subsumed or "possessed" the very wellspring of human wealth creation with the commodification of labor power, it internalized its very own fount of regeneration and self-expansion. Of course, the subsumption of the labor and production process as the chrematistic production of surplus value did not stop capital from pillaging or colonizing in its peripheries as it got the chance. *But the latter no longer defined it.* To the extent Harvey argues that the defining feature of the neoliberal era is a kind of primitive accumulation or "accumulation by dispossession" akin to the days preceding the historical consolidation of capital in its heartlands, then what he is in effect confirming is my claim that our current "surrogate economy" entails the retreat of capital to the interstices of the world from whence it emerged.

For Harvey, global "dispossession" opens up an expanded compass of new "class" positions ranging from the indigenous populations "freed" from their land and resources, through the all manner of "dispossessions" of property and savings following on the heels of the meltdown of 2008–2009, to the fashion by which intellectual property rights pirate everything from music cultures to genetic resources from their people and places of origin. In Harvey's words:

> The political unification of diverse struggles within the labour movement and among those whose cultural as well as political-economic assets have been dispossessed appears to be crucial for any movement to change the course of human history. The dream would be a grand alliance of all the deprived and dispossessed every-where.[23]

The indications of such a grand "ruptural" alliance emerging, however, are not promising. Harvey, rather, sees anti-systemic challenges splintering to deal with discrete "dispossessions".

One example he cites is the proliferation of NGOs from the onset of the neoliberal era. While these organizations provide invaluable service in key issue areas of advancing social betterment, en masse, as reflected in the role of NGOs in the World Social Forum, their calls for change have had limited resonance. Harvey asserts, "revolutionary change by NGO is impossible". Then there are the "autonomist" and anarchist grassroots organizations (GROs). These include the panoply of "horizontally networked" organizations including solidarity economies, LETS, collectives, and so on discussed earlier and to be returned to. Harvey sees their "self-organizing powers" as necessarily factoring into "any anti-capitalist alternative". He notes as well, the radical propensity of some groups to directly and even violently confront current state power structures. But the inability of this amorphous collection of oppositions to "scale-up their activism into organisational forms capable of confronting global problems", according to Harvey is the bane of their transformatory efficacy. Third, Harvey sees a raft of social movements such as the Landless Workers' Movement (MST) in Brazil, often led by an "organic" intellectual à la Antonio Gramsci, that might coalesce with like movements in the right circumstances to foment a broader struggle. Fourth, there are the "identity" movements, women, gay, race, and so forth. Finally, there is the labor movement, though Harvey is not especially sanguine about its prospects. And from what was said above, Harvey's views here are justified. In the end, despite his nod toward decentralization in building the new socialism of the future, as cited in the previous chapter, Harvey concludes his review of potential anti-systemic challengers with the dictum "that there is no way that an anti-capitalist social order can be constructed without seizing state power".[24] This, of course, leads one to a pessimistic view of "ruptural" strategies because, with the exception of the labor movement, each of the foregoing agencies eschew organizational ties with political parties that have traditionally been seen as the vehicle through which the state would be "seized".

However, there is something rather befuddling about Harvey's take on transformatory action given his coining of the oft-quoted concept of "accumulation by dispossession", in that he does not seem to fully grasp the implications of his own analysis. After all, the "seizing" of state power in Marxist theory was predicated upon the view that the state sat atop a "real economy". The real economy the state sat atop was the production-centered economy operated by the market principle of capital. And, from the late nineteenth century through to the mid-twentieth-century "golden age", while the market principle of capital predominated, the planning principle of the state was marshaled to a greater and greater extent in support of capital to ensure the material economic reproducibility of society. It was the "seizing" of this production-centered economy, based largely upon heavy industry and rudimentary planning, at least during the period in which actual "ruptural" socialist revolutions in history took place, that Nobel Laureate Joseph Stiglitz, cited in Chapter 5, maintained offered "a short window of time" for socialists to transform society by expanding the scope of the planning principle of the state.

But in the current "surrogate economy" the largely integrated industrial and manufacturing systems of the capitalist era have been gutted and disarticulated across the globe. Moreover, along with the predominance of global agrochemical industries, and commandeering through Washington Consensus policies of third-world agricultural resources to feed the wealthy, global food provisioning has also been disarticulated through "cool chains" that place each and every one of us ever more at the mercy of giant MNCs with their international food distribution networks. Remember, prior to the 1970s around 90 percent of global food production was consumed within the country where it was produced.[25] This is nowhere near the case today. As the grip of capital on human material existence loosened through the neoliberal decades, the material economic viability of human society has thus increasingly been called into question because the general norms of economic life are less and less satisfied by the market principle of capital. Nor has the planning principle of the state compensated for the loosening grip of capital. Except for the aforementioned prison/security/military industrial complex, fiscal policy is anathema to the neoliberal state that concentrates its energy on fomenting casino play and mopping up the mess so as to prolong the game. But even if a progressive force captured the state à la Harvey, the economy they were once able to centrally manipulate with macroeconomic fiscal tools no longer exists.

Again, the reason why anti-systemic local struggles, movements, GROs of various stripes are in surplus in the neoliberal era is precisely to replace economic principles of material reproduction such as the market principle of capital and planning principle of the state, which no longer ensure the livelihood of their communities, with ones like *reciprocity* or "baseline communism", that do. In the age of capital as indigenous or peasant societies were displaced or "dispossessed", craft forms of work and the communities they thrived in destroyed, capital exerted a *centripetal* force drawing the displaced into its treadmill of accumulation and value augmentation. Today what exists is "dispossession" pure and simple without "accumulation". Harvey's term in this sense is misleading. The retreat of capital to the interstices of the world operates with a *centrifugal* force impelling production into guarded apartheid enclaves of "special economic zones" (SEZs), MNC wealth into "offshore" tax havens, PFI and MNB finance into "shadow banks", from where capital can mount hit and run attacks on remnants of real economic life and wealth creation. Harvey's notion of "dispossession" in this reading is a rather polite way of describing what I see as a "Merchant of Venice" dynamic of wealth expropriation and rent seeking that will scrape the flesh from the bones of humanity if not stopped.

We can thus extrapolate from the foregoing to put to rest but one more convoluted, though much radically hyped scheme for "ruptural" change, that of Michael Hardt and Antonio Negri. As with Guy Standing and his "precariat", Hardt and Negri play off Marx's notion of class-in-itself becoming class-for-itself as its collective struggles and consciousness drive it to perform its HM role, with their self-styled notion of a "multitude". As they put it: "The first is multitude *sub specie aeternitatis* . . . this multitude . . . is *ontological* . . . The other is historical multitude or, really, the not-yet multitude".[26] For Hardt and Negri, to recapitulate the point made in the quote by Hardt alone, cited in Chapter 1, "the various forms of labor throughout the global economy are today becoming common . . . Producing in common presents the possibility of the production of the common, which is itself a condition of the creation of the multitude".[27] Then, echoing Marx's line from *Capital* Volume I that socialization inhering in production explodes the capitalist integument leading to the "expropriation of the expropriators", so Hardt and

Negri declare, "Sovereignty . . . has always been a relationship grounded in the consent and obedience of the ruled. As the balance of this relationship has tipped to the side of the ruled, and as they have gained the capacity to produce social relations autonomously and emerge as a multitude, the unitary sovereign becomes ever more superfluous".[28]

Dressed in a new chic language such views nevertheless remain temporally frozen in an historical period when forces of the commodity economy did evidence a centralizing force as social wealth accumulated as capital came to constitute a new form of "possession". The belief among early revolutionaries of the Soviet era in particular, that they were riding the wave of "a few rough structural principles" to paraphrase Eric Hobsbawm in Chapter 3, is what lent to "socialist hopes the certainty of historical inevitability". And contributed to the over half century of eliding the morning after question as the development of the "common" in the new form of capitalist "possession" was conceived as the antechamber of socialism. It also led to a paucity of engagement by socialists in creative thinking about the institutional configuring of the progressive socialist society of the future in terms of its material economic viability and promotion of human flourishing. Hardt and Negri seem to be peddling the same snake oil with the argument that "forms of labor throughout the global economy are today becoming common". Especially, when such is hardly the case. Indeed, as capital retreats to the interstices of the world more and more "forms of labor" are being exploited in ways that bear little relation to the reproduction of the "common" livelihood of the direct producers and their societies. And this cuts for Hardt and Negri's political prognostications as well. Panagiotis Sotiris observes,

> it would be a mistake to take the current aspects of the composition of the labour force as given and think that they can be directly transformed into a radical political composition . . . The "traces of communism" in the collective practices, demands and aspirations of the contemporary labour force go hand in hand with the pervasive effects of fragmentation, insecurity, precariousness, along with various forms of ideological miscognition.[29]

Finally, let us take up the third strategy type, what Eric Olin Wright refers to as "interstitial strategies". Wright's notion of "interstitial strategies" builds upon Marx's conception, discussed above, of *forms* of capital such as money, prices, wages, "markets" having an existence in the ancient world external to the modalities by which precapitalist societies reproduced their livelihood. The subsumption of the transhistorical metabolic interchange between human beings and nature by capital did not entail a single great cataclysm. Rather, it involved the dual process of the historical limitations being reached by the precapitalist feudal economy and the corrosive effects on the feudal carapace of encroaching value forms carried by the commercial "money" economy. Only when the externalities of value forms were internalized by society, and labor power converted into a commodity, could we say that capital, with its market principle of economy, was in the historical saddle wielding human society as a byproduct of its abstract chrematistic of value augmentation.

As in the case of past epochal historical transformations, human society and its ability to reproduce its material existence finds itself trapped in a kind of twilight zone where the old society has exhausted its historical role and elements of the new society are just beginning to take root. But, there are notable differentiating features attendant to the current period of change. As the feudal order putrefied, the ideology of the divine right of kings proved little match for the new claims to science advanced by the bourgeois. Today, however, though capital has long exhausted its historical role, the ideology of the scientificity of neoclassical economics and shrill chants by neoliberals over TINA exert a powerful opiate-like force, narcotizing young minds in ways that ideologies of the past could never do. Further, as feudal bulwarks crumbled, and its economic principle of *redistribution* through interpersonal relations of domination and subordination loosened its grip on society, the market principle of capital rapidly filled the vacated spaces. Today, as capital beats its retreat to the interstices of the world, the planning principle of the state has been recruited by capitalists without their capitalist economy with such force to create a "Merchant of Venice" expropriation and rent-extorting machine that is extracting a tribute of every last drop of real wealth from humanity. Lastly, the activities of those in command of the state are fomenting the destruction of the biosphere itself as it has sustained human life.

In this light, "interstitial strategies" may be seen as paralleling the retreat of capital to the interstices of its old world clutching its final quantum of abstract mercantile wealth, where "interstitial strategies" entail reinforcement of all those endeavors operating in the interstices of the current "surrogate economy" with variegated principles of *reciprocity* and small-m markets and so forth, devoted to concrete goals of human material economic provisioning and survivability, eco-sustainability, and human flourishing. In books cited in the previous chapter the sheer extent worldwide of combinations of LETS, "solidarity economies", GROs, cooperatives, and the list goes on, has been shown. In fact, even in the US, as displayed by Gar Alperovitz, "more than 130 million Americans – 40 percent of the population – are members of one or another form of cooperative, a traditional organizational form that now includes agricultural co-ops dating back to the 1930s, electrical co-ops prevalent in many rural areas, insurance co-ops, food co-ops, retail co-ops . . . health care co-ops, artist co-ops, credit unions . . . and . . . many more".[30] Alperovitz also points out that even energy across the US, in fact 25 percent of it, is currently "supplied by locally owned public utilities and co-ops". And that these "socialist" economic forms not only offer high-quality services like broadband internet but are at the forefront of environmental sanctity.[31] Alperovitz, in his excellent book, touches base with anarchists like Murray Bookchin who argue for the reembedding of economic life in smaller local communities as a way of reviving genuine participatory democracy. Alperovitz calls his remaking of the US as a congeries of communities "a pluralist commonwealth". This includes, he suggests, not only communitywide stabilizing efforts but also cooperatives, worker-owned companies, neighborhood corporations, small- and medium-sized independent firms, municipal enterprises, state health efforts, new ways of banking and investing, regional energy and other corporations, and in certain critical areas national public firms and related democratic planning capacities.[32]

Unfortunately, Alperovitz, though he is certainly not alone here in Left writing, never considers the specific economic principles that his "pluralist commonwealth" will run on. In the previous chapter, I presented a model that does exactly that, explaining the material reproductive, progressive, popular empowering, eco-sustainable pedigree of each in the context of their organization and interrelationship as they coalesce toward realizing socialist goals of extirpating all forms of alienation in work and engendering human flourishing. In particular, I lay emphasis on the qualitative use value *community* foundation of the socialist society for reasons similar to defenses of community foundations of the future by anarchists such as Bookchin and progressive writers like Alperovitz. With the important difference that I specify how the economic substructure of the community will be operated and how that economy will relate to other communities or forms of organization as put forward, for example, by Alperovitz in the quote above. But one issue I did leave hanging is something that Alperovitz does begin to address. I talked about a socialist "state" or "region" as the geospatial scale for operationalizing the tri-sector model of socialist society but was not forthcoming with specifics. Part of the reason for the omission is that much will be determined by the conditions under which the socialist transformation takes place. However, in line with the discussion here of "interstitial strategies" it is important to discuss visions of this.

Alperovitz, sticking with the US example, alludes to the long history of thinking about types of regional decentralization even by US governmental authority figures. Particularly during the 1930s Depression era leading academics had speculated as to how the devolution of both economic life and political authority to states or regions might best contribute to ameliorating crisis conditions.[33] There is a longstanding movement in the state of Vermont, for example, to secede from the US union. Its legal argument is based on foundational readings of the US Constitution that claim a more voluntarist interpretation of the initial accession of states to the union. More importantly, its economic argument is based precisely upon the uniqueness and solidarity of Vermont community life. And the belief that the predatory forces euphemized as "globalization" are strangling that life and disembedding material reproductive capacities from Vermont communities.[34] Cities in Vermont have taken the lead in thinking about a "new economic model" and new community/state-serving institutions like a public bank to "divert Wall Street rather than occupying it".[35] Nor is Vermont alone in seeking to delink and exit from globalization. Its advocates of secession point to numerous projects where states have successfully dismembered such as the Czech and Slovak republics and the plethora of independence movements from Canada through Britain and Spain seeking similar outcomes.³⁶ Indeed, the Marinaleda socialist cooperative in Spain is a living example of the management of a little piece of the kingdom of freedom in the here and now.

There also is growing recognition on the part of wide swathes of the Left that the exit from globalization and building of a socialist future will necessarily commence today with some kind of "interstitial strategy". Panagiotis Sotiris declares:

> Demands for de-linking from processes of internationalization of capital and from international commodity and money flows have often been presented as a futile exercise in isolation, since it is supposedly impossible to think in terms of self-sufficiency . . . Some degree of self-sufficiency, de-centralization and locality are indispensable aspects of any potentially socialist policy . . .
>
> That is why we need to rethink what internationalism means. Instead of fantasies about a global insurrection or revolution, which in the end easily turn into reformist calls for a more responsible international community, I think that making the crucial social and political rupture in a potentially "weak link" remains the most important form of internationalism and has the potential to send tectonic political shifts and create waves internationally.³⁷

And we should be clear that the notion of "small scale" advanced here is actually not that small. If we think about existing federal structures such as the US or Canada, a European country could easily fit geospatially in a single large US state or Canadian province bringing to bear the material and resource accouterment of such. State or provinces in these terms, depending upon their size and resource endowments, will easily provide ample scope for hosting one or more tri-sector community models. These tri-sector communities I have outlined with their quantitative goods sectors are large enough to contain within them the material wherewithal to provide much of the quality medical care, renewable energy, public transportation and communications infrastructure, and so on, for example, that constitute mainstays of civilization few will want to part with. Further, socialist communities will be quick to establish regional mutual support systems where one or another tri-sector community grouping lacks elements of the necessary resource base as has occurred in Latin America recently with the Bolivarian Alliance for the Americas (ALBA) founded by Cuba and Venezuela, and Bank of the South. Martin Hart-Landsberg views ALBA as a kind of "middle-ground" strategy of delinking for engaging "in the coordinated planning and production required to overcome existing economic distortions and weaknesses".³⁸

To, be sure, besides the unrepentant Leninist on the Left, there are those among other components of the broad potential transformatory constituency such as sections of Greens, who are skeptical of any process of change that does not involve state structures. In clear opposition to the position of Bill McKibben, David W. Orr, for example, has this to say:

> We are between the proverbial rock and hard place. There is no good case to be made for smaller governments in the long emergency unless we wish to

sharply reduce our security and lower our standards for the public downward to a libertarian, gun-toting, free for all – Thomas Hobbes's nightmare on steroids. On the contrary, it will be necessary to enlarge governments both domestically and internationally to deal with the nastier aspects of the long emergency, including relocating people from rising oceans and spreading desserts, restoring order in the wake of large storms, managing conflicts over diminishing water, food, and resources . . .[39]

Well, we *are* certainly caught between a rock and hard place but Thomas Hobbes real "nightmare on steroids" is the militarized, authoritarian "Leviathan" state defending the stranglehold on global provisioning systems of "big MNC" and "big MNB" and the concentrated wealth of über rich in their fortified "green zones". While this is the topic for another book, it is easy to see the attachment to the state on the part of the person on the street given the way the bourgeois state across the capitalist era became the locus of individual citizenship, issuing our passports, negotiating political arrangements with other states, conferring upon populaces rights of citizenship, eventually even assuming some responsibility for education, health care, old age retirement, and so forth. But, as with the exhaustion of capitalism, so the bourgeois state of old no longer exists. Wright, himself, dismisses "interstitial strategy" precisely on the ground that he still sees the state as a "capitalist state" lording over the old devil we know, capitalism.[40] But the writing is already on the wall with erstwhile advanced capitalist states abdicating piece by piece everything from citizenship rights through mobility to bourgeois legal procedures. With powerful, armed to the teeth Leviathans, holding the global gun over what constitutes an "emergency" and what does not and who will access scarce water resources and who will not. Jean-Claude Paye captures it thus:

> The imperial structure . . . encompasses the totality of life . . . the relationship between society and State is reversed . . . The idea of popular sovereignty, as the source of the State's legitimacy, is obsolete. It is the government that grants or takes away citizenship and legitimizes society, that forces the latter to conform to its model or, if necessary, criminalizes it.
>
> Organic sovereignty characteristic of the national form of State and based on the organization and control of people's sovereignty, disappears. It gives way to the . . . split between the mechanical and external moment of the political order, symbolized by the idea of governance, and a structure of political and military command constructed around the American executive power.[41]

And time is of the essence. The American emperor, here, has no "real" economy. And as its developed state acolytes increasingly expose their economies to the Wall Street "Merchant of Venice" dynamic of casino play and expropriation they will abdicate more and more of their own. Remember, the whole edifice including the state or "big government" is held up by a Himalayan mountain of debt and credit issuance based on paper money as Richard Duncan, cited in Chapter 1, sees it. For Duncan, this credit/fiat money-based structure, what I refer to as a "surrogate economy", is on the cusp of debilitating collapse. In fact, for Duncan, already, "*Austerity* means collapse".[42] Under such conditions, he suggests, there is no guarantee that states will be able to maintain property rights particularly of homes and lands, for example, of vulnerable middle classes and small business owners. There is evidence that in some US cities, such property "redistribution" is now underway. Therefore, it will not be to the state, but our communities and neighbors (do we even know them?) that we, unlike the über rich with their private armies and paramilitaries and connections to the MNC operators of the prison/security/military industrial complex, will have to rely on for survival. This is what the case for local economies advanced by Greens, eco-anarchists, eco-Marxists, ecosocialists, and so forth ultimately rests on – survival to build into progressive, eco-sustainable human flourishing.

As alluded to at the end of Chapter 6, the optimal and most rational program for change initially entails some combination of what Richard Duncan suggests and that advocated by Thomas T. Sekine,[43] which would be for "big government", instead of printing money to foment casino games predicated upon debt and leverage, to print its state fiat money for grants to progressive regions and communities ready with plans to begin constructing redistributive, eco-sustainable, renewable energy, socialist tri-sector community models engineered to enhance human flourishing. This would involve a combination of Wright's "symbiotic metamorphosis" and "interstitial metamorphosis". However, the kinds of "haircuts" Duncan suggests for asset holders to make such redirected "big government" investment work is likely not going to go down well on Wall Street and its global satellites nor in the halls of the prison/security/military industrial complex invested into to defend the casino game.[44] This brings us back to some combination of "interstitial strategy" with potential "ruptural" change as demonstration effects of socialist success reverberate across the globe. But it all has to move quickly.

Notes

1 Richard Wolff, *Democracy at Work: A Cure for Capitalism* (Chicago, Il: Haymarket Books, 2012) Chapters 6 and 7.
2 See John Stonestreet, "Spain Barter Economy Wins Followers in Grip of Crisis", *Reuters*, 20 February 2012, http://www.reuters.com/article/2012/02/20/us-spain-barter-idUSTRE81J0NJ20120220.
3 See Simon Broll, "Making Money: New Currency Brings Hope to Debt-Stricken City", *Spiegel Online*, 16 March 2012, http://www.spiegel.de/international/zeitgeist/theater-group-launches-local-currency-in-german-city-a-821769.html.
4 See the website The Real Utopias Project, http://www.ssc.wisc.edu/~wright/RealUtopias.htm.
5 Eric Olin Wright, *Envisioning Real Utopias* (London: Verso, 2010) in particular, on this, pp. 128–49.

6 Ibid., p. 304.
7 See Westra, *Political Economy and Globalization*, p. 48.
8 Ibid., pp. 337ff.
9 Greg Albo, "The Crisis and Economic Alternatives", *Socialist Register 2013: The Question of Strategy* (Pontypool, Wales: Merlin Press 2012) p. 5.
10 Ibid., pp. 5–8, 14–18.
11 See also Westra, *Political Economy and Globalization*, pp. 78ff.
12 Ibid., p. 139.
13 Makoto Itoh, "From the Subprime to the Sovereign Crisis: Why Keynesianism Does Not Work?" The Uno Newsletter, http://www.unotheory.org/files/2-9-1.pdf.
14 See, for example, the critique of Krugman by Saral Sarkar, "Krugman's Illusion: We Becoming Richer, But Not Damaging The Environment", *Saral Sarkar's Writings* (blog), 28 April 2014, http://www.eco-socialist.blogspot.jp/2014/04/krugmans-illusion-we-becoming-richer.html.
15 Naomi Klein, *The Shock Doctrine: The Rise of Disaster Capitalism* (New York: Metropolitan Books, 2008).
16 Luke Cooper and Simon Hardy, *Beyond Capitalism: The Future of Radical Politics* (Winchester, UK: Zero Books, 2012) pp. 30–3.
17 Wright, *Envisioning Real Utopias*, p. 307.
18 Harvey, *The Enigma of Capital*, pp. 242–3.
19 Standing, *The Precariat*, p. 7.
20 Ibid., p. 106.
21 Cooper and Hardy, *Beyond Capitalism*, pp. 63–73.
22 What follows draws upon my discussion in Westra, *Political Economy and Globalization*, pp. 128ff.
23 Harvey, *The Enigma of Capital*, pp. 244–7.
24 Ibid., pp. 251–8.
25 Westra, *Evil Axis of Finance*, p. 200.
26 Michael Hardt and Antonio Negri, *Multitude: War and Democracy in the Age of Empire* (New York: Penguin Press, 2004) p. 221.
27 Ibid., p. 338.
28 Ibid., p. 340.
29 Panagiotis Sotiris, "From Resistance to Hegemony: The Struggle Against Austerity and the Need for a New Historical Bloc", *The Bullet*, Socialist Project E-Bulletin No. 988, 26 May 2014, http://www.socialistproject.ca/bullet/988.php#continue.
30 Gar Alperovitz, *What Then Must We Do? Straight Talk about the Next American Revolution* (White River Junction, VT: Chelsea Green Publishing, 2013) p. 35.
31 Ibid., pp. 58ff.
32 Ibid., pp. 144–5.
33 Ibid., pp. 145, 153.
34 See Thomas H. Naylor, *Secession: How Vermont and All the Other States Can save Themselves from the Empire* (Port Townsend, WA: Feral House, 2008).
35 Warren Johnston, "Toward a New Economic Model: Vermont Aims for More Local, Sustainable System", *Valley News*, 10 November 2013, http://www.vnews.com/home/9206399-95/toward-a-new-economic-model-vermont-aims-for-more-local-sustainable-system
36 Naylor, *Secession*, pp. 98–9.
37 Sotiris, "From Resistance to Hegemony".
38 Hart-Landsberg, *Capitalist Globalization*, p. 180.

39 David W. Orr, "Governance in the Long Emergency", *State of the World 2013*, pp. 287–8.
40 Wright, *Envisioning Real Utopias*, pp. 335–6.
41 Jean-Claude Paye, *Global War on Liberty* (New York: Telos Press Publishing, 2007) p. 252.
42 Duncan, *The New Depression*, p. 170.
43 Sekine, "Fiat Money and How to Combat Debt Deflation", unpublished.
44 Duncan, *The New Depression*, pp. 121ff.

Index

Adaman, Fikret 114, 115, 117, 118, 121, 128, 155
agrochemical industry 86, 87, 88, 97, 124, 149, 156, 163, 166, 189
agroecology 156, 158
Albert, Michael 114, 115, 119, 124
Albo, Greg 160, 161, 163, 165, 166, 167, 182, 183
Albritton, Robert 35, 37, 38, 43, 44, 49, 50, 91, 99, 120, 146
alienation 78, 113, 119, 120, 124, 127, 137, 138, 157, 160, 162, 164, 165, 177, 193
All Country World Index (ACWI) 96
Alperovitz, Gar 192, 193
alternative hedonism 158
assets under management (AUM) 15
attention-deficit/hyperactivity disorder (ADHD) 85

Badiou, Alain 1, 2, 3, 6
bank for international settlements (BIS) 16, 21, 25
baseline communism 143, 144, 146, 147, 151, 170, 190
Bell, John R. 48, 49, 51, 109
Bello, Walden 8
Bettelheim, Charles 66, 67, 70, 73
Bhaskar, Roy 29, 30, 31, 33, 131
big bank 18, 22, 88, 93, 142, 151, 163, 180, 183
big government 12, 13, 17, 18, 19, 21, 22, 87, 88, 93, 142, 151, 163, 180, 183, 184, 195, 196
big MNC (see also multinational corporation) 22, 88, 93, 142, 163, 183, 195
biospheric despoilment 22, 23, 83–3, 84, 89, 91, 182

Blackburn, Robin 63
Bolivarian Alliance for the Americas (ALBA) 194
Bookchin, Murray 154, 167, 168, 170, 193
Britain 10, 18, 27, 44, 46, 53, 100, 129, 150, 193
business cycles 64, 71, 122, 127, 128, 130, 184

calculation (economic) 101, 110–14, 115, 116, 117, 119, 145, 164
Capital 5, 7, 23, 24, 32, 34, 36, 37, 38, 39, 40, 41, 43, 44, 45, 47, 54, 57, 58, 60, 61, 63, 64, 71, 80, 81, 103, 105, 108, 109, 110, 111, 120, 129, 133, 135, 136, 150, 158, 159, 175, 176, 186, 188, 190, 197
capitalism 3, 4, 5, 6, 7, 9, 10, 13, 14, 19, 22, 23, 28, 29, 31, 32, 34, 37, 39, 45, 46, 47, 49, 52, 53, 54, 55, 57, 58, 59, 63, 64, 65, 67, 68, 69, 71, 72, 74, 75, 76, 78, 79, 82, 89, 91, 94, 99, 100, 102, 110, 112, 113, 114, 115, 119, 120, 122, 123, 125, 127, 129, 130, 131, 137, 138, 140, 142, 144, 146, 147, 148, 150, 161, 164, 165, 172, 177, 178, 179, 180, 181, 182, 183, 185, 186, 195
capitalists without capitalism 20, 21, 25, 180, 183
carbon dioxide (CO_2) 82, 84, 85, 86, 94, 95, 97, 98, 167
carbon dioxide removal (CDR) 95
China 17, 18, 19, 21, 82, 86, 87, 88, 131, 156, 157, 179, 184, 185, 187
class 2, 4, 6, 9, 10, 13, 20, 27, 28, 40–1, 47, 65, 66, 67, 73, 74, 75, 77, 88, 103, 124, 138, 140, 144, 146, 148, 160, 163, 165, 172, 177, 178, 185, 186, 187, 188, 190, 196

Index

climate change 22, 23, 77, 79, 82, 84–5, 87, 88, 89, 94, 95, 98, 184
Cockshott, W. Paul 114, 115, 116, 118, 123, 129, 154, 155, 164
Collier, Andrew 31, 32, 45
commodification of labor power 9, 10, 12, 13, 15, 39, 40, 47, 48, 51, 70, 71, 78, 99, 120, 121, 137, 141, 145, 146, 150, 151, 163, 164, 178, 179, 181, 184, 185, 187, 188
concentrating solar power (CSP) 95, 96, 97
consumerism 48, 50–2, 53, 69, 73, 79, 85, 93, 99, 122, 129, 130, 137, 142, 147, 181, 183, 184
contradiction 5, 36, 37, 38, 39, 40, 41, 42, 47, 64, 79, 91, 110, 127, 147, 161, 181
Cooper, Luke 187
corporate capital 50, 51
Cottrell, Allin 114, 115, 116, 118, 123, 129, 154, 155, 164
critical realism (CR) 29, 30, 32, 33, 34, 35, 43, 131,
Crouch, Colin 16, 22
Cuba 156, 166, 194

Dejima (protruding island) 101, 170, 171, 172
deoxyribonucleic acid (DNA) 108
Department of Defense (DoD) 97
Devine, Pat 114, 115, 117, 118, 121, 128, 155
discovery (economic) 114–15, 124, 129
Duménil, Gérard 68, 73, 74
Duncan, Richard 18, 19, 20, 180, 196

economics 3, 27, 28, 34, 120, 129; bourgeois 28, 32, 79, 90, 91, 108, 111, 115, 178; Buddhist 100; classical 138, 161; environmental 89, 93; formalist revolution in 109; heterodox 27; mainstream 3, 16, 28, 89; Marxian 4, 10, 55, 69, 82, 109, 111, 121, 135, 144, 147; neoclassical 3, 6, 27, 29, 30, 31, 37, 43, 45, 63, 89, 96, 98, 101, 108, 113, 119, 120, 121, 124, 125, 128, 135, 145, 161, 192; vulgar 28, 29, 58, 91
economic substructure (base) 8, 55, 54–6, 58, 59, 69, 75, 120, 136, 142, 147, 170, 172, 181, 182, 183, 184, 193
economic theory 3, 4, 5, 28, 29, 32, 34, 35, 36, 43, 45, 71, 108, 127, 142; dialectical 42, 43, 44, 45, 46, 47, 49, 52, 53, 54, 55, 56, 58, 59, 64, 69, 70, 71, 74, 75, 76, 77, 78, 79, 83, 90, 91, 92, 98, 99, 103, 109, 110, 116, 119, 127, 128, 129, 131, 136, 137, 144, 150, 172, 174, 178; Marxian 7, 10, 27, 29, 37, 55, 57, 58, 75, 117, 118, 124, 131, 135, 136, 137, 142, 145, 146, 147, 177, 178
ecosocialism 3, 148, 158, 160
energy return on investment (EROI) 96
Engels, Friedrich 2, 7, 36, 59, 64, 68, 74, 108
entrepreneurial profit 42
European Union (EU) 87, 90, 154, 168

Federal Reserve Bank (FED) 21
feudalism 69, 141, 146
Fine, Ben 27, 28, 29, 31, 32, 33, 37, 44, 45, 52, 55, 109
finance, insurance and real estate sector (FIRE) 16, 184
finance capital 47, 50
forces of production 11, 20, 54, 64, 65, 73, 126, 127, 164, 178, 184
foreign direct investment (FDI) 15
Foster, John Bellamy 148, 151, 152, 161, 174
Fullbrook, Edward 21

Germany 129, 181
Graeber, David 101, 138, 143, 144, 145, 146, 147, 151, 165
Green 3, 23, 37, 82–3, 89, 90, 94, 98, 100, 103, 128, 147–8, 152, 160–1, 164, 182, 194, 196
greenhouse gas (GHG) 84
green zones 195
Great People's Communes (GPCs) 156
grassroots organization (GRO) 189, 190, 192

Hahnel, Robin 114, 115, 119, 124
Hamilton, Clive 84, 94, 95
Hardy, Simon 187
Harvey, David 6, 11, 144, 167, 168, 170, 186, 188, 189, 190
Hayek, Friedrich 115, 117, 119
Heinberg, Richard 97, 98, 130, 131
historical analysis 47–8, 49–52, 53, 55, 56, 71, 73, 92, 137
historical materialism (HM) 5, 7, 29, 44, 54, 55, 56, 57, 59, 63, 64, 65, 66, 68, 69, 70, 71, 72, 73, 74, 75, 76, 77, 109, 112, 118, 119, 120, 135, 136, 137, 139, 141, 144, 177, 178, 183, 184, 190
Hobbes, Thomas 195

Hodgson, Geoffrey 115, 116, 117, 118, 121, 124, 127, 128, 130, 131
Hudis, Peter 57, 63, 91, 112, 154

imperialism 6, 27, 45, 47, 48, 49, 50, 51, 52, 53, 65, 68, 71, 73, 79, 92, 99, 130, 137, 142, 147
information and computer technology (ICT) 13, 19, 24, 85, 93, 114, 129, 130, 131, 155, 159, 161, 164, 165, 174, 184
idle money (Idle M) 14, 15, 16, 17, 18, 22, 39, 93, 171, 179, 180
industrial capital 39, 42, 45, 46, 54, 99, 122
International Monetary Fund (IMF) 18, 24, 25
I owe you (IOU) 17, 18
Intergovernmental Panel on Climate Change (IPCC) 84, 85, 104
Itoh, Makoto 73, 111

Japan 18, 19, 21, 27, 101, 113, 181
Jurassic Park (film) 108

Kautsky, Karl 5, 37, 63, 64, 72, 102
Klein, Naomi 184
Kourkoulakos, Stefanos 35
Kovel, Joel 148, 149, 150, 151, 161, 167

Lange, Oskar 111, 115, 119
Landless Workers' Movement (MST) 189
land grabbing 88
law of value/labor theory of value 39, 40, 48, 50, 51, 111, 118, 120, 116
Lenin, V. I. 8, 65, 66, 72, 76, 82, 111
levels of analysis 45, 47–8, 52, 53, 55, 56, 73, 74, 92
Lévy, Dominique 68, 73, 74
Levy Economics Institute 14
liberalism 48, 52, 53, 99
local exchange/ employment and trading system (LETS) 142, 152, 153, 155, 165, 170, 173, 180, 189, 192

Mandel, Ernest 67, 73
Marinaleda 154, 158, 160, 194
market and state debate 8, 10, 77, 122
market socialism 3, 112–14, 119
Marx, Karl 2, 3, 4, 5, 6, 7, 8, 9, 10, 11, 16, 20, 27, 28, 29, 32, 34, 35, 36, 37, 38, 39, 40, 41, 43, 44, 45, 46, 47, 48, 54, 55, 57, 58, 59, 63, 64, 65, 67, 68, 69, 70, 71, 72, 74, 75, 76, 78, 82, 90, 91, 92, 93, 99, 101, 102, 103, 108, 109, 111, 112, 116, 117, 121, 124, 125, 126, 127, 129, 130, 131, 135, 136, 137, 138, 139, 141, 142, 143, 144, 146, 147, 148, 150, 151, 154, 157, 158, 159, 160, 165, 172, 174, 177, 178, 181, 184, 185, 186, 188, 190, 191
mercantilism 48, 49, 52, 53, 185
merchant capital 39, 40, 46, 179, 185
Middle East 1, 2, 76
Milonakis, Dimitris 27, 28, 29, 31, 32, 33, 37, 44, 45, 52, 55, 109
motivation (economic) 23, 59, 78, 79, 123, 124, 125, 128, 137, 144, 145, 157, 158, 162
multinational bank (MNB) 15, 190, 195
multinational corporation (MNC) 7, 12, 13, 15, 19, 20, 22, 25, 51, 53, 73, 74, 85, 86, 88, 90, 93, 128, 129, 142, 163, 183, 184, 187, 190, 195, 196,
multitude 2, 190–1

National Aeronautics and Space Administration (NASA) 85
necessary labor 40, 41, 58, 69, 72, 116, 120, 121, 140, 141, 145, 154, 159, 160, 165, 178, 179, 184
neoliberalism 6, 7, 13, 16, 22, 27, 75, 142, 167, 168, 180, 181
neuroeconomics 146
Newman, Daniel 167
new economic policy (NEP) 111
new international economic order (NIEO) 87
non-equity modes (of control) (NEM) 13
non-governmental organization (NGO) 188
Norris, Christopher 30, 136
Nove, Alec 112, 113, 114, 128, 129

ontology of socialism 76–9, 137, 147, 155, 162, 165, 170
Organization of Economic Cooperation and Development (OECD) 15, 17, 18, 25
originate-to-distribute banking (OTD) 16, 93, 142, 184
Ostrom, Elinor 167, 168, 171

Paye, Jean-Claude 195
Pepper, David 152
persistent organic pollutants (POPs) 85
petrofood 86
photovoltaic (PV) 95, 96, 97, 161, 167
planetary boundaries 83, 86, 88, 89, 94, 166, 184
Polanyi, Karl 32, 34, 50, 52, 101, 124, 138, 139, 140, 141, 143, 144, 145, 146, 147, 151

Polanyi, Michael 117
primitive accumulation 188
primitive communism 139, 140, 141, 143, 144, 146, 151
prison/security/military industrial complex 184, 190, 196
private financial intermediaries (PFIs) 15

qualitative use value community (sector) 155, 156, 157, 159, 160, 163, 165, 169, 170, 171
quantitative use value sector 162, 163, 164, 165, 166, 168, 169, 171, 172, 173

reciprocity 79, 139, 140, 141, 142, 143, 144, 147, 151, 153, 155, 162, 165, 170, 171, 173, 180, 190, 192
redistribution 52, 139, 141, 142, 147, 162, 170, 173, 192
reification 32, 34, 36, 37, 45, 54, 55, 58, 77, 119, 120, 131, 144
relations of production 10, 11, 19, 20, 34, 42, 54, 55, 58, 64, 75, 93, 121, 126, 127, 136, 138, 140, 144, 151, 157, 164, 165, 170, 178, 185
representative concentration pathway (RCP) 84
Rescher, Nicholas 135
research and development (R&D) 85, 129, 130
Resnick, Stephen 67, 73
Revisionist Controversy 182
Ricardo, David 14, 28, 154
Russia 65, 66, 72

Schumacher, E.F. 100
Schweickart, David 113, 119, 120, 177
Scott, James C. 141
Sekine, Thomas T. 14, 29, 31, 36, 43, 45, 48, 49, 50, 51, 92, 109, 110, 116, 127, 140, 196
slavery 69, 141, 146
Smith, Adam 37, 100, 101, 102, 120
socialism 2, 3, 6, 8, 29, 44, 48, 57, 59, 63, 64, 65, 66, 67, 68, 69, 70, 71, 72, 73, 74, 76–9, 82, 100, 102, 110, 112, 114, 115, 116, 118, 119, 121, 122, 123, 124, 128, 131, 136, 137, 140, 141, 146, 148, 149, 151, 152, 156, 157, 158, 160, 164, 165, 167, 172, 181, 183, 186, 189, 191; Soviet-style 22, 63, 66, 68, 71, 157
socially necessary labor 72, 116, 121, 154
special economic zone (SEZ) 190

solar radiation management (SRM) 95
Soper, Kate 158
Sotiris, Panagiotis 191, 194
Soviet Union 2, 7, 48, 67, 69, 71, 82, 111, 112, 118, 119, 130, 135, 156, 166
Speth, James Gustave 89, 90, 93, 98, 100
stage theory 47–8, 49, 52, 55, 56, 69, 71, 73, 74, 79, 92, 99, 102, 137, 147, 183
state 2, 7, 8, 9, 19, 11, 12, 14, 17, 18, 19, 20, 22, 23, 28, 46, 47, 50, 51, 52, 63, 65, 66, 69, 70, 71, 76, 88, 112, 129, 140, 141–2, 151, 181, 184, 189
state capitalism 67, 69
state macroeconomic policy 7, 12, 15, 51, 93, 122, 141, 183, 190
Stiglitz, Joseph 122, 123, 131, 189
superstructure 46, 47, 49, 50, 52, 53, 54, 55, 56, 59, 69, 71, 75, 79, 92, 109, 120, 122, 129, 130, 136, 137, 147, 167, 170, 179, 180, 181, 182, 183
surplus labor 40, 41, 55, 67, 69, 120, 121, 145, 159, 160, 165, 185
Sweezy, Paul 67, 70, 71

treasury bill (T-bill) 17, 18
there is no alternative (TINA) 7, 63, 192
total primary energy supply (TPES) 84, 95
town and village enterprises (TVEs) 157
Transatlantic Trade and Investment Partnership (T-TIP) 90
transformational model of social activity (TMSA) 33
Trans-Pacific Partnership (TPP) 90
tri-sector community 168, 169, 172, 193, 194, 196

United Nations Framework Convention on Climate Change (UNFCCC) 84
United States (US) 1, 2, 13, 14, 15, 16, 17, 18, 19, 20, 21, 24, 25, 27, 49, 50, 67, 82, 87, 89, 90, 95, 96, 97, 98, 104, 106, 129, 156, 166, 167, 177, 179, 180, 181, 184, 192, 193, 194, 196
Uno, Kozo 36, 39, 45, 109
urban state sector 165, 166, 173
usury/loan capital 16, 39, 42, 179

value and use value 37, 38, 39, 40, 41, 42, 43, 44, 45, 46, 47, 48, 50, 53, 64, 77, 78, 79, 83, 91, 92, 93, 94, 96, 99, 102, 103, 110, 116, 119, 121, 122, 123, 127, 130, 131, 136, 137, 138, 139, 142, 145, 147, 148, 150, 151, 153, 155, 156, 157, 158, 159, 160, 161, 162, 163, 164, 165, 166,

168, 170, 171, 172, 173, 178, 181, 182, 184, 193
van der Ploeg, Jan Douwe 153, 158
Vermont 193–4
von Mises, Ludwig 111, 114, 115, 117, 119, 128

Washington Consensus 17, 18, 87, 88, 156, 189
Waterworld (film) 84
Williams, Chris 149, 151

Wolff, Richard 67, 73
World Bank (WB) 18
World Trade Organization (WTO) 18
World War I (WWI) 17, 48, 49, 111
World War II (WWII) 7, 12, 47, 48, 49, 50, 52, 68, 85, 87, 109, 111, 112, 122, 128, 129, 167, 177, 180, 181, 183, 187
Wright, Eric Olin 182, 186, 195, 196

zero interest rate policy (ZIRP) 21, 22
Žižek, Slavoj 1, 8

eBooks
from Taylor & Francis
Helping you to choose the right eBooks for your Library

Add to your library's digital collection today with Taylor & Francis eBooks. We have over 45,000 eBooks in the Humanities, Social Sciences, Behavioural Sciences, Built Environment and Law, from leading imprints, including Routledge, Focal Press and Psychology Press.

Choose from a range of subject packages or create your own!

Benefits for you
- Free MARC records
- COUNTER-compliant usage statistics
- Flexible purchase and pricing options
- 70% approx of our eBooks are now DRM-free.

Benefits for your user
- Off-site, anytime access via Athens or referring URL
- Print or copy pages or chapters
- Full content search
- Bookmark, highlight and annotate text
- Access to thousands of pages of quality research at the click of a button.

ORDER YOUR FREE INSTITUTIONAL TRIAL TODAY

Free Trials Available

We offer free trials to qualifying academic, corporate and government customers.

eCollections
Choose from 20 different subject eCollections, including:

- Asian Studies
- Economics
- Health Studies
- Law
- Middle East Studies

eFocus
We have 16 cutting-edge interdisciplinary collections, including:

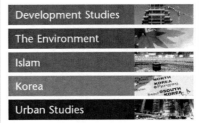

- Development Studies
- The Environment
- Islam
- Korea
- Urban Studies

For more information, pricing enquiries or to order a free trial, please contact your local sales team:

UK/Rest of World: **online.sales@tandf.co.uk**
USA/Canada/Latin America: **e-reference@taylorandfrancis.com**
East/Southeast Asia: **martin.jack@tandf.com.sg**
India: **journalsales@tandfindia.com**

www.tandfebooks.com